Manfred von Richthofen

In memory of my grandfathers – Arthur Hillier (1893–1962) and Albert Graves (1885–1980) and their sons – Ronald Hillier (1922–84) and Bernard Graves (1926–93) – who, like Manfred von Richthofen and millions of others, fought for their countries with courage, steadfastness and little regard to the costs involved.

Manfred von Richthofen

The High Price of Glory

Tim Hillier-Graves

First published in Great Britain in 2024 by
Pen & Sword Military
An imprint of
Pen & Sword Books Ltd
Yorkshire - Philadelphia

Copyright © Tim Hillier-Graves, 2024

ISBN 978 1 03610 026 1

The rights of Tim Hillier-Graves to be identified as the Author of this work has been asserted by him in accordance with the Copyright, Designs and Patents Act 1988.

A CIP catalogue record for this book is available from the British Library.

All rights reserved. No part of this book may be reproduced or transmitted in any form or by any means, electronic or mechanical, including photocopying, recording or by any information storage and retrieval system, without permission from the Publisher in writing.

Typeset in INDIA by IMPEC eSolutions
Printed and bound in the England by CPI Group (UK) Ltd, Croydon, CR0 4YY

Pen & Sword Books Ltd. incorporates the Imprints of Pen & Sword Archaeology, Atlas, Aviation, Battleground, Discovery, Family History, History, Maritime, Military, Naval, Politics, Railways, Select, Transport, True Crime, Fiction, Frontline Books, Leo Cooper, Praetorian Press, Seaforth Publishing, Wharncliffe, White Owl and After the Battle.

For a complete list of Pen & Sword titles please contact

PEN & SWORD BOOKS LIMITED
47 Church Street, Barnsley, South Yorkshire, S70 2AS, England
E-mail: enquiries@pen-and-sword.co.uk
Website: www.pen-and-sword.co.uk

or

PEN AND SWORD BOOKS
1950 Lawrence Rd, Havertown, PA 19083, USA
E-mail: uspen-and-sword@casematepublishers.com
Website: www.penandswordbooks.com

Contents

Acknowledgements   vii

Introduction   xi

Chapter 1   A Prussian Dawn   1

Chapter 2   The Lamps Go Out   26

Chapter 3   A Pressing Need for Heroes   59

Chapter 4   Fight for the Sky   89

Chapter 5   From Fledgling to Hawk   118

Chapter 6   In the Devil's Iron Grip   149

Chapter 7   Into the Void   190

Chapter 8   Immortalised   220

Chapter 9   Cause and Effect   256

References   269

Index   271

Acknowledgements

This book is about the physical and mental costs borne by young men in war, with particular emphasis on that suffered by air crew. To accomplish this, I have purposely chosen one specific pilot to study, perhaps the most famous of all, Manfred von Richthofen. This was a quite deliberate choice, because here we have a man not only shouldering the burden of combat when leading a large group of other young men into battle each day, but also the crippling cost of being a celebrity. In this role he was shamelessly exploited by Germany's leaders as an image of knightly virtue to urge a war-weary nation to carry on fighting despite the appalling costs involved, when suing for peace would have been a more sensible course of action to take. So, the pressures exerted on him were a magnification of those suffered by all combatants. This makes his life an important conductor when it comes to analysing the effects of combat fatigue and its consequences on young men at war.

To do this I was privileged to meet or correspond with many veterans of both world wars over many decades. Each added a great deal to my understanding of aviation and combat fatigue, so their contribution to this book is invaluable. Some, in fact, flew with von Richthofen and others against him, so could provide eyewitness accounts of his life and his ability to lead and survive for so long.

In addition to this wealth of material contained in these first-hand accounts we have von Richthofen's own papers, plus a hastily written memoir published in 1917. These, and a brief supplement written later, offer us many valuable insights into his life and what it meant to be a fighter pilot on the Western Front. Some doubts have been expressed about the biography's provenance, with a suggestion that it may have been ghost written to enhance its propaganda value. This may well be so, but I tend to think the book was most probably a collaborative effort in which von Richthofen played a considerable part. If nothing else, he was a man of integrity and so it is unlikely that he would have let something be published in his name that didn't reflect his thoughts and feelings accurately. On this basis it remains an invaluable document, as does his mother's own book *Mein Kriegstagebuch*, which was published in 1937, and many letters written by family, friends and military comrades.

Below I have listed all those who have helped me during many years of research by the war in which they fought, although some served in both.

1914–18 War

Albert Graves, Arthur Hillier, Cecil Lewis and Tim Hervey, who both flew with Albert Ball VC, Carl-August von Schoenebeck and Hans-Georg von der Osten, who flew with von Richthofen, David Lewis, Arthur Gould Lee, Ronald Adams, Leonard 'Tich' Rochford, Joseph Fall, Thomas Cassidy and Albert Heurteaux, who flew with the French Ace Georges Guynemer.

1939–45 War

Hank Adlam, Gordon Aitken, Bill Atkinson, Ron Ayrton, Douglas Bader, Richard Bigg-Wither, Tom Blackburn, John Blade, Alan Booth, Geoffrey Brooke, Eric Brown, Roy Brown, Stan Buchan, Don Cameron, Arthur Cargill, Peter Carmichael, Freddie Charlton, Ken Chapman, Bill Christie, Don Chute, John Cooper, Brian Cork, Mike Crosley, Robert Cunliffe, Mike Davey, Stuart Eadon, Rick Emberton, John Empsom, Stan Farquhar, Colin Facer, Chaplain

Edward Fawkes, Bill Fenwick-Smith, Bill Foster, Rowan Fullerton, Richard Goadsby, Lionel Godfrey, Pat Godson, Bernard Graves, Boone T. Guyton, Michael Hancock, Norman Hanson, John Hawkins, Ronnie Hay, Bill Hargreaves, Ben Heffer, John Herbert, Johnnie Johnson, Cliff Jones, Donald Judd, Peter Jupe, Dennis Kirby, James Kirk, Vic Lowden, John Lowder, Norman Luard, Dick Mackie, Alex Macrae, H. Mattholie, John Maybank, Ross McBain, Neville McNamara, Alistair Michie, Dave Millington, Noel Mitchell, Eric Monk, Ivor Morgan, Keith Munnock, Gerry Murphy, Barry Nation, Dick Neal, John Northeast, Dennis Papworth, Jack Parli, Hugh Popham, Richard Philips, Derek 'Rennie' Renvoize, Dick Reynolds, Douglas Richardson, Mike Ritchie, Dennis Robinson, Peter Roe, Jack Ruffin, Gerry Salmon, Fraser Shotton, Clifford Singleton, Doug Smith, Fred Starkey, Ian Stirling, Peter Swift, Mike Tritton, Fred Turnbull, Peter Ward, Bob Walsh and Al Watson.

To this list can be added the many men who wrote biographies about their lives and war experiences. In some cases, these were written in German and Dutch and later translated, sometimes crudely, into English, losing much along the way. Here I have taken the liberty of tidying up the translations to make them flow more evenly, hopefully in a way the writer originally intended.

In Britain we are lucky to have many institutions that preserve material meticulously for all to see and research. First and foremost among these is the Imperial War Museum, where so many people work to ensure the past, and the people who contributed so much to it, are not forgotten. The same may be said of the RAF Museum at Hendon and the National Archives at Kew.

Last, but not least, I was greatly assisted by four historians of note who made it their lifetime's work to collect information about Great War aviators and von Richthofen in particular. They are Charles Donald, Pasquale Carisella, Ed Ferko and Douglas Whetton. All four men, who are all no longer with us, were very generous in their help and very graciously sent me masses of material over the years. All this is featured here in this book and a second, photographic volume about von Richthofen.

To all the people who helped me I give my most profound thanks.

Introduction

> Artillery fire and aerial activity had been increasing steadily, and on 21st April the German ace, Richthofen, was brought down behind enemy lines, quite near some men of the Sixth, who tried to reach the plane before enemy fire destroyed it.
>
> War Diary of 6th 'Cast Iron' London Regiment, 58th Division, 1918

For several weeks the 6th had seen much hard fighting at Villers-Bretonneux, as the German Army tried to achieve a breakthrough. The village, though precious little of it remained, had become a killing ground for the Germans, with artillery fire, machine guns, gas and bayonets decimating their numbers as each attack was beaten back. In the centre of all this the 'Cast Irons' had stood firm, but by the 19th, following an attack in which 'they were drenched in poison gas and lost heavily', they were withdrawn from the front line for a short rest. It was a break that also allowed their losses to be made good and for them to be served hot meals, the first for a long time. While this happened the regiment acted as a mobile reserve ready to face a long-expected attack along Morlancourt Ridge. It was here on the 21st that some of the men saw a single red triplane, containing von Richthofen, come down late that morning:

> We envied the boys in their aircraft and often thought about what it would be like to fly home after a battle to a bath and a fresh bed. Being stuck in a fetid trench for twenty-four hours a

day, with all matter of muck being thrown at us by 'Jerry', was hardly conducive to a happy life. So we watched the airmen and resented the home comforts they enjoyed simply flying for a couple of hours each day.

When the weather was clear we watched them fighting, sometimes in large numbers. It helped pass the time and we cheered when a Bosch was shot down, although silence would descend as a pilot, no matter what their nationality, became detached from a burning aircraft and plunged to earth, often writhing in flames themselves. Then we didn't envy them, especially when they crashed nearby and we could see for ourselves their dead, badly damaged bodies. British, French or German made no difference, they were all young lads trying to do their best in an impossible situation. If we could we treated all their remains with respect.

I and my platoon were on Morlancourt Ridge on the 21st preparing to move back to the trenches at Villers, when Richthofen came down though we didn't realise it was him immediately. As his aircraft had crash-landed quite heavily I was ordered to lead a party of men forward to take him prisoner, treat any wounds he might have had or simply lay him out if dead, collecting any papers that might prove of interest to the Intelligence Corps at HQ. Groups of Aussies were there already and had begun their usual scavenging activities, especially when word that it was Richthofen in the aircraft got round.

By the time I reached the crash site the pilot had been confirmed dead, so we only remained for half an hour or so, there being no more we could do. Before departing, I spoke to an AEF sergeant who handed me a piece of wood as a souvenir; the wings by then being stripped down with knives, bayonets and anything else to hand. Later on I used my carpentry skills to fashion this into a clothes brush, which I still use to this day.

I then took a close look at the pilot and his face in particular, which was badly knocked about and bloodied. I had seen many German dead by then, green and rotting away in no man's land for the most part, so it was interesting to see someone more recently killed and wonder what sort of man he had been and ponder the grief soon to descend on his family and friends.

By this stage of the war Richthofen was well-known to us all, and every time we saw an enemy aircraft it was him flying it, such was the strength of his reputation. We also knew that he was an undoubted killer with far too many of our men dead or injured as he took his path to fame. However, he seems to have fought cleanly and bravely so probably deserved our grudging respect.

Sergeant A.E. Graves (No. 322248), 6th London Regiment

To me its seems remarkable that von Richthofen should be so well-known by a soldier on the other side of the lines, who spent his life in muddy trenches, dodging German bullets and shells, plagued by rats and lice. Yet even sixty years later, when I spoke to my grandfather and recorded his memories, he recollected with great clarity witnessing von Richthofen's final moments and then observing his body and crashed red triplane from close quarters. How did this come about, especially in such a bloody, no holds barred war? In a world where secrecy was paramount and the art of propaganda practised with such venom by both sides, eager to demonise an enemy, such a thing shouldn't have been possible. But here we have a platoon of young British men, accompanied by a lot of Australians, clearly knowing his name and the fact that he was responsible for the deaths of so many of their comrades.

Yet, even on the day of his death, *The Times* in London reported his seventy-ninth and eightieth victories, as though it was an international sporting match where an opposing player had scored a couple of goals or hit a hundred runs, not the lives of two young

Allied pilots, one of whom was killed. But it had been this way since late 1916 when von Richthofen's rise to fame had begun. In a very short time he went from being an unknown pilot to a fighter ace of great standing. In the process he became a national hero whose growing reputation was exploited by a propaganda machine eager to prop up a population grown tired of war. And with an ever-increasing clamour for peace being heard in the Reichstag, shortages of food, malnutrition and little prospect of victory, Germany's leaders had to encourage a war-weary nation to carry on the fight until victory might finally be grasped. It was for this great and utterly pointless endeavour that a carefully managed vision of Von Richthofen's knightly virtues, fighting a sort of medieval joust high above the trenches, was conceived.

For one young man to shoulder such a burden was a very tall order indeed, especially when still required to fight and lead many other men at the front in ever worsening conditions. Inevitably, it was a game of chance that relied too heavily on his flying skills, his luck holding and his ability to tap into any reserves of strength he could muster as exhaustion set in. Eventually the law of averages prevailed and he was killed in a fruitless search for an elusive 'victory', joining hundreds of thousands of fellow Germans to their graves. If he had survived, and gone home for a prolonged rest, he could have continued to inspire others to fight, but when such a personification of courage dies hope tends to die with them.

Von Richthofen's elevation to war hero was rapid, unprecedented and on a different scale to other German champions, before or since. During the Great War the deeds of fighter pilots such as Oswald Boelcke and Max Immelmann had captured the public's imagination. When both were killed there was an outpouring of grief, but this doesn't seem to have lasted for long as new heroes emerged to take their place, including von Richthofen. Here, promoted by a carefully orchestrated PR campaign, he moved centre stage and his fame simply grew and grew, surprisingly crossing the front line into the enemy camp in a way still difficult to comprehend. I suppose it is finding some way of explaining this strange paradox that lies at the heart of this book.

To try and understand von Richthofen's life I travelled to France, Belgium, Germany and Poland to see for myself where he lived, fought, died and now rests. I hoped to find traces of the world in which he lived, though found very little except regenerated land where many terrible battles were fought, a dilapidated childhood home and old family estates, destroyed or bullet-marked memorials and, finally, a well-tended grave where he was finally laid to rest with members of his family. In some ways what I saw was a metaphor for all that happened in Germany between 1914 and 1945, but the result was disappointing nonetheless.

The truth, as I soon realised, lay in tapping into the memories of those who had experienced air warfare at first-hand. Only they could conjure up a true picture of those times when flying into the wide blue yonder each day, to fight for your country, with your life on a knife-edge, was for a time their sole reason for living. It was only they who truly knew the cost of war – mentally, physically and spiritually. In von Richthofen's case the costs were too high and in trying to understand how deeply he was affected by all he experienced it was the contact with those who knew or fought against him that proved so important.

I realise that eyewitness accounts can at times be coloured by age and failing memory, but those I met or corresponded with knew this and peppered their thoughts with words such as, 'I think this or that happened, but I'm not entirely sure of my dates or the sequence of events.' This may be so, but I always believe that when reliving an ancient time, it is the spirit found in memories not the minutiae of facts that matter. If you want a detailed knowledge of the way an aircraft is built or want to discuss a fighter pilot's 'score' you have to go elsewhere. If you want the truth about personality, the corrosive effects of fear, how bravery is sustained in the face of near impossible odds and much more, it is the spirit contained in the memories of those who were there that count most. For they saw life in the raw, shared the terrors and intense excitement, survived in one way or another, to live with loss and, sometimes, a belief that these precious years may have been sacrificed unnecessarily.

Having collected a great deal of information and read many books on the subject, it seemed to me that now is the time to present a new account of Manfred von Richthofen's life. However, the result is only part biographical because my aim here is to unravel a dichotomy. To do this meant focusing on fame and how it is exploited by those whose motives are not always simple or honourable – among whom I would list politicians, military leaders or those who simply wish to benefit from another person's efforts or sacrifice. Manfred von Richthofen's life encapsulates these issues, but there are two other, equally significant elements to consider when forming a view. First of all, we have the debilitating effect of combat fatigue and how this affected his behaviour and may have led to his death. Then, there is the militaristic nature of his Prussian birthright. It was this culture and its celebration of martial prowess that would determine the course of his life, as it did for many in his family. It was a society and caste founded on Bismarck's vision of a strong, united Germany, soon reinforced by Wilhelm II when becoming Kaiser in 1888. As such, its all-pervading influence on the life of its most famous son cannot be underestimated or ignored.

So, our story begins in the 1870s when Germany first came into being and grew into a country that bred and nurtured one young Prussian boy. And then, having set him on a militaristic course, propelled him to greatness and a destruction witnessed by one very tired, khaki-clad 'Tommy', serving with the 6th London Regiment, who remembered that day for the rest of his life.

Chapter 1

A Prussian Dawn

> As a little boy of eleven I entered the Cadet Corps. I was not particularly eager to become a Cadet, but my father desired it, so my wishes were not consulted. I found it difficult to bear the strict discipline and to keep order ... I was never good at learning things ... I had a tremendous liking for all sorts of risky tricks.
>
> MvR

As a Prussian, Manfred von Richthofen was born into a world of caste and strict social order, where a father's wishes did indeed take precedence over many things. It had been this way for so long that few questioned its beginnings. Like the wind blowing, its existence was simply accepted as a fact.

Prussia had grown over many hundreds of years, in the careful, calculating hands of the Hohenzollern family, from the small state of Brandenburg, centred on Berlin, to something much larger. By the early nineteenth century it was a country of size and stature, entering the international scene most famously at the Battle of Waterloo in 1815. Here three corps from the Prussian Army, led by Field Marshal Gebhard von Blücher, arrived at a strategically opportune moment and in so doing turned the tide of this battle and European history.

By then Prussia had grown considerably and now included such territories as East and West Prussia, Pomerania, Posen, Westphalia, and Silesia. But it hadn't been an easy process and could have easily come unstuck in any one of a number of wars that reshaped the continent. In fact, Waterloo had been preceded by a period in which

Prussia almost ceased to exist. With Napoleon's domination of central Europe almost complete, the French Army's triumphs at the twin battles of Jena and Auerstedt on 14 October 1806, which led to the one-sided Peace of Tilsit a year later, changed things considerably. Here the Prussian king, Friedrich Wilhelm III, was forced to cede half his territory to France and, in the process, subjugated all Prussian people to French rule in these occupied lands. And so it lasted until October 1813 when Napoleon was defeated at the Battle of Leipzig. So important was this victory that it became a milestone, not only on the path to Prussian survival and revival, but also German nationhood.

Until the creation of this unified country could take place, Prussian influence continued to grow, guided by its Chancellor, Otto von Bismarck. His aim was clear and his method of achieving it was best summed up in a speech he made to the Prussian House of Representatives in 1862:

> The position of Prussia in Germany will not be determined by its liberalism but by its power ... Prussia must concentrate its strength and hold it for the favourable moment, which has already come and gone several times ... Not through speeches and majority decisions will the great questions of the day be decided ... but by iron and blood.

Bismarck, in these most forthright words, set out his plan of the future and the direction in which his country must go. It was a message that he would reaffirm when Germany came into existence following the Franco-Prussian War that erupted in 1870. A rapid victory by the Northern Confederation of German States over 'the old enemy' set off a spontaneous wave of patriotism throughout all German lands, not simply Prussia. This encouraged Bismarck, who had carefully stage managed many events, to push ahead with his plans for closer ties with these neighbouring states. In the glow of this nationalistic fervour, any opposition to his plan soon dissipated and agreement was reached. With that the new German state was proclaimed at the Palace of Versailles in January 1871, with Wilhelm I anointed Kaiser, so extending the House of Hohenzollern's authority even further.

It was during this triumphant period of Prussian and German history that Manfred von Richthofen's parents were born and grew to maturity, profoundly influenced by all that was going on around them in this new fledgling state. Manfred's father, Albrecht, was born on 13 November 1859, the eldest son of Karl Oscar Lothar von Richthofen (apparently known as Julius or Jules to his family) who owned and worked an estate at Romberg near Breslau in Silesia. Albrecht's mother, Hulda Eva von Teichmann, hailed from the Mecklenburg region of Northern Germany and was undoubtedly attracted to the notably handsome, well-established Karl, who would have been considered 'quite a catch' for any young woman at the time. Their eldest child, although a career managing the family estate might have beckoned, chose instead to enter the Corps of Cadets and joined the 12th Regiment of Uhlans. How Karl greeted this news is not recorded, but it was an honourable career to follow so it was probably accepted with little criticism or reserve.

Manfred's mother, Kunigunde von Schickfus und Neudorff, came from an equally privileged background, her father Leopold owning Baumgarten, a substantial estate to the south of Breslau. It was while under the tutelage of Baron von Falkenhausen of Wallisfurth that Leopold fell for and married Maria Theresia von Falkenhausen, one of the Baron's four daughters. The marriage produced Kunigunde on 27 November 1868 and her sister, Elfriede, two years later.

Sadly, their mother died in 1881, when only 33, having contracted scarlet fever. So ended what seems to have been an idyllic childhood in which the only real trauma for Kunigunde had been witnessing her father march off to fight in the Franco-Prussian War. In due course the Baron remarried and, as seems to happen quite often in these situations, the step-parent and stepchildren did not appear to have enjoyed an easy relationship. Very quickly Kunigunde was packed off to a boarding school in Berlin by Louise, her new mother, and, when free of this closeted and impersonal life, was actively encouraged to marry. In the circumstances this was probably the best thing for her to do, especially in an age when women of her class were not expected to enter a profession or be free of a man's influence. Nevertheless, she did harbour an ambition to make her own way in the world by becoming a qualified governess, only for her father to exert parental control and push her towards marriage instead. For a clearly intelligent, strong-minded, young woman this may have been a bitter pill to swallow.

The route to a good marriage for young woman such as Kunigunde was similar to that followed by families in the upper reaches of British society at the time. Eligible young women would be promenaded at social events, such as balls and garden parties, where eligible young men would be present. In this case possible suitors would have had to have title, rank or wealth. Snaring a man with all three would have been considered a major triumph. In Kunigunde's case Albrecht von Richhtofen, by then a handsome young cavalry officer, appeared to have all three and so passed muster very quickly. So a romance began, helped by a shared passion of equestrianism.

Marriage soon followed, but if it was expected that Karl von Richthofen's wealth would cascade down to his son and new wife, a surprise might have been in store. With two other sons, Friedrich and Walter Lothar, to support, plus his wife, the income from his assets seems to have proved inadequate. And when Karl died in 1893 there seems to have been insufficient funds in his estate for Albrecht to receive an inheritance of any sort. So, he and his wife had to manage on an army officer's pay, and, inevitably they struggled as their family grew larger.

Kunigunde, who may have married with some sort of dowry and allowance, could have sought additional support from her father but chose not to do so. As a result, they were continually short of funds and she was unable to live the life she had once enjoyed. The stresses and strains caused by this would have been only too obvious and probably caused many rifts in their day-to-day lives. It undoubtedly didn't help that he 'understood little about practical life and even less about money', as she later wrote. But they were proud aristocrats who struggled on hoping to maintain a picture of refinement, though genteel poverty may have been a better description. Such is the way of life in the 'privileged' classes and in Prussia those of noble birth, no matter how wealthy, came to be known as 'Junkers'.

It was a name with a meaning that gradually changed over the years as the class extended its influence over life in Prussia and then the newer state of Germany. This happened to such an extent that it was later said that 'if Prussia ruled Germany, the Junkers ruled Prussia, and through it the Empire itself', such was the sway they had on events in Germany and Europe in the nineteenth and twentieth centuries. In this, they were little different from Britain's ruling class, where great power rested in the hands of a tiny minority of vastly wealthy men and their families. The advance of true democracy would only come slowly in both countries, with each liberalising and democratising step forward resisted by those with a vested interest in maintaining the status quo.

From very early in the life of Prussia, the Junkers monopolised all pastoral matters east of the River Elbe, where, as landed autocrats they owned most of the arable land, applying a culture of serfdom to their workers. These estates, many of them vast, were passed down through the generations, some growing ever larger and inevitably became an inheritance enjoyed mostly by eldest sons. As a result, younger sons tended to miss out and turned instead to the civil and military services for employment when school days came to an end. Here the Junkers tended to dominate the senior ranks of both services, as von Bismarck's career clearly demonstrates, and became the bulwarks and defenders of the Hohenzollern dynasty. In these vital positions they can be said to have controlled the Prussian Army as well as wider political life in Germany in the years leading up to the Great War.

To the impartial observer the Junkers are now seen as an ultra-conservative, reactionary and anti-democratic, hugely influential group of men. True or not, their influence over internal affairs was rarely liberal and seemed more concerned with perpetuating feudalism. As such, it was increasingly out of step with changing attitudes, where true democracy and greater freedoms for the individual were rapidly gaining ground. If the Junkers moved at all to accept and legislate for these changing values it was done so grudgingly. From 1890, with the autocratic Kaiser Wilhelm II on the throne, who believed strongly in his divine right to rule, progress became, if anything, even slower. While this was happening, Germany's military might continued to grow, as did the Kaiser's desire to create an Empire to match those of Britain and France. In so doing, he allowed militaristic and territorial ambitions to become more firmly embedded.

Although Prussia represented a patriarchal view of society, this was not the complete picture as the nineteenth century gave way to the twentieth. Women's suffrage still had a long way to go, especially in terms of establishing equality as a legal entity, but some advances had been made as Kunigunde von Richthofen's life makes clear.

Here was an educated and determined young woman denied a career and held by established convention, clearly more capable than her husband and having to manage their lives in a way that he was unable to do. In a different age she would undoubtedly have entered university and become a professional in some field, achieving much in the process. As it was she managed their home and the lives of their children most capably, ensuring, as far as she could, that the strictures of society were followed and they achieved their full potential in any field of work they chose to pursue. They might be limited in these things by their own personality and ability to study, but she instilled ambition in them and, with Albrecht's undoubted help, a strong sense of duty and commitment to country and family. Nevertheless, nurture must always go hand in hand with nature and no matter how well children are directed, their idiosyncrasies will rise inevitably to the surface, for good or bad.

Normally it might be safe to assume that a child would grow up in a way that mirrored the world around them, absorbing the manners, attitudes and etiquette of their caste. This would be especially so when born into a very privileged family, such as those existing in Prussia. However, it was a state with a varied ethnic mix of people that reflected the way the 'empire' of the Junkers had grown when acquiring land and property from neighbouring states. For example, there were strong Polish, Slavic and Jewish elements, plus people who came from other parts of Germany, Western Europe and Denmark. The Slavs and Poles tended to work the land as labourers or became servants to the wealthier families. These duties, although important in day-to-day life, had little social status. So, they still tended to be regarded as serfs, although this form of peasantry was formally abolished by Frederick II of Prussia in the 1760s. But old habits die hard and each new Junker generation would, undoubtedly, have inherited this superior view of the world and treated their underlings accordingly.

Much the same thing was happening in Britain, despite more liberal voices calling for reform and a rebalancing of society. E.M. Forster, in his book *Howards End*, observed this world as it was in the first years of the twentieth century and the attitude of Britain's ruling class to the less well-off. Forster, through the medium of one of his characters. wrote: 'Don't take up a sentimental attitude to the poor. The poor are poor, and one is sorry for them, but there it is.'

With these few words Forster perfectly describes the way in which the disadvantaged were seen and how social divisions were perpetuated simply for the benefit of the few. In this Britain and Prussia had much in common. So the attitude and character of those enjoying the privileges of noble birth in each country would have been of a particularly superior kind. As a result, there existed a clear master and servant relationship, which the von Richthofen children would have known only too well and perpetuated in their attitudes, sense of entitlement and the way they lived their lives. Only time would tell how they would react when more liberal attitudes began to prevail, as they did when war came in 1914.

Albrecht and Kunigunde's relationship, although one seemingly based on mutual attraction, soon began to show cracks, with the lack of income at its root. Any differences they had would have been exacerbated as their children began to arrive, which they did during August 1890 when their daughter Elisabeth Therese Elfriede (known as Ilse to the family) was born. At this stage the couple were living, very frugally by the standards they had come to expect, in Kleinburg, on the south-eastern edge of Breslau, close to where Albrecht's regiment, the Kurassier Rgt Groffer Kurfurst Nr 1, was quartered. There has been some speculation that the apartment in which they lived was in a large building on the Kaiser-Wilhelm Straße (Nos 92 to 96); a wide boulevard where the wealthiest families lived, often in very expensively built villas. If so it was while living in this community that Manfred Albrecht was born on 2nd May 1892 and his brother, Lothar Siegfried, two years later on 27 September 1894, all the children apparently being raised in the Lutheran faith.

On the choice of his first Christian name Manfred later wrote: 'I have been named after my uncle Manfred who, in peacetime, was Adjutant to His Majesty and Commander of the Corps of the Guards.'

Mention of this relation is interesting, but such is the way with noble families where power and influence are inevitably intertwined. Yet this was only one such connection that Manfred and his family enjoyed that may have aided his advancement in army circles and his ever-increasing fame when war came.

If his parents had struggled to make ends meet early in their marriage, then with three young children to raise things could only get worse. Being a fairly senior officer in an elite cavalry regiment meant that Albrecht had, for etiquette's sake if nothing else, broader social obligations to meet that went beyond simple soldiering. Many of his fellow officers would have had substantial private incomes, in addition to their pay, to see them through, but the von Richthofens had no such estate or benefactor and struggled. So it is little wonder that Kunigunde later reported that the constant 'penny pinching' left her depressed and, as the person responsible for managing such a limited budget, bitter at times. With the pressure of motherhood, the load on her must have become intolerable and affected the way her children grew and responded to the world around them. Even very young children have the capacity to sense when things aren't going well and respond accordingly. In Manfred's case this seems to have bred a seriousness of mind and a strong sense of responsibility along with other character traits.

In the early years of Manfred's life, and perhaps in an effort to ease the financial burden, the family moved to a house in the country. Here there was more space to live, seemingly at lower cost and where the pressure on Kunigunde might be less. But the new home required servants, the children a governess, plus horses and carriage for transport, as befitted descendants of two noble families. To this would be added the costs Albrecht incurred as a soldier, plus the purchase of hunting privileges over nearby land for his sport. Living beyond their means is an appropriate description of the situation in which they found themselves. It was hoped that a move back to Breslau might rein in their expenses, but their plight only seemed to worsen following a winter exercise, as Manfred later recorded:

> My father (now a Major) was the most conscientious soldier imaginable. He began to suffer from a hearing difficulty and had to resign. He had contracted ear trouble when saving one of his men from drowning, and though he was wet through and

through he insisted upon continuing his duties as if nothing had happened, wet as he was, without taking notice of the rigours of the weather.

Although the date of this incident is unclear, beyond being in the late 1890s, the impact his compulsory retirement had on family life was clear. Although Albrecht's income as an officer was hardly sufficient for their needs, living on a pension would have been considerably more difficult. Thrift and frugality, a continuing feature of their married life, would have had to be practised even more keenly. However, a hearing impairment didn't stop Albrecht seeking other work and he found employment in nearby Schweidnitz procuring horses for the army and, in particular the cavalry. This inevitably meant a move away from Breslau and a new home, where the von Richthofen's fourth and last child, Bolko Karl Alexander, was born on 16 April 1903.

Sadly, on 11 October in the same year, the happiness of this new arrival was negated by the death of Kunigunde's father, Leopold, at the age of 65. A period of mourning followed, during which his estate would have been dispersed according to his will. His widow, Louise, and his daughters appear to have been beneficiaries. Kunigunde was left sufficient to enable them to buy a substantial house in Schweidnitz and, hopefully, ease their financial problems, for a time at least. However, it is reported that Kunigunde was very conscious of the fact that her standard of living, although high for the time, was far below that enjoyed by her family.

By this stage Manfred had passed through the fashionable phase of the time that urged mothers to dress small boys in flowing clothes, with their hair allowed to grow long and, hopefully, curly. Rather charmingly, Kunigunde later said of Manfred that his hair 'shone like spun sunlight', so moved was she by the sight of her young son. However, custom also dictated that by 2 or 3 a son should be dressed in more boyish clothes and have their hair cut short, as though preparing for a military life.

With his sister as his only companion, until Lothar arrived, home schooling with a governess would probably have been a closely managed process. In a class full of children, the mind was free to wander, not so when there were only two involved with an eagle-eyed tutor in attendance. Needless to say, the quality of their education rested largely on the skills of this one person. Manfred's lack of academic prowess and educational achievements later on suggest the grounding he received may not have been sufficient for his needs.

During this time the church was central to family life and Kunigunde later reported that the family regularly attended the Friedenskirche in Schweidnitz. It is not known how deep Manfred's faith was and whether it was a duty more than a calling. However, he kept a Lutheran hymn book, inscribed by his mother, with him for the rest of his life, which suggests some emotional or philosophical connection.

Other extra-curricular activities would have focussed on open-air pursuits and would have added greatly to his understanding of Prussian culture. One photograph, in particular, catches the tone of his young life. It shows him and his sister being drawn along in a cart pulled by a white goat, with Manfred taking the reins and one of Karl von Richthofen's liveried footmen in attendance. Such a scene would be enacted in many noble homes at the time, with riding and hunting being almost compulsory pursuits for boys.

These were things at which Manfred excelled, undoubtedly schooled by his father and encouraged by his mother. And in this environment Manfred's personality began to form. Like most small children, his realm was a narrow one in which the outside world did not intrude to any great extent. Nevertheless, many things were happening all around him that left unchecked by wise minds would doom Europe to another war and Manfred's generation to an unnecessary slaughter.

In many ways Bismarck had set the pattern for this long before Kaiser Wilhem II forced his resignation in 1890 and assumed direct control of Germany's future. Unfortunately, he lacked Bismarck's cleverness or his broad and far-seeing strategy that had made him the master of the finely tuned game of diplomacy. Instead, Wilhelm tended to choose special advisors who simply flattered him for their own benefit or others with few of the Bismarck skills. In reality the Kaiser should have remembered the old Chancellor's speeches to the Reichstag in which he often spoke of the dangers in setting off a European war. He cautioned that if this happened Germany might have to fight on two fronts and face insurmountable odds. He then underlined his desire for peace and the futility of a conflict with the words:

I am opposed to the notion of any sort of active participation of Germany in these matters, so long as I can see no reason to suppose that German interests are involved, no interests on behalf of which it is worth our risking – excuse my plain speaking – the healthy bones of one of our Pomeranian musketeers.

Wilhelm showed no such caution and by 1898 had set in motion a massive expansion of his navy, so challenging Britain's domination of the high seas. At the same time, his army had also increased in size, making both France and Russia increasingly nervous of German ambitions and so drawing them closer together in an attempt to counter any threat this rapidly expanding 'empire' posed. Inevitably, battle lines were being drawn across Europe that would lead to war.

The downside of all of this was that the German government's budget went into deficit as it spent more and more money on the army and navy. As a result, its national debt grew to a massive 490 billion marks by 1913. Despite this, the Kaiser's policies found support among his subjects, carefully fostered by propaganda that asserted Germany was at risk from its European neighbours if it didn't arm itself adequately. It was a message that appealed to his people's sense of patriotism and seems to have achieved a broad consensus.

While this was happening, and to appease social reformers in the Reichstag, new legislation was occasionally enacted to improve the lives of many impoverished Germans. Sadly, this doesn't seem to have been for truly altruistic reasons but more a response by the Junkers and industrialists who wanted to limit the influence of reforming socialists, whose voices were growing louder each year. So, the Kaiser supported the introduction of some modest reforms in order in to keep the working classes loyal to the German state. Most prominently, these included a law that banned Sunday working and the employment of children under 13. Then in 1901 industrial arbitration courts were introduced to settle disputes between workers and employers. In an autocratic country where a master and servant way of living was held sacrosanct this was a major step forward. The trouble for the Kaiser was that once a reforming door is open the clamour for more freedoms and rights inevitably follows and this he was seemingly ill-prepared to meet. His brand of conservatism had come face to face with newly born socialist principles, which made confrontation, at some stage, inevitable.

All this was accompanied by huge demographic changes across Germany as agriculture gave way to heavy industry as the major employer of labour. Coal mining remained a significant industry, especially with demand increasing to meet the country's growing industrial needs, but now such things as chemicals, motor vehicles and armaments were also being produced in vast quantities. By 1910 there were 10.86 million workers employed in these industries, most of them migrating from the countryside to towns and cities to do so. Such was the rate of growth that Berlin doubled in size between 1875 and 1910 and cities such as Munich, Essen and Kiel also grew rapidly. By 1910 there were forty-eight German towns with populations over 100,000 when in 1871 there had only been eight. However, there was no clear plan to provide adequate accommodation for these workers, most of whom could only find overcrowded slums to live in. Soon the clamour for better living conditions grew louder and a once docile workforce grew more aggressive in demanding greater social justice.

The extension of voting rights to all adult men, when Germany came into being in 1871, meant that this large group of workers could change the nature of the Reichstag in their favour. And so, large numbers began voting for the reforming German Social Democratic Party, which in 1912 finally held the largest number of seats. By forging an alliance with the Central and Progressive Parties they could have forced through many reforming issues, but for most of the time they were unwilling to act together in opposition, which left the government largely free to do as it wished. Sadly, this meant that the established hierarchy of German society remained unchanged with the Kaiser's all-powerful autocracy left largely unchallenged or controlled. As the situation in Europe gradually deteriorated, and battle lines were drawn, this had unfortunate consequences.

Despite this the Kaiser seems to have remained a much-admired figure in Germany, if not the rest of the world. In achieving this the growing power of the press proved crucial, sustaining, as it did, an almost blind belief in Kaiser and country. But Germany wasn't alone in this because the art of propaganda had become, by the early years of the twentieth century, a much-practised art by democracies and dictatorships around the world.

In his book *Munitions of the Mind* Philip Taylor offers a considered view of this phenomenon:

> Propaganda, it is felt, forces us to think and do things in ways we might not otherwise have done had we been left to our own devices. It obscures our window on the world by providing layers of distorting condensation. When nations fight, it thickens the fog of war. It has become the enemy of independent thought and an intrusive and unwanted manipulator of the free flow of information and ideas in humanity's quest for

peace and truth ... It suggests the triumph of emotion over reason in a bureaucratic struggle by the machinery of power for the control of the individual. It is a 'dirty trick' utilized by 'hidden persuaders' in order to control our behaviour to serve their interests rather than our own.

True or not, propaganda had, as Manfred grew to maturity, become a much-used and often abused art that played on people's prejudices, ambitions, likes and dislikes in various ways. On one level it was merely a means of selling goods, and on a deeper, more profound level it became a means of marshalling hatred and fear to achieve a political, cultural or racist aim. It was a technique most terrifyingly and expertly exploited by the Nazis in the 1930s and '40s and led directly to the death camps and the slaughter of millions of innocent people.

In the early 1900s this 'art form' had found its feet aided by a burgeoning press ever eager to sell its papers and make a profit. At the same time, printing and photographic techniques were advancing rapidly, making newspapers and magazines much cheaper to produce and distribute. And with high literacy rates across all classes in Germany, readership quickly grew and this encouraged even more publishers to begin trading. But this wasn't something solely confined to the Reich, it also existed in Britain, France and the USA, where the press wielded immense power.

At the same time, the twentieth century witnessed the birth of moving pictures and the development of the cinema. It didn't have the immediacy of newspapers, and in many producers' eyes was more an art form than a means of spreading information. In truth, its power was, as yet, barely understood and the means of reaching the public still at a very early stage in the lead-up to the Great War. However, this was changing rapidly and by 1916 the number of picture houses had grown in Germany from one in 1906 to nearly 2,000, with admissions growing rapidly each year and running into many millions by the time war broke out.

With such a perceived power to influence opinion it wasn't long before the film industry was partially nationalised with the creation of Universum Film AG (UFA) in 1917. This was a move, it has to be said, partly taken in response to the very effective use that the Allied powers were making of films for propaganda purposes. Under the direction of the Germany's all-powerful military machine, Vaterland films were produced in ever-increasing numbers. These matched the Allies in output and in the way they disparaged the enemy, and, it was hoped, would sustain a belief in the rightness of Germany's cause and promote a will to keep fighting.

As the von Richthofens moved to their new home in Schweidnitz during 1903, much of this still lay in the future, but the social, political, military and cultural changes taking place across Germany were slowly casting a spell over their lives. However, Manfred, now a budding 11-year-old, had more pressing matters to concern him because that year his father's decision over his future, in which he had no say, became a reality. So, after a year spent at a school in Schweidnitz, he was despatched to the Cadet Institute at Wahlstatt to begin his initiation into the army. His life as a Prussian officer had begun.

Why Albrecht took such a strong line over the future of his eldest son is unclear, so is open to conjecture. Was it the act of a man whose own military career had been frustrated by illness and who saw in Manfred a means of achieving his thwarted ambitions? Or was it based on a deep understanding of his son's character, coupled to the realisation that he lacked academic prowess, which Manfred seems to confirm in his memoirs? Lothar would eventually follow suit, but his entry to military life was delayed by Kunigunde's concerns over his fragile state of health. Ilse, as a woman, had even less choice and was sent to a finishing school in Lössnitz in Saxony for two years in preparation for her entrance into upper-class society and then, presumably, marriage.

Twelve years later, when Kunigunde was delivering her youngest son to Wahlstatt, she reminisced about Manfred's time there.

She appears to have had no qualms about sending him to such an institution when so young and harboured no doubts about the benefits of its education. This suggests that her oldest son had kept quiet about the discomforts he had suffered there and bears witness to a certain stoicism in his personality. Her reaction to the place was, as we shall see, the complete opposite to Manfred's:

> The spirit of the institution pleased me greatly. The children had to learn to be clever and healthy, while they diligently did gymnastics ... this art became very useful to him in cadet school. Several times he excelled.

The reality for Manfred was rather different and, as a result, he failed to shine, perhaps being unready for the strict regimentation and bullying endemic in institutions such as this and exercised by both teachers and older pupils alike. Nowadays this sort of behaviour would be condemned, but not then because it was believed that new recruits needed to be 'toughened up' to face the hardships of military life. Sadly, the results were almost always the opposite to those intended. Such treatment only bred fear and resentment of the system that allowed it to thrive and hatred of the cruel perpetrators of these practices. It was allowed to continue because the victims were brought up in a society where you were expected to suffer in silence and make a virtue of reticence and constraint.

Manfred was a boy of spirit and independence, who when at home had grown used to riding and hunting, with this freedom to roam becoming an important part of life. But now all this was subordinated to a much stricter, less sympathetic regime. His response to these new restrictions was, inevitably, a poor one, as he later reported:

> I did just enough work to pass. In my opinion it would have been wrong to do more than just sufficient, so I worked as little as possible. The consequence was that my teachers did not

think overmuch of me. On the other hand, I was very fond of sport, particularly I liked gymnastics, football etc. I could do all possible tricks on the horizontal bar.

I had a tremendous fondness for all sorts of risky tricks. One fine day I climbed, with my friend Frankenberg, up the well-known steeple at Wahlstatt by means of the lightning conductor and tied my handkerchief to the top.

In many ways Manfred's reaction was similar to many of those boys of his own age and class who were passing through public schools in Britain at the time. One of their number, Kingsley Martin the author, later wrote that:

Inattention, stupidity, bad work or other forms of wickedness could only be expatiated by an exemplary whipping ... No boy was expected to be concerned with music or the arts, or politics or the world around us ... We were bored beyond belief, so we ragged when we dared and dozed where we could.

Manfred's acts of great daring were characteristic of a strong personality demonstrating a desire to challenge the system when he felt he could, and prove he wouldn't buckle no matter how extreme the pressure. How his father viewed his 'misdemeanours' is unclear, but he seems to have loved his children so would probably have adopted a kindly approach, as far as possible, to keep his son moving along the right line. And this seems to have worked, though may have taken longer than he had hoped. So, by the time he left Wahlstatt in 1909 Manfred had begun to learn the benefits of order and discipline, but not to a slavish level as befits men or women with little power to lead. Instead, he began to combine a mastery of himself and an ability to look more broadly and, in doing so, began to demonstrate true leadership qualities, albeit untested by the rigours of war. It was as Benjamin Franklin put it succinctly, 'He that cannot obey, cannot command,' and now Manfred began putting this principle into practice.

These growing signs of maturity became more apparent when he successfully passed out of Wahlstatt and progressed to the Royal Military Academy at Lichterfelde in the south-west corner of Berlin, within a few miles of Sanssouci, the Kaiser's summer palace in Potsdam. This institution, known as the Preußische Hauptkadettenanstalt, opened in 1882 and attendance, as one might expect, was particularly prized by aspiring young officers from Junker families. And the presence of this prestigious Academy soon drew many famous members of that class to the district. In so doing they created a community that provided a ready supply of high-society functions for the young men to enjoy. Nevertheless, Manfred doesn't appear to have participated in these events to any great extent and seems to have found life at the Academy only marginally better than Wahlstatt:

> I liked it better [than Wahlstatt]. I did not feel so isolated from the world, and began to live as a human being … (But) my experience there reminded me too much of the Corps of Cadets, and consequently my reminiscences are not agreeable.
>
> My happiest memories of Lichterfelde are those of great sports when my opponent was Prince Friedrich Karl. The Prince gained many first prizes against me in running and so forth, as I had not trained as carefully as he had done.

Here von Richthofen's mention of Karl is revealing. His full title was Prince Tassilo Wilhelm Humbert Leopold Friedrich Karl of Prussia and he was born on 6 April 1893. From early in life he shone as an all-round sportsman, competing in football, tennis and athletics and even participated in British tennis tournaments under the pseudonym F. Karl. Being a talented rider, he was selected to be part of the German men's equestrian team at the 1912 Olympics in

Stockholm and won a bronze medal for show jumping. So it is little wonder that Manfred should have looked up to him and, perhaps, sought to emulate his achievements, even hoping to become an Olympian himself. As chance would have it, they would meet again much later when both were fighter pilots, by which time Manfred's deeds had easily exceeded those of his nemesis in sport.

In many ways, passing through a difficult phase in your life can be made easier by a bond of friendship, better still if these friends are of like mind and background. If so, Manfred was lucky to have met Hans von Schweinichen, with whom he passed through Wahlstatt and Lichterfelde. So close was their friendship that Kunigunde would later write that:

> He had been Manfred's best friend since the Cadet Corps. At their confirmation they knelt together in front of the altar. We parents sat together at this ceremony. The two of them remained inseparable at Lichterfelde and the Sunday holidays were mostly spent together – in this friendship there was no disagreement or discord, it would last forever.

Manfred recorded little about his time at the Academy, but from what he wrote it seems safe to assume that he wasn't particularly happy there and was relieved to leave in 1911. Nevertheless, Lichterfelde helped shape him in ways that may have not been apparent to him at the time, though would become so later on. As a shy, introverted person he didn't immerse himself in the social life of the college, as many fellow students did, and didn't give in willingly to the strong discipline that was imposed, but he does seem to have recognised the benefits of applying himself more fully to his studies. As a result, he was reported to have worked harder, though not enough so to see him through his last crucial ensign's examination, in which he fell short. Aware of Manfred's limited academic skills, this probably came as no surprise to Albrecht and Kunigunde, but his long-suffering parents may have wondered what to do next. Exam failure did not preclude him from beginning his service career with a suitable regiment, but he could only transfer to one as a non-commissioned officer until he could pass his exams and qualify for a commission.

The one compensation for any unhappiness he felt at being at Wahlstatt and then the Academy was the time he was able to spend at home on leave. Here he could allow family life and horse riding to fill his days and revel in the freedom these pursuits offered him. And it was here that a passion for hunting continued to grow. Even as a child he had demonstrated his ability with a gun and by the time he was a teenager had become an expert shot, taking down any bird on the wing with an instinctive knowledge of deflection shooting. It was a skill that would be key to his success as a fighter pilot.

In many ways the country life suited him far better than soldiering. If he could have become a landed 'squire' running an estate, where his natural talents could have flourished, he might have found a more rewarding career. But this wasn't to be and a military life beckoned with its many fateful implications for the young men of his generation.

So, the search for a suitable regiment began. Inevitably for someone of his caste this meant the cavalry, even though some far-sighted individuals had by then realised that future wars would be dominated by artillery and the machine gun, not gallant cavalry charges. Nevertheless, hidebound traditionalists in Germany, Britain and France remained firmly wedded to this concept and failed to appreciate that the nature of war was changing. It proved to be a lethal and wasteful error, but in the heady days of these pre-war years being a member of a famous cavalry regiment was still glamorous and attracted great kudos.

Whether through family influence or the recommendation of his instructors at the Military Academy isn't clear, but he received a posting to a Uhlan (light cavalry) regiment as a sergeant in 1911. Disappointment at being left behind by his comrades, and losing a year's seniority in the process, seems to have stung him into action. So, when he sat the ensign's exam again, after a further period of study at the Military Academy, he achieved the pass mark and could be commissioned. His sense of relief was still palpable when writing in 1917:

> Of course I was very impatient to get into the Army. Immediately after passing my examination I came forward and was placed in the 1st Regiment (Emperor Alexander III) of Uhlans (at Easter 1911). I had selected that regiment. It was garrisoned in my beloved Silesia and I had some acquaintances and relations who advised me to join.
>
> (Autumn of 1912) At last I was given my epaulettes. It was the most glorious feeling; the finest I have ever experienced.

Although on active service with the Uhlans, life in such a regiment in peacetime was more akin to being a member of a gentlemen's club. There would have been parades and occasional military manoeuvres to rehearse, but this left a lot of time to enjoy life in the mess, riding and hunting. So it is hardly surprising that when recalling this period of his life Manfred chose to write about this other side of military service:

> My father brought me a beautiful mare called Santuzza. She was a marvellous animal, as hard as nails. She kept her place in a parade like a lamb. In the course of time I discovered that she possessed a great talent for jumping, and I made up my mind to train her. She jumped incredible heights ... In this venture I received much support and co-operation from my comrade von Wedel, who had won many a prize with his charger Fandango.
>
> We two trained our horses for a jumping competition, then a steeplechase at Breslau. Fandango did gloriously. By

taking a great deal of trouble with Santuzza I hoped to achieve something. However, on the day before she was due to compete I wanted to jump all the obstacles on our training ground once more. In doing so we slipped. Santuzza hurt her shoulder and I broke my collar bone.

I also had a good charger. The unfortunate animal had to do everything, racing, steeplechasing, jumping and Army service. There was nothing that the poor beast had not learned. His name was Blume and we had some real successes. The last prize I received riding that horse was when I rode for the Kaiser Prize in 1913. I was the only one who went over the entire course without making a single mistake. In so doing, I had an experience which I shouldn't wish to repeat. In galloping over a piece of heath land I suddenly stood on my head when the horse stepped into a rabbit hole. When falling, I broke my collar bone (again). Despite this fracture, I rode on for another 40 miles without making a mistake and arrived keeping time.

This must have been an ideal time for von Richthofen. His duties wouldn't have been too onerous, he finally had officer status, was free to enjoy countryside pursuits whenever he could and was living close to home, with all the benefits that this offered. And after attending a massive military parade in Berlin during late 1913, his life must have seemed set fair for a bright future. Yet in the background the pressures that had been building in Europe for many years were about to explode into a war of unimaginable violence. Only time would tell how Manfred would respond to this, but at least his personality and his physical accomplishments seemed to have fitted him well for such a life.

He was a keen and skilful horseman and a first-rate shot, although only proven against targets that could not shoot back. He had learnt the benefits of order, discipline and obedience, but, in doing so never lost the ability to think for himself or challenge authority when he thought it was wrong. It was also undeniable that he had a store of resilience and strength of character to help him survive life in the army and in combat, if it became necessary.

Perhaps the most revealing picture of Manfred's character at this time comes from his mother when describing his preparations for war in the summer of 1914. She wrote:

> Seven hundred marks arrived from Manfred. I shall save it for him. He leaves no debts behind him – so he writes – but he still had something saved up. That is totally his way. All his affairs are always in such a condition that he can account of every hour. He is always clear, orderly and prepared.

For Kunigunde, grown used to the worry of living with a husband who 'understood little about practical life and even less about money', these were greatly valued qualities indeed. But she was an astute woman who saw much more than this in her eldest son and he had, slowly but surely, become her confidant on many matters and a rock to which she could cling in difficult times. Later on she would write:

> Boyish frolics always occur around Manfred, he is so refreshing, but it does not define his character, something else prevails in him – mainly zest for action, paired with an iron will and unswerving purpose. I intentionally say 'purpose', because I believe that he always had a strongly defined aim in mind, which he would attain, and do so in whatever field he wished to follow. Frantic daredevilry was by no means Manfred's way. His way of living was first balance – then risk. He would correctly assess a situation, make a plan in his clear mind, then allow nothing else to confuse him … He could make lightning-fast decisions, and always knew what he wanted to do. In spite of his youth, I liked to discuss matters with him, as one would usually do with the head of the family.

Manfred saw things amazingly clearly. He always gave correct advice with perfect equanimity, which scarcely seemed to fit his age. It was wonderful to talk something over with him. When one heard his opinion, one could calmly handle the matter. Manfred was always right – that was also Lothar's irrevocable view too. He loved Manfred more than himself … he would have sacrificed his life for his brother's without hesitation … Lothar had a contempt for death. He was of unprecedented courage. In this respect, he stood not one step behind Manfred.

There is no doubt that Manfred inspired the love and loyalty of his family, but as a fighter pilot, then as a commander, could he do the same with men, under severe stress, in need of strong and inspiring leadership? Only time would tell, but the signs were there that after many difficult years of education he had the character, physical strength and skills to do so.

Chapter 2

The Lamps Go Out

Even an historian as well informed as A.J.P. Taylor found it difficult to explain the causes of the Great War. After many decades of thought he came to this far-seeing, but unsatisfactory conclusion:

> Each country fought ostensibly to defend itself, yet sought also to conquer and to make great gains. The statesmen were overwhelmed by the magnitude of events. The generals were overwhelmed also. Mass, they believed, was the secret of victory. The mass they evoked was beyond their control. All fumbled more or less helplessly. They were pilots without a chart, blown before the storm and not knowing where to seek harbour.
>
> There was tension of course, when five Great Powers face each other in unbridled national sovereignty. This tension (in 1914) was no greater than in previous years, rather it was less. Germany and Britain were on more friendly terms, their naval rivalry dwarfed by agreement on the Baghdad railway and a future partition of the Portuguese colonies. France too, was moving towards friendship with Germany. In April 1914, a general election in France had returned a pacifist majority of Radicals and Socialists. The German industrialists did not want war. They were convinced with good reason, that Germany would soon become the leading Power in Europe from sheer economic strength ... Good judges guessed that the future pattern would be an alliance of the three Western European Powers – France, Germany and Britain – against

the Russian colossus. Everything was running in Germany's favour. Why spoil it by war?

Why indeed? The madness of it all is only too apparent to us today, but it happened nonetheless, soon wasting the lives of millions of young men along the way. And yet when war came it was greeted with widespread celebration. Such sentiments, which were given wide press coverage in all the warring nations, appeared deeply felt. But to sustain this effort beyond initial enthusiasm, a provoking language of animosity and self-righteousness soon flowed into the vocabulary. And with this, propaganda entered a new, very dangerous phase. Gradually descriptions of enemy actions and behaviour became more enflamed and if there was some truth in the accusations being bandied about then the substance was soon lost in exaggeration and fiction.

When the Archduke Ferdinand of Austria was assassinated in June 1914, and political dominoes began to fall, Germany struck first, to avoid a prolonged war on two fronts, setting in motion a strict, seemingly irreversible, long-planned timetable for war. And with its army sweeping through Belgium and France, the Kaiser and his generals quickly forfeited the moral high ground and were judged aggressors.

With stories of murdered civilians, rape, ill-treatment of refugees and many more horrors, real or imagined, soon filling many column inches, the German cause quickly lost support. As the war progressed things only grew worse as Germany sought to force a decision using increasingly brutal methods before their reserves ran out – poison gas, unrestricted submarine warfare and the targeting of civilians being the worst. For a country that had prided itself on being civilised and cultured such methods were abhorrent and, ultimately, self-defeating. On one level it created the image of the German 'Ghastly Hun', which the Allies then exploited to the full. On another level, it ensured that Germany could expect harsh treatment if and when defeated.

To counter the effect of so much bad publicity, Germany's leaders had few options to explore in a bid to turn international opinion in their favour. In fact, the damage was probably irrevocable and all they could do, with any real chance of success, was try and keep their own people committed to the fight as casualties mounted and opposition to the war grew. It was here that the cult of the hero played an increasingly important part.

In his autobiography Manfred hints at some of the muddle and disorder that existed in the summer of 1914, before war was finally declared and his regiment was guarding Germany's eastern border near Ostrovo, on the Prosno River:

> For several months all were accustomed to war talk. We had so often packed our service trunks that the whole thing had become tedious. No one believed any longer that there would be war. We who were close to the frontier believed least that there would be a war.
>
> On the day before military operations began we were sitting in the Officers' Club eating oysters, drinking champagne and gambling a little. We were very merry. No one thought of war … Suddenly the door opened. It was Count Kospoth, the administrator. He looked like a ghost and had come to the frontier to convince himself that the rumours of an impending war were true … We learned from him that all the bridges in Silesia were being guarded by the military and that steps were being taken to fortify various positions.
>
> We soon convinced him that the possibility of war was absolutely nil and continued with our festivities. On the next day we were ordered to take to the field.

Without a clear picture of what was happening, and while the German Army pushed toward the west, those stationed in the east, to guard against any invasion by the Russian Army, watched and waited. This meant sending out scouting patrols to establish the enemy's strength, a task that clearly appealed to Manfred:

> Every one of us knew to the smallest detail what to do, and what to leave undone. At the same time, nobody had a very clear idea what the first thing should be.
>
> We young cavalry lieutenants had the most interesting time. We were to study the ground, to work forwards to the enemy and destroy any important targets.
>
> Having my orders, I rode at the head of my men for the first time against the enemy at midnight. A river marked the frontier and I expected to be fired upon when reaching it. To my astonishment I passed over the bridge without incident. During the next morning we reached the church in the village of Kieltze, which was well known to us through our frontier rides, without having had any adventures and without seeing anything of the enemy.
>
> The question was now, 'what should I do in order not to be noticed by the villagers?'. My first thought was to lock up the 'pope' (the local Catholic priest). So we fetched him from his house, much to his surprise and locked him in the church tower and took away the ladder. I promised him he would be executed if the population should show any hostile intentions. A guard was placed on the tower to observe the neighbourhood.
>
> Up to the fifth night everything was quiet. Then the lookout came rushing to the church calling 'the Cossacks are here!' The night was as dark as pitch and it was raining a little. As a precaution we had pulled down the wall around the churchyard and through this breach we led the horses, the darkness being so great we were perfectly safe as we advanced fifty yards. I went forward with the lookout to the place where we believed he had seen the Cossacks.

When I got there I felt a strange feeling, for the street swarmed with Cossacks. Most had lanterns and were acting incautiously and were very noisy. I estimated that they were 20 to 30 in number. One had left his horse and gone to find the priest, who I had let out the day before. It quickly flashed through my mind that we were betrayed! So we had to be doubly careful. We could not risk a fight, because of our small number. After a few hours our visitors rode away again.

Next day I thought it wise to change our quarters and, on the seventh day I returned to my garrison where everyone stared at me as if I was a ghost. This wasn't due to my unshaved face, but because of a rumour that Wedel and I had fallen at Kalisch. The place, the time and all the circumstances of my death had been reported with such a wealth of detail that the account had spread throughout Silesia. My mother had already received visits of condolence.

With the vast distances involved, coupled to the slow pace of the Russian war machine in assembling a large enough force to do the Germans serious damage, the Eastern Front remained a backwater for a time. It wouldn't last, but while it did the war in the west might, it was hoped by the German High Command, be fought to a successful conclusion. However, the French, now aided by the British, were proving a tough nut to crack. Although the Germans made rapid progress, there was sufficient Allied resistance to make the campaign increasingly difficult and costly. Losses rose and those who survived would soon grow weary. Inevitably, the rapid victory that German strategy had dictated grew ever more elusive. To maintain pressure reserves were needed and these could only be found from conscripts still being called up or regular troops from the east. Within days Manfred's Uhlans were transferred to the fast-moving and still mobile Western Front, leaving, it seems, only three active corps and three reserve divisions to face the Russians until reinforcements became available:

> We travelled night and day, first through Silesia and then Saxony. Apparently we were going in the direction of Metz. At every station there were huge crowds of men and women who bombarded us with cheers and flowers. The nation had been seized by a wild enthusiasm for the war. The Uhlans were particularly admired ... We were very wild and happy until we disembarked at Busendorf, near Diedenhofen ... The heat was so great that our horses almost collapsed. On the next day we marched northwards in the direction of Luxemburg and through Esch then approached the first fortified towns of Belgium [taken some days earlier].
>
> We marched and marched, sending patrols far ahead, until we arrived at Arlon. I had a funny feeling when crossing an enemy frontier for a second time. Obscure reports of franc tireurs etc had already come to my ears ... Later on I heard that the inhabitants had behaved treacherously several days previously towards our cavalry, and later on to our ambulances. (As a result) it had been necessary to place quite a number of these men 'against the wall'.

Manfred's attitude to these deaths is an interesting one, although it has to be said that there is no evidence that he was personally involved in these killings. My country right or wrong is a dubious concept at the best of times, more so when it includes killing civilians in a country where German forces had no right to be – morally or legally. In reality these were callous murders and yet the young Uhlan seems to have thought them necessary, even warranted acts. Clearly they weren't and one is left to ponder the way propaganda had shaped and distorted his attitudes and those of his comrades.

The extent of the brutality shown to the civilian populations of Belgium and France by the German Army was shameful and rightly drew widespread condemnation. Very early in the war hundreds of civilians were killed in this way. By then the raison d'être behind this cruelty was becoming only too clear, with massacres occurring where the invading army suffered setbacks. Victims were disingenuously accused of being franc-tireurs or 'civilian snipers', with most Germans believing this to be true, due to wholly misleading press reports. Yet many of those killed were women, children and old men who were unlikely to have been anything but innocent victims. The massacres also went hand in hand with a strategy designed to show civilians how helpless and vulnerable they were. To make matters worse, people were made to cheer the troops and witness local dignitaries being publicly abused and, in some cases, killed.

The German advance got under way on 18 August and soon crossed into Belgium, with the first ten days seeing the worst violence meted out to non-combatants. The troops, exhausted by long forced marches and often under the influence of alcohol, committed a series of massacres, burning and pillaging towns and villages on the way, then deporting any survivors. The hardest-hit places were Aarschot on 19 August, then the small industrial town of Tamines on the Meuse, where 383 inhabitants were killed. Dinant came next on 23 August, leaving 674 people, or one tenth of the population, dead. This level of barbarity then engulfed the university town of Louvain, where the historic library was burned down and 248 civilians killed. Further south, hundreds of people were executed in the Belgian Ardennes and the killing went on with, among other murderous acts, sixty people killed in Gerbéviller on 24 August.

As the German armies moved further into France, the violence began to diminish, although there were occasional flare-ups. In September dozens of civilians were killed in East Flanders as the invading troops clashed with the Belgian Army. Weeks later, the German attack on the French and Belgian defenders at Diksmuide in West Flanders led to mass killings with, on 19–21 October, 161 civilians being shot plus some other brave souls killed when they rushed to act as human shields for their loved ones.

When mobile warfare came to an end, with invaded territories in Belgium and northern France under a more organised military occupation, the massacre of civilians appears to have ended, although the persecution of local people continued, in one form or other, until the end of the war. But the cost of German brutality during 1914 had been a heavy one indeed with 906 victims reported dead in France and 5,521 in Belgium. So, it is little wonder that Allied propaganda coined words and phrases that vilified the Germany soldiers in the years that followed.

With the main thrust of the invasion now well into France, von Richthofen and his men found themselves on the left wing of the assaulting force. From Arlon they advanced south-west to Virton hoping to make contact with the enemy and scouting ahead to find out where they were. With battlefield communications barely advanced since the Franco-Prussian War, fresh intelligence about enemy dispositions and movements was meagre to say the least. To help them each side could boast a few fragile aircraft to observe troop movements, but the means of communicating this information to those on the ground were crude to say the least and left much to chance. So novel was this arm of the service that von Richthofen later wrote that:

> I had no idea about the activity of our flying men. At any rate, I got tremendously excited whenever I saw an aviator. Of course, I had not the slightest idea whether it was a German or enemy airman ... The consequence was that every aeroplane we saw we fired upon.

Such a reaction is not surprising as very few people had seen an aeroplane in action before 1914. This would soon change as aircraft designers, under the impetus of war, built machines of ever greater complexity to observe the enemy and be able to strike them with an increasing array of weapons. With the war becoming gradually embedded in trenches, from the Belgium coast to the Swiss border, the aircraft's role, though still in its infancy, was beginning to become a crucial part of life on the battlefield. As the conflict became static and siege-like in nature, it is hardly surprising that von Richthofen looked skywards as a worthier place to fight his war. For the moment, though, he remained earthbound as the Kaiser's army sought to force a decision in the west and in a forest near Virton he found an enemy who could fight back with skill and determination.

> We approached the edge of the forest … The soil indicated that a short time ago considerable numbers of hostile cavalry must have passed by … We followed this trail at a rapid trot for an hour. As we approached the exit I felt certain that there we would meet the enemy. Therefore, caution! To the right of our narrow path lay a steep rocky rise many yards high. To the left, a narrow stream and on its far side a meadow 50 yards wide, surrounded by barbed wire. Suddenly all trace of horses' hoofs disappeared over a bridge into the bushes. My leading men pulled up when our exit from the forest was found blocked by a barricade.
>
> Immediately I realised that I had fallen into a trap. I saw movement among the bushes behind the meadow and noticed dismounted enemy cavalry. I estimated that they were about 100 in number. Nothing was to be done except go back … a second later we heard the first shot, which was followed by intensive rifle fire from the woods. I had told my men to join me immediately when they saw me raising my hand and beckoned them to follow. Possibly they misunderstood my signal. The horsemen who were following me believed I was in danger and came rushing forward at great speed to help me escape. As we were on a narrow path one can imagine the

confusion that ensued. The two men ahead rushed forward in a panic ... the last I saw of them they were leaping the barricade and were no doubt taken prisoner.

I myself turned my horse round and gave him the spurs, probably for the first time in his life. I had the greatest difficulty making the Uhlans rushing towards me understand that they must not advance any further, but turn back and get away. My orderly was at my side. Suddenly his horse was hit and fell [leaving the man trapped underneath]. I jumped over them, while horses were rolling all around me. There was a chaotic muddle ...

I was delighted when, two days later, I saw my orderly standing before me ... he could tell me little about the fate of our comrades who had been left behind.

For most people their first time under fire is a terrifying experience. Our instincts dictate a fight or flight reaction that can be hard to control no matter how resilient the person. The seasoned combatant falls back on all they have rehearsed in training and in previous battles. So, they react more quickly, regroup when necessary and fight back in carefully measured steps. The inexperienced tend to panic and take to their heels and this is what von Richthofen did, seemingly leaving his men to their fate. However, his reaction was both a natural and understandable one, and his retelling of the story very frank and without an attempt to save face. It was a mistake he would not repeat on the ground or in the air.

For the moment though, his war was a microcosm of a conflict on a scale that still beggar's belief. With millions of men on both sides fighting pitched battles where thousands upon thousands of soldiers perished or were maimed each day, a little skirmish in a forest near Virton was of little consequence. Yet, as the third week of the war passed, the breakthrough and triumph the German High Command thought would be theirs appeared increasingly out of reach.

Speed and surprise are essential in a battle if a quick victory is to be achieved. But in a war where most soldiers had to march long distances, much of it over rough ground, and mobility depended on horse-drawn transport, an attack can soon get bogged down in the face of stiff resistance. After defeats that forced many French, Belgium and British troops to retreat, they regrouped and stood their ground. They still gave way when forced to, but did so grudgingly, having inflicted heavy losses on the enemy. As exhaustion set in the Germans became more desperate and threw ever more men into the battle, but did so in a welter of confusing tactics that offered the defending forces opportunities to exploit and hit back.

Germany's First Army under General Alexander von Kluck, which was to the right of the advance through France, could go either east or west of Paris. However, if von Kluck chose to go east he could be attacked on his flank. If he went to the west he would open up a gap between himself and the Second Army, commanded by General Karl von Bülow, which the Allies might exploit. While he considered these options the German advance wavered and lost momentum. With a strong garrison guarding Paris, von Kluck eventually decided to go east of the city in the hope that he could then encircle the French armies in the field before the troops in Paris, under the command of the city's Military Governor, Joseph Gallieni, could intervene. But the French general, armed with reports from the few aeroplanes operating in the area, saw von Kluck's exposed flank, and proposed striking it when the German had committed himself to an eastwards thrust. Yet in delaying his attack he gave his opposite number a chance to review his strategy and, suspecting a trap, von Kluck turned west again to counter this developing threat, so opening up a huge gap between his and von Bülow's armies.

Such a critical moment in a battle has to be exploited quickly, but the Allied effort lacked co-ordination and did not take full advantage of this unexpected opportunity, perhaps fearing a trap. Nevertheless, with the British Army first piercing the gap between von Bülow and Von Kluck's armies and on their flanks the Paris garrison in good fighting trim, the main French force fought hard and pushed forward. The German High Command, seeing this resistance build, feared defeat, panicked and ordered a general retreat. As a result, and as A.J.P. Taylor's later analysis shows:

> Everywhere the Germans began to roll back. High Allied officers talked of being in Germany within a month, or even three weeks. The Allied advance, in fact, lasted five days. On 14th September the Germans reached the Aisne. They were exhausted, could march no more; they were joined by some fresh troops, released by the fall of Maubeuge. The Germans scratched holes in the ground, set up machine guns. To everyone's amazement, the advancing Allies hesitated, stopped. The campaign was over. One man with a machine gun, protected by mounds of earth, was more powerful than the advancing masses. Trench warfare had begun.
>
> The war of movement ended when men dug themselves in. They could be dislodged only by massive bombardment and accumulation of reserves – a warning which always gave the other side time to bring up reinforcements ... The opposing lines congealed, grew solid. The generals on both sides stared at these lines impotently and without understanding. They went on staring for nearly four years.

While these world-changing events were taking place, Manfred's unit were slowly advancing into France. Having regrouped after their skirmish at Virton, he continued scouting for the enemy before re-joining his regiment, as he later recalled:

> The enemy was retiring and we were following him. Consequently, we could pass the night with reasonable security. Not far from the enemy there was a monastery with large

stables, where the monks were extremely amiable ... We settled down as though on manoeuvres, as if we were in the house of a pleasant host and friend. Though at the same time it should be noted that three days later we hanged several of our hosts to the lanterns because they could not overcome the desire to take a hand in the war. But that evening they were extremely amiable.

In the middle of the night somebody suddenly flung open the door and shouted 'Sir! The French are here!' ... 'How many are there?' 'We have shot two dead, but we cannot say how many more there are, because it is pitch dark.' I heard Leon [his friend and fellow officer] in a sleepy voice say, 'All right. When more arrive call me again.' Half a minute later both of us were asleep again.

As a matter of fact, the French had passed the monastery during the night and our look-outs had fired on them. As it was dark nothing further happened.

With confusion appearing to reign across the battlefield, many men, in small or large groups, were adrift, uncertain where they were and, more importantly, where the enemy might be. Sometimes this could lead to some strange encounters, as von Richthofen soon discovered when seeking to re-join his regiment, his scouting mission at an end:

We rode over the battlefield and discovered, to our surprise, that it was populated not by German soldiers, but with French Red Cross men. Here and there were French soldiers. They looked as surprised at seeing us as we did seeing them. Nobody thought of shooting. We cleared out as quickly as possible, and gradually it dawned on us that our troops, instead of advancing, had retired. Fortunately, the enemy retired at the same time in the opposite direction, otherwise I should now be in captivity ... Late in the afternoon I reached my regiment [apparently having lost 10 men].

A keen sense of disappointment, at retreating then going to ground, would have been unavoidable, but at least, after a few brief moments of glory, Manfred was still alive, remaining on the Western Front as both sides tried to outflank each. Neither could achieve an advantage and within weeks the line of trenches ran from the English Channel to the Swiss border, on the German side guarded by barbed wire with strengthened points containing machine guns, capable of dominating the battlefield and defending captured ground in depth.

In this way they could command the battlefield and make any attempted Allied advance a costly business indeed. There would be some movement back and forth, as each side attacked or counter-attacked, but the cost in human life was terrible and achieved no material benefits until 1918. Little wonder that the troops who suffered death, injury and terrible hardships came to regard the war as an unnecessary sacrifice or, as my late grandfather put it, 'the genocide of a whole generation of young men by those who should have known better'. For a man who spent three years in the trenches this is a view that has to be respected and valued.

So the armies went to ground and by slow degrees Manfred and his Uhlans found themselves entrenched in front of the immensely strong French fortifications at Verdun. Suddenly it was a war where the cavalry had little use for their horses. There was some compensation for this in the award of an Iron Cross (Second Class) for his patrol work early in the war. But with many millions of these medals bestowed during the war it was hardly an event of great significance, beyond showing that you had been in battle and given a good account of yourself.

Perhaps of greater importance was the fact that Manfred had not been found wanting when faced with a determined enemy. No one knows how they will react in these circumstances and are fearful that they might eventually cut and run when facing bullets and cold steel. According to the memories of many survivors, their instinctive response, when under fire for the first time, was to hide and seek safety. Some never overcame these feelings, while others learned to control their instinct for survival, then stand and fight not once but many times over. After a few months in battle, where he might have been killed or wounded on a number of occasions, Manfred had discovered that he too could do this and flourish as a soldier. Nevertheless, it soon became apparent to him that a static war in the trenches was not how he wished to fight, not because he wanted safety but because he craved action.

The other issue he was forced to explore at this time was loss and the grief that follows the death of friends and comrades. For those experiencing combat for the first time this can be a particularly shocking experience, made worse by witnessing these things first-hand. Facing battle together bonds a group of people. It is a union that can make fighting and the horrors of war slightly more tolerable, but it could come at a terrible cost, as my maternal grandfather, Arthur Hillier, a territorial serving with the Post Office Rifles on the Western Front from 1915 to 1918, recalled:

> I was the only one of my original draft who survived in service until the end of the war and this was without all the others who came and went between times. It was a lonely business being a survivor. You had to harden your heart to the sudden death of friends, whose bodies you might have to live with for days if a battle was raging. In the mud and squalor this was bad enough, but during the heat of the summer the stench was overpowering, as were the swarms of flies and the hundreds of rats all feeding on the corpses.
>
> After a while you ceased making friends, to save yourself mostly, and became distant and remote from those around you. This could work up to a point, but you couldn't really escape the horrors for long and your spirit broke. The brave, and those with a strong sense of duty, carried on longer, of

course, but even they would eventually reach their limit and need to be freed of these terrible responsibilities. Sadly, with such terrible losses on both sides this proved very difficult to achieve and many tired men, who should have been at home, died unnecessarily as a result.'

In a letter to his mother on 27 March, Manfred gives a hint of the sense of loss he was beginning to feel:

I have had no news of Lothar for a month [at that moment he was actually lying in a hospital bed in Berlin having been taken seriously ill]. His cavalry division was put into action and has had very heavy casualties. Hugo Freier of the 4th Dragoons was killed. He was a good friend of mine. We were in the same class in the cadet corps since the Sexta. That's always the way, the nicest people are the first to fall and die. 'Weeds never die'. After this remark you may certainly think, well, surely Manfred is immortal then ... So many good people have fallen around me, that only by a miracle have I been spared enemy bullets.

Although still in the early stages of the war, Manfred had seen a great deal of action and was beginning to experience the draining effects this can have on mind and body. Luckily, he hadn't experienced the trauma of a wound and so had yet to realise how this could affect the individual as well. Inevitably much worse lay ahead, and many more friends would die or be maimed, before he would truly understand the meaning of the words 'it was a lonely business being a survivor'.

Manfred was also learning that warfare required broader skills than he possessed. In a letter to his family he referred to his lack of experience: 'If I emerge alive from this war, it will be more by luck than judgement.' Perhaps he was becoming aware that all the classes he'd attended at military school, to which he seems to have paid insufficient attention, were more important than he had first supposed. Life in the trenches, to which he was now unavoidably committed, quickly reminded him that the cavalry was not the be all and end all of military life and this new type of warfare required much more from its officers and men if they were to succeed or simply survive. Nevertheless, he still baulked at trench life and, as winter approached, wrote:

> I am a restless spirit ... At the beginning I was in a spot where nothing happened. Then I became a despatch-bearer ... The fighting men despised me and considered me a 'Base-hog'. I was not really at the base and I wasn't allowed to advance within 1,500 yards of the front trenches. There below ground I had a bomb-proof, heated abode. Now and then I to go forward into the front line, which was a great physical exertion. I had to trudge uphill and downhill, criss-cross through an unending number of trenches and mire-holes until at last arriving at a place where men were firing ... my position seemed to me a very stupid one.
>
> It had not yet become clear to me what it means to dig trenches. Of course, we knew the names of various ditches and holes through the lessons we had received at the War Academy. However, the digging was considered to be the business of the engineers. Other troops were supposed not to take a hand. However, here at Combre, everyone was digging industriously ... It was funny that in many places the French were only five yards away from us. I could hear them speaking and see them smoking cigarettes ... We conversed with them, but also tried to annoy them in many ways, especially with hand grenades ... After these morning visits to the front line the more tedious business began and I had to attend to the telephone again.
>
> In this way I passed several months when one fine day our front became very active. A small attack was planned. I was

delighted, for now at last I should be able to do something more important. But I was to be disappointed! I was given another job [as a staff officer with the 18th Infantry Brigade which kept him out of the action] and had had quite enough.

As a result, Manfred wrote to his commanding officer requesting a transfer to more active duties. He is reputed to have written: 'My dear Excellency, I did not go to war in order to collect cheese and eggs, but for another purpose ...' In his biography he refutes this claim, asserting that this was a rumour spread by 'evil tongues'. True or not, he seems to have made his feelings known to those in authority, but initially found his request rebuffed, although later on they relented and a transfer was approved.

It was at this point that the Air Service is mentioned for the first time by Manfred, although he doesn't explain his reasons for wishing to become an airman. He simply states that, 'eventually they fulfilled my wish. Thus I joined the Flying Service at the end of May 1915.' Such a momentous decision must have come after a period of contemplation and discussion with aviators he may have known. But he provides no clue to the way his thoughts developed. True, he may have seen a few aeroplanes hovering overhead as the battle waxed and waned and wondered about life up there in the clouds. He may even, as my grandfather did, have envied the apparent 'cushiness' of pilots' and observers' lives, returning to base after each operation to a degree of comfort unknown in the trenches. But is this enough to justify such an important change in his life?

On 21 May Manfred returned home on leave to see his mother and discussed his transfer with her. Kunigunde later wrote:

Manfred came to Schweidnitz early in the morning, having telegraphed a few days before. The garden gate was still locked. Suddenly he stood at my bedside laughing. 'How did you get in here, Manfred?' ... 'Over the fence.'

We got up with utmost haste and gathered ourselves together for breakfast. Manfred has grown somewhat broader, looked fresh and energetic. The sun shone, the birds in the Virginia creeper sang in chorus. We went into the garden and sat under the old nut trees. I never tire of listening to Manfred's stories. I mentioned the many victories and that the war must finally be coming to an end. Then Manfred said, 'I don't believe we will win this war.' There stood the sentence, stated plainly and objectively. I didn't believe that I had heard him correctly. And Manfred then added, 'You have no idea how strong the enemy is.' ... 'But we keep on winning!' 'Have you not heard anything about our retreat on the Marne?' ... 'No, we knew nothing at all about that', and Manfred concluded with the words 'At best, it will be a stalemate.'

We then spoke of this and that, exchanged opinions and arguments, his mature, sensible views always surprised me. Then standing still in front of me, Manfred said, unexpectedly that 'I am going to join the fliers.' There was something very fine and joyful in his voice, as he spoke. I understood nothing of it and could imagine little, yet I knew that once he had spoken it was already a fact to him and the choice was irrevocably made. I therefore said nothing against it – we would get used to it, in respect of Manfred and in spite of his youth. After that I listened with greater interest, as he told me about what he knew of this new weapon. As we went from the garden into the house, I felt with certainty that a new and great task had taken root within him.

The key to his choice undoubtedly lay in the tedium of trench life where a squalid, anonymous death could come at any moment of the day or night. For a man imbued with a strong sense of duty, a daredevil attitude to life and the outlook of a cavalryman, life and death in the mud of Flanders would have held little appeal.

Better to be in the open, high in the heavens having some choice in the matter of your fate. His training, a strong moral obligation to Kaiser and country, carefully nurtured since birth, and his own desire to be more involved in the war, all came into play and the fledgling Air Service must have seemed the perfect solution. It also helped that aeroplanes were gradually being used in a scouting and reconnaissance role usually undertaken by the cavalry, which on a static battlefield had become impossible. In such a confined, claustrophobic war a detailed knowledge of enemy movements and intentions was essential. Although restricted by poor weather for much of the year, aircrew could still accomplish more in this way than any troops on the ground.

There may also have been one other reason behind his wish to become an aviator. Manfred appears to have been a career-minded, ambitious man. Advancement would have been important to him, as would the collection of awards and decorations – their kudos would not have been lost on him. In November 1914, for example, he wrote that, 'I would have liked to have earned the Iron Cross First Class, but have had no opportunity to do so.' And later on, in another letter, he added, 'I am trying hard to win the Iron Cross. Unfortunately, we Uhlans have been attached to the infantry. I write unfortunately because I feel certain that Lothar has already been in big cavalry charges such as we shall never ride in here.' Although very close to his brother, he seems to have been concerned that Lothar would soon acquire more decorations before he had the opportunity to do likewise. This sense of competition would have acted as a spur to action and the Air Service seemed to offer him the opportunity he sought for glory.

By 1915 aviation had moved on apace. It wasn't a war-winning weapon yet, but it had the potential, if used correctly, to influence events on the ground. Aerial observation was in its infancy, with few yet fully aware of the advantages it offered by comparison to observers in baskets slung beneath tethered balloons or men on the ground. If left unmolested these aircraft were free to wander over the lines, gathering much more information in the process. They could also, if equipped with transmitters, direct gunfire accurately onto targets. With this strategic role developing, these eyes in the sky were making movement on the battlefield in daylight increasingly difficult, so making it necessary for these activities to be carried out under the cover of darkness. Day was turning into night, with all the inconveniences this change would cause – delays in moving supplies and men forward, confusion because no light could be shown when this was happening and the need to muffle the sounds that seemed to travel so much further in darkness, betraying any movement on the ground. Small wonder then that the role of the aircraft was growing more important and measures to counter its growing influence were continually being developed.

Although offering huge tactical advantages, aeroplanes were also something that captured the public's imagination. It had been this way since the Wright Brothers took their first flight at Kitty Hawk on 17 December 1903. In the intervening years it was a fascination that grew and grew, with journalists, newsreel editors and advertisers making full use of its potential to draw a crowd or sell a product. With pilots only numbering in their hundreds by 1914, these people became the object of hero worship and much else besides. With the coming of war, and the added frisson of danger it offered, this appeal became an important propaganda tool to be exploited whenever the opportunity arose.

Highly publicised endurance flights and air races became the peacetime diet for these enthusiasts. Louis Blériot's cross-Channel escapade of July 1909 was a high spot to be enjoyed by many, but he was just one of a growing number of aviation celebrities. Some of these pilots, such as Hubert Latham, Karl Jatho, Charles de Lambert, John Seymour, John Moisant, Roland Garros and Samuel Cody, came and went quite quickly. Tommy Sopwith, Harry Hawker, Geoffrey de Havilland, Glenn Curtis and Anthony Fokker lasted much longer, having successfully made the transition from pilot to aircraft designer and constructor.

While fixed-wing flying machines were the order of the day in most industrialised countries at this time, aviation in Germany had tended to be dominated by Count Ferdinand von Zeppelin and his dirigibles. When his first airship, LZ1, took its first flight in July 1900, it quickly attracted much attention and in the years before the Great War more and more appeared, with some being acquired by the army. In some ways this success acted as a distraction to those prepared to invest or develop in other types of aircraft, so in these early years Germany tended to lag behind France, Britain and the United States. It wasn't until 1909 that this began to change with the help of August Euler, then in his thirties.

Initially Euler was fascinated by motorbikes and cars, before becoming interested in aviation. As a keen entrepreneur he set up a company to build Voisin aircraft under licence in Germany and during 1908 began production. In December 1909, he was awarded German Pilot's brevet No. 1 and soon began operating a flying school to encourage others to take up the 'sport'. In 1910 he set a German flying record by staying airborne for three hours six minutes and eighteen seconds, which drew much-needed attention to this industry. Nevertheless, Germany's military leaders appeared to show little or no interest in aeroplanes, preferring to increase the number of Zeppelins it possessed instead.

In 1911 the rate of change in Germany increased when a military aircraft competition was held in France to choose the best designs for use by the French Army. All this was observed by more enlightened souls in the German Army, who realised how far their own air arm was lagging behind. Although much scepticism remained among traditionalists in senior circles, an advance was made nonetheless and Germany's slowly developing aero industry came to life. Soon the number of flying schools increased and the Albatros and Aviatik companies began to expand their works, with Daimler and Mercedes investing more heavily in new engine designs. But still the sceptics sought to slow this progress and it was hoped that a series of war games in 1913 would allow aviators to show what aircraft had to offer.

Sadly, they failed to impress the watching VIPs, a situation made worse when reconnaissance aircraft failed to discover two divisions they were sent out to track. With Germany's industrial might and many clever design engineers available, a nod from the army and greater funding at this stage could have seen Germany steal a march on their competitors and enter the war possibly enjoying a clear advantage over their enemies. As it was they were no better or worse than their opposite numbers in Britain and France. Despite this, when war broke out, the German Air Service could boast forty-nine flying sections of six aeroplanes each, plus eighteen training units, making a total strength of 296 machines, although only 218 of these were deemed fit enough for war service. France was slightly better placed in terms of numbers, while the British could muster 272, though at least half of these were thought incapable of even crossing the Channel to reach the battlefield, let alone fly in combat.

One of the problems created by this laissez-faire attitude was the lack of clarity over what aircraft could and should be able to do. At this stage reconnaissance was their primary purpose, but little thought appears to have been given to the way aircraft should evolve to allow the aircrew to fulfil this duty more effectively. And even less thought seems to have been given to the specialist training men needed to undertake this work, beyond the attainment of basic flying skills. Added to this, and as befits a Junker society based on caste, the pilot was considered to be the chauffeur, more often than not, a non-commissioned officer, while the observer had officer status.

In all this, the point that seems to have escaped many commanders was that aviation required new tactics and new skills. No longer could the established ways of running an army apply. The sky was a new place to fight, being three-dimensional in nature, whereas ground troops operated in a two-dimensional world. To put it simply, there was a clear difference between the limited horizontal scanning applied by scouting cavalrymen and the all-encompassing vertical panoramas seen by airman. This poor appreciation of the problems involved and possible solutions meant that both aircraft and men were poorly prepared for what lay ahead.

When war broke out the few aircraft available to the German Army were basically cobbled together solutions not purpose-built for the task. Some were biplanes and some, like the Igo Etrich-designed Taube, were monoplanes, but each had their own limitations. Invariably the pilot sat behind the observer, where the general view was greatly restricted by the position of wings, struts and wires, and they were unable to operate in poor weather. On the Eastern and Western Fronts, where the weather was so variable, this proved to be a significant dis-advantage. Their operational ceilings were also low, which made them vulnerable to enemy gunfire. So it was, perhaps, unsurprising that senior commanders, including General Erich Ludendorff, paid aviation little attention and even, it is reported, held it in contempt. But things did begin to change as the war progressed, helped in part by the arrival of better aircraft and better-trained men.

As the science evolved, so did tactics. Early in the war airmen on both sides tended to leave each other alone as they went about their business. For the most part they lacked the weapons to do otherwise, but, as the role of reconnaissance aircraft became more crucial in such a static war, matters began to change. It was obvious that too much was being observed by these overhead snoopers and common sense dictated that they be deflected from their task. At first pilots and observers went armed with rifles and pistols, but met with little success, and then machine guns began to be fitted and casualties increased on both sides, but not sufficient to deter the enemy to any great extent.

The solution to this problem seemed to be single-seater fighters armed with machine guns, whose sole purpose was to destroy enemy observation aeroplanes whenever and wherever they found them. However, without a safe and effective method of firing their guns through propellers, so taking full advantage of a fighter's greater speed and manoeuvrability, pilots still found destroying enemy aircraft difficult, though not impossible. In doing so there was much experimentation. Guns were fitted in various offset positions to overcome the problem, though there was always a danger of them hitting their own wings. And some designers tried the 'pusher' configuration, with the engine positioned behind the pilot, and achieved some success this way. But despite this straight-ahead shooting, through the propeller, was still believed to be best way of hitting an enemy.

Oddly enough, the Swiss-born engineer Franz Schneider, who served his apprenticeship with the Nieuport company in France before moving to the Luft-Verkehrs-Gesellschaft (LVG) in 1912, had come up with a solution – an interrupter gear linked to a fixed, forward-firing machine gun. In addition, he also found a way of mounting a gun so that it could fire through the hollow shaft of a revolving airscrew. These inventions and much more were patented, but for reasons that aren't entirely clear, were ignored by Germany's military leaders. Perhaps if he had fitted an aircraft with his interrupter gear and demonstrated its potential things might have been different, but the idea seems to have lain dormant and ignored.

The French airman, Eugene Roland Garros, tried a different approach. Having become an important figure in aviation in the years before the war, he took all his accumulated knowledge of long-distance flying into the French Air Force. It seems that he was initially posted to Escadrille No. 23 flying Morane-Saulnier aircraft before transferring to Escadrille No. 26. With an ever-growing awareness of the need to destroy enemy observation aircraft, Garros soon attempted to shoot them down with handheld weapons. Having achieved little or no success, he turned to the aircraft designer

Raymond Saulnier for advice and visited him at his works late in November 1914 to discuss the problem.

By this stage, like Franz Schneider at LVG, Saulnier had designed and patented a form of interrupter gear, but this had yet to be tested successfully, so at that moment in time it was of little immediate help to Garros. So he sought an alternative and with the help of his mechanic, Jules Hue, began to develop another solution. In this case they decided to fit protective wedges to a slightly narrowed propeller blade to deflect the occasional round that might otherwise have shot through and destroyed the propeller. This they fitted to a Morane-Saulnier parasol monoplane and began operations. Success didn't elude him for long and on 1 April 1915 he claimed his first 'victories' when shooting down two Albatros two-seater observation aircraft north of Buc and south-west of Paris, and at least two more enemy aircraft later in the month.

The Germans were quick to note all this and wonder what might have been happening to their aircraft. However, fortune soon favoured them when, on 18 April, Garros' aircraft was forced down behind enemy lines. Quickly overcome by German soldiers, he was unable to set fire to the Morane before being captured, allowing it to be salvaged intact and for its secrets to be revealed. Very quickly the crude but functional method of firing through the propeller was evaluated to see if it might be adapted for use on German aircraft.

Anthony Fokker, a Dutch national, who trained as a pilot in Germany during 1911 and then went on to establish a training and aircraft manufacturing business at Schwerin, to the east of Hamburg, became actively involved in this issue. Despite being in breach of his country's neutrality, he'd begun, by 1914, to make a profitable living by building and selling aircraft to the German Army. He was, according to some accounts, a very astute businessman who knew how to wine, dine and flatter officials in the hope of encouraging trade. So it was perhaps unsurprising that by 1915 his status had grown considerably and new orders for aircraft were gradually forthcoming. This enabled him to expand the works at Schwerin and take on many additional workers. As a coming man he found that he could begin to wield some influence, so it is not surprising that army officials chose to seek Fokker's advice on the question of machine guns firing through propellers when Garros' 'secret' had been revealed.

By this stage of the conflict the German Air Force was being reorganised to make it more effective in waging war. Before then, rather like the Royal Flying Corps in Britain, its efforts had been poorly co-ordinated, even amateurish. As the role of aircraft began to be appreciated, and their numbers increased, Colonel von Eberhardt, on behalf of the army's commanders, recommended that a Feldflugchef be appointed to make the service more effective. In March 1915 Major Hermann von der Lieth-Thomsen was appointed to this post and took over the army's Inspectorate of Aviation (Idflieg) in the process.

Lieth-Thomsen was born on 10 March 1867 in Flensburg, of Danish extraction, and was commissioned into the Prussian Army during 1888. Here he became a Pioneer Officer due to his knowledge of engineering. Nine years later, having firmly established his reputation, he was transferred to the Engineer and Fortress Department of the General Staff, one of the Prussian military agencies that kept a watching brief on military aviation. In January 1908, the German General Staff created a technical section to follow foreign and domestic developments in aviation, motorised transport and telegraphy and appointed von der Lieth-Thomsen, by then a captain, to lead it. Shortly afterwards his group came under the control of Erich Ludendorff, who headed the army's mobilisation department, which gave it much added weight.

At the beginning of the First World War Lieth-Thomson had already gained experience of aircraft and aviation. Having impressed his superiors with the depth of his knowledge, his appointment to the Supreme Army Command as Feldflugchef came as no surprise, despite his fairly junior rank of major. In due course he became the

Chief of Staff to the Commanding General of the Air Force, Ernst von Hoeppner, and was duly promoted to colonel.

All this was as a result of Ludendorff's growing concern that the Air Service lacked effective command and needed a general officer to wield authority over all the army's ground and air units, in the field and at home. Ludendorff, by then Quartermaster General to von Hindenburg, Chief of the General Staff in 1916, chose Hoeppner to lead the service and, at the same time, changed its name from Fliegertruppe to Luftstreitkräfte. To help him in his mission to improve the service, Hoeppner was given the title of Kommandierender General der Luftstreitkräfte (or Commanding General of the Air Service, otherwise known as Kogenluft), and promoted to lieutenant general. In this role he was directly responsible to both Hindenburg and Ludendorff – two men who became so powerful that they virtually dictated the course of the war at home and abroad. Under them Hoeppner and Lieth-Thomson could do largely as they wished in building up the Air Service and promoting its cause through carefully placed propaganda. For von Richthofen this would, in time, have life-changing consequences.

For the moment, Hoeppner, ably assisted by Major Siegert and Hauptmann Helmuth Foerster, as adjutant, had much to do in simply developing the service, mobilising the aviation industry and directing a very active re-equipment programme. He and his team provided the impetus necessary to make these things happen and very soon the question of aircraft armaments fell on his desk and led him to Fokker, whose work he would already have known.

As luck would have it, Fokker, like Saulnier and Schneider, had been giving the matter some thought before Garros had been brought down. This probably convinced Lieth-Thomson that he was the man to take this work forward. So, this is what Fokker did, completing development of his own form of interrupter gear within days, apparently assisted by Heinrich Luebbe, the watchmaker and engineer. This was then fitted to a Fokker M.5K monoplane, which the Dutchman personally demonstrated to staff officers at Döberitz, to the west of Berlin. Subsequently, he was asked to take this invention to France, where it could be shown to front-line officers. By then LMG.08 machine guns had been similarly fitted to a Fokker E.2/15 and E.3.15 and it was these two aircraft that he took with him to the battlefield for test purposes, with one more added later.

In his autobiography, Fokker recalled these demonstration flights in a most dramatic and, some say, misleading way. By then he was writing for a peacetime audience who might have serious concerns about his wartime activities, which were hardly those of a man coming from a strictly neutral country. Being seen to be pressed into action, but then drawing a line beyond which he refused to go might be seen as a commendable response. However, the reality seems to be that he demonstrated few, if any, scruples while searching for fame and fortune. In his 1929 account he makes much of his 'host's' demand that he demonstrate his aircraft in action over the Western Front. Nothing less would do in convincing them to order the monoplanes. As a result, on seven occasions he went up, clothed in a German uniform, without meeting an enemy aircraft. Then on the eight attempt, when flying in the vicinity of Douai, he came across a French Farman two-seater:

> As the distance between us narrowed, the aircraft grew larger in my sights. My imagination could picture my shots puncturing the gasoline tanks which would catch fire. Even if my bullets failed to kill the pilot and observer, the ship would fall down in flames. I had my finger on the trigger ... I had no personal enmity towards the French. I was flying merely to prove that a certain mechanism I had invented would work. By this time, I was close enough to open fire, and the French airmen were watching me curiously, wondering, no doubt, why I was flying up behind them. In another instant, it would all be over for them.

Suddenly, I decided that the whole job could go to hell. It was too much like 'cold meat' to suit me. I had no stomach for the whole business, nor any wish to kill Frenchmen for Germans. Let them do their own killing!

When landing he reported being confronted by German officials eager to know why he had returned without accomplishing his mission. An argument ensued, but Fokker was unmoved and it was finally agreed that he would train another pilot in the use of the gun and Lt Oswald Boelcke was selected for this task. Shortly afterwards, when Fokker had departed for his works in Schwerin, he was informed that the young German, on his third flight in the Fokker, had brought down an enemy aircraft.

However, other accounts offer a rather a different version of these events. In these it is recorded that, after the successful live firing trials at Döberitz, Lieth-Thomson and his staff simply wanted the Dutchman to show front-line officers what the monoplane could do. On 23 May he began his tour by demonstrating his aircraft to Crown Prince Wilhelm, then commander of 5th Army, at Stenay. Once completed Fokker briefed a number of pilots on the aircraft's capabilities, then allowed them to take one of them up. In this he was assisted by the experienced aviator Lt Otto Parschau, who was already skilled in handling a monoplane. As a result, he was ordered to accompany Fokker during the rest of his tour, so smoothing the path for the Dutchman as he sought to impress front-line pilots and their commanders.

By this stage of the war Parschau, who was born on 11 November 1890 in Klausen, East Prussia, had become an important figure in German aviation. In so doing his career had been shaped carefully to a model that would be used to mould the life and career of von Richthofen in particular.

Parschau was a professional soldier who had been awarded his commission in 1910 when serving with the Infanterie-Regiment Nr.

151. At some point he was attracted to flying and began training as a pilot, receiving his licence on 4 July 1913. When war broke out he soon found himself flying a two-seater observation aircraft over the front line in the Champagne area before serving in Flanders and Alsace-Lorraine. Then, shortly afterwards, he was posted to the Eastern Front, rapidly becoming an expert and respected reconnaissance pilot.

In the early days of the war Parschau had begun flying an unarmed Fokker A.III monoplane on occasions, in his case one privately purchased in 1913 by fellow officer Oberleutnant Waldemar von Buttlar. Due to the parlous state of aviation in the German Army in 1914 this aircraft was requisitioned for military service, by which time it had been painted a distinctive shade of green by von Buttlar. In due course, and as Parschau's name and reputation spread, this aircraft attracted the soubriquet Parschau's 'Green Machine' and received much publicity in the process; another hint of what lay ahead for von Richthofen.

From Stenay, Fokker and Parschau travelled to Douai, seemingly invited by Major F. Stempel, the 6th Army's Air Corps staff officer, to brief some of the pilots operating on that front. Here they conducted a number of demonstration flights, sometimes with another pilot squeezed into the cockpit to aid familiarisation. One of the units involved was Feldflieger Abteilung 62 (FFA 62), commanded by Hauptman H. Kastner. Under his leadership it had grown in experience flying armed two-seaters, its success quickly attracting much attention and press coverage. Among its pilots No. 62 could number Oswald Boelcke and Max Immelmann, both of whom would soon make good use of the new Fokker. But first they, and other selected pilots, had to help prove the monoplane and its gun could be operated successfully by average front-line pilots. This they did and the delivery of the first new machines began in July 1915.

All this leaves one question hanging in the air. Did Fokker fly one of his aircraft in combat or did he leave it to Boelcke to undertake this task, preferring to remain oddly neutral in the matter? In his book *Fokker:*

The Creative Years, A.R. Weyl states that Fokker's story simply 'strains credulity to the limit ... his fanciful account can impress only those who know nothing of the discipline and fanatical pride of officers of the German Flying Corps'. Perhaps, of greater significance is the fact that Boelcke, recently promoted to Oberleutnant, only claimed his first 'victory' on 4 July 1915 when flying a two-seater LVG. It wouldn't be until 19 August that his second success would be achieved, this time flying a new Fokker E1. By this time fellow pilots Lt Kurt Wintgens, of FA-6b (Bavaria), and Immelmann had been credited with downing enemy aircraft – on 15 July and 1 August respectively. This suggests that the story reaching Fokker about Boelcke's success in June was, at best, an exaggeration, in which case his whole account of flying in combat for the Germans is left open to question.

Nevertheless, there is no denying the important part Fokker played in the development of Germany's air arm. And as the years unfolded he continued to exert an ever-growing influence on fighter production and, as an astute businessman, and adept user of propaganda, enveloped von Richthofen, as he became more famous, in his rapidly expanding empire.

For the moment, though, the introduction of these monoplanes soon turned the tables on the Western Front. Allied casualty rates began to soar and reconnaissance operations became increasingly more difficult. The situation became so serious that some aircrew referred to this period as the time of the 'Fokker Scourge'.

For Parschau the next few months marked the beginning of even greater fame, this time as a fighter pilot. In the process he was appointed to FFA 62 as an instructor to teach other pilots the tactics to be employed when flying monoplanes. In the months that followed Parschau carefully shaped the careers of men such as Boelcke and Immelmann while becoming an 'ace' himself, destroying six enemy aircraft between October 1915 and 2 July 1916. The next day he shot down an enemy observation balloon, before transferring to FFA 32, where he gained his eighth victory on 9 July 1916, on the eve of being awarded the Pour le Mérite. But in such a dangerous business the risk of death or injury was a constant companion and on 21 July 1916 Parschau was wounded during a combat with Royal Flying Corps aircraft over Grévillers. Although managing to force land behind German lines, his injuries were so severe that he expired on the operating table. So died a gallant man, one of the first of a growing number who would briefly blaze like shooting stars cross the sky, making a vivid impression before dying in the service of their country.

Ultimately the real success of the monoplane and interrupter gear lay in making Fokker's name, which allowed his company to go from strength to strength. Such was the extent of orders he received that by the end of the war his company had built 3,350 or more aircraft for the German Air Force. Along the way he became a close associate and, occasionally, a friend of the leading fighter pilots, who he sought to influence in one way or another in the pursuit of more business. Von Richthofen, as he became a national hero, inevitably became one of the celebrities that Fokker sought to exploit.

As Manfred made ready to transfer to the Air Service in May 1915 much was happening in the background in Berlin, Schwerin and on the Western Front that would profoundly affect his life. And so, he set off for flying school eager to learn his new trade, uncertain whether he would make the grade or be returned to life and death in the anonymity of the trenches.

Chapter 3

A Pressing Need for Heroes

When Europe went to war many expected that 'it would all be over by Christmas'. Why this was so is now hard to fathom. Perhaps, it was simply hope triumphing over reality – although there was precious little for these hopes to cling to that autumn.

With the main belligerents able to field many millions of men, it was obvious to some that neither side could hope to force a decision, so a stalemate would follow that could only be broken by a negotiated peace. Others saw the financial consequences of rich economies quickly being sucked dry of resources as trade dried up and hoped that reason would triumph before bankruptcy prevailed. But reason was in short supply in 1914 and national pride, carefully manipulated by propaganda, ensured that a mutually destructive war would continue impervious to the realities of life. With the madness of lemmings, the two enemy camps slipped into their trenches, marshalled their machine guns and artillery and then let the slaughter begin.

As they did so, other ways of breaking the stalemate were considered and put into action. The Royal Navy, with its huge dominating fleet, sought to blockade German ports and stifle the supply of food and raw materials to a point at which the enemy starved and its industry could not produce the goods needed to continue the war. The German Navy retaliated by putting more and more U-boats into service hoping to achieve the same aim and starve Britain into submission, though would not risk its High Seas Fleet in the same pursuit until very briefly in 1916.

These tactics had much to commend them, but were essentially part of a long-term strategy that was unlikely to produce results in years, let alone months. And their use, though logical enough, eventually proved counterproductive in so far as the will to continue fighting was concerned. Each side would paint the other as assailants deliberately adopting a way of fighting that targeted the innocents in each land. Nothing was more likely to anger right-minded people and rouse them to greater effort than this.

So, the war ground on, each side borrowing heavily to keep the factories going and their people fed, while ways of breaking the deadlock were sought and practised with varying degrees of failure and success. It was a carefully stimulated madness best summed up with these biting, but perceptive words written during the war, 'God is with us, cried the Germans, God is with us, cried the British, God is with us, cried the French, God is very busy, cried God!' A hell had been created that each side thought had been shaped by the other, so sustaining a vision of outrage, until the losses grew so large as to make hope evaporate and a sense of reality slowly return.

The von Richthofen family reacted to all these things much as people in all the warring nations were expected to do – with stoicism, unquestioning patriotism and an acceptance of the rightness of their country's cause. But for Kunigunde this was coupled with a growing sadness at the loss of so many young men from Manfred and Lothar's circle of friends. These were issues she described very clearly in her memoirs:

> A victory report! And a pleasant one that has swept away at one stroke so many depressions that the war was inflicted on us. U-9 has torpedoed three enemy cruisers ... the jubilation over it is universal. Now we must go forward on all fronts until victory is ours.
>
> East Prussia must endure the devastation of the Russian hordes ... The casualty figures are increasing; already one sees

much black clothing. This is a time that demands great inner fortitude.

Admiral Graf Spee reported a victory over a British Squadron off the coast of Chile. Two English ships were sunk, a third fled ... On 11th the flags sank to half-mast in the grievous knowledge that von Spee's squadron have been annihilated by the English. If the numbers had been equal the outcome would have been otherwise ... The trust in our navy is boundless.

The war has entered a new phase. England's objective, to starve out Germany, gave birth to the U-boat war. The English merchantmen sail under neutral flags. Therefore, a whole area of the sea had to be declared a war zone. The neutrals were allowed 14 days in which to warn their steamers. In the fight over food, it really came down to life or death. The women and children, the elderly and helpless are also dragged into the war.

U-29 is lost – presumably its captain, Otto Weddigen, stopped an armed English ship sailing under a neutral flag and it sent him to the bottom.

1914 – Wolfram von Richthofen is dead, shot by a sniper. Friedel Leutsch has fallen, killed by grenade fragments while on patrol. Walter Kaewel, the son of our Lord Mayor, is dead. Uli Tettenborn has fallen. Siegfried, the 17-year-old son of Herman von Richthofen, has died, shot through the mouth. Graf von Konigsmarck has been killed in enemy territory ... 1915 – Karl-Anselm Prittwitz has fallen. Rochow is said to be dead as are Prince Ratibor and Count Matuschka [from Lothar's regiment then fighting on the Eastern Front] ...

The war aroused many conflicting emotions, each nurtured by carefully placed press reports in which each side continually accused the other of cruelty, duplicity and dishonour. So, while Kunigunde saw the English as responsible for the war of blockade, she remained silent on the torpedoing of the passenger liner RMS *Lusitania* with the death of so many civilians. Then there was the aerial bombing campaign against Britain that began in January 1915 and the first use of poison gas by the German Army in April the same year, with its appalling consequences. All-out war had arrived, and with it truth became a rare commodity in both camps as each side prepared its men, women and children for a long and bitter struggle.

In 1915, with the land war stagnating and casualties mounting, the German people began to look skywards for new heroes to admire and revere. Airship crew became the first of these with their bombing raids on Britain, but losses and a sense that their civilian targets were not honourable one's limited their propaganda value. Then on the Western Front combat between military aircraft began and soon conjured up images of great gallantry. Man pitted against man in a heroic battle for survival in the clear blue sky, conjured up a vision of daring and valour that most found impossible to resist. But in 1915 the power of this propaganda was barely glimpsed, and its exploitation remained muted. This would soon change when the German Army began receiving its Fokker monoplanes with their forward firing machine guns, and putting them into service on the Western Front. There numbers may have been small by comparison to what would follow, but their effect was overwhelming for a time.

While this was happening Manfred began his training as an observer. If he was aware of Fokker's work, and the development of the monoplane, he remained silent. In any case, at this stage he would have been more concerned with his new duties and wondering whether flying was for him, rather than any possibility of becoming a fighter pilot. And in late May he joined Flieger-Ersatz-Abteilung No. 7 based near Cologne, with twenty-nine other candidates, to have his fitness for observer duties evaluated. It was a crucial moment that could so easily have ended his flying career as soon as it started. The early signs were not good, as he later recorded:

The next morning at seven o'clock I was to fly for the first time ... I was naturally very excited, for I had no idea what it would be like. Everyone whom I had asked about his feelings told a different tale. The night before I went to bed earlier than usual to be thoroughly refreshed ... We drove to the airfield and I climbed into an aircraft for the first time. The draught from the propeller was a dreadful nuisance. I found it impossible to make myself understood by the pilot. Everything was carried away by the wind. If I held up a piece of paper it disappeared. My safety helmet slid off. My muffler fell off. My jacket was not sufficiently buttoned up. In short, I felt very uncomfortable and before I knew what was happening, the pilot accelerated away at full speed ... We went faster and faster. I clutched the sides of the cockpit. Suddenly, the shaking was over and the aircraft was in the air and the earth rapidly dropping away from under me.

As the flight continued he gradually began to settle down overcoming his initial bewilderment:

I had been told where we were to fly and I was to direct the pilot... but I lost all sense of direction above our own aerodrome. I had not the slightest idea where I was. I began to look over the side very cautiously at the country ... The houses seemed to have come out from a child's toy box ... Cologne was in the distance, the cathedral looked like a little toy. It was a wonderful feeling to be so high above the earth, to be master of the air. I didn't care a bit where I was, and felt extremely sorry when my pilot thought it was time to descend ... In an aircraft one possesses a feeling of complete security ... At the same time, flying affects one's nerves when racing at full speed through the air, particularly when the aeroplane dips and when the engine stops running and the tremendous noise is followed by an equally tremendous silence ... I counted the hours to my next flight.

Few, if any, did not experience the sense of being lost when flying for the first time. Early familiarisation flights with an experienced pilot soon corrected this in most cases, but for some they never adapted to this new world and were rejected by their instructors. If they continued they would undoubtedly have been a danger to themselves and to others. Von Richthofen doesn't record how many of the thirty trainees in his group failed these initial tests, but there would have been some. And so the weeding out process began in earnest and many more would soon fall by the wayside.

Many accounts written later by successful pilots and observers elude to the 'air blindness' experienced by von Richthofen and that they believed for a time that it could never be overcome. Even when they were qualified and reached a squadron, the problem persisted as Richard Cork, a Second World War naval ace, remembered:

Losing my bearings completely in the air and apart from the River Thames couldn't recognise a great deal even though it was a bright day! It was a feeling that persisted when first flying in combat – everything happened so quickly and enemy aeroplanes seemed to appear from nowhere. I soon 'got my eye in' and things became easier, but there was a great danger for some time that you wouldn't see the enemy that killed you.

Leonard Rochford, a Great War naval ace, in a letter to the author, mirrored these thoughts and took the theme a little further:

All I could do at the beginning was grab anything close to hand and hope for the best. Even though I had carefully thought through all that I might face, nothing had prepared me for the panic and anxiety I felt as we left the ground. All seemed alien and very strange. During my first few flights I was genuinely concerned that I would be 'washed out', but gradually things settled down and I learnt to fly.

Crossing to France and joining a squadron for the first time [in his case No. 3, later becoming 203] soon revealed how little I knew and how little I saw when flying. Suddenly I was being asked to fly in formation, constantly watching the leader, fly safely and search the sky for the enemy at the same time. Like all newcomers all this seemed to be beyond me and so everything happened rapidly and without warning. I was lucky to survive and was genuinely shocked when later in the mess so and so would say 'did you see the two green Albatros the leader attacked or the two seater we shot down'. I hadn't seen them though remembered the rattle of gunfire, which I thought was the others warming up their guns.

Slowly but surely I learnt to scan the sky and see the enemy close to and afar, though would occasionally still be caught out by a high-flying enemy aircraft carefully stalking me. But by then my reactions were much quicker and my tactics for avoiding trouble fairly sound.

Even those who rose to the top as fighter pilots experienced this same sense of panic when flying in combat for the first few times. The Canadian William Avery Bishop, who would later claim seventy-two enemy aircraft shot down, wrote very candidly:

> The way I clung to my companions reminded me of some small child hanging to its mother's skirts while crossing a crowded street. I remember also that I felt like a child when it goes up a dark flight of stairs and sure something is going to reach out of somewhere and grab it. I was so intent on my clinging part that I paid very little attention to anything else.

And things were viewed in a similar way from the other side of the lines, as Hans-Georg von der Osten, who later flew with von Richthofen in Jasta 11, recorded:

> It took me some time to become competent in the air. Good eyesight was essential for both pilots and observers. If you could not see an enemy some way away you were lost. When aloft you had to search the sky constantly, twisting and turning your head until your neck ached. Even then you could find yourself taken by surprise. This is where the great pilots came into their own. They seemed to see everything for many miles all around – above and below, near or far – and act accordingly. And they did so when at the head of a Jasta or a Geschwader with all the attendant needs, both practical and tactical, of the men they led.

There was no easy path to acquiring visual acuity when learning to fly and many failed or quickly became victims to 'unseen' enemies simply because they were slow in losing their air blindness. Looking back, many of those who survived and prospered recorded vision in the air as one of the most important elements in combat flying and concluded it was not a natural state and could only be developed as a pilot slowly grew in experience. As von Richthofen took to the air for the first time he probably doubted, like all trainee aviators, whether he could ever develop the skills necessary for survival let alone become a truly effective flier.

After his initial alarm Manfred appears to have settled into the routine of flying in the sky over Cologne fairly quickly, leading Kunigunde to report that 'he passed his class successfully. Flying is ceasing to be contrary to his nature; already after his first flight he was so inspired that he would have liked best of all to sit in the aeroplane the whole day.' But the ability to see all around him was only one of the skills he was beginning to acquire as he prepared for front-line service.

Although not a pilot yet, he had to understand aircraft handling and exactly what a machine could do. Then there was map reading and navigation skills to develop, learning to spot things of interest on the ground that might be of use to intelligence officers, bombing practice, handling a machine gun and how to clear stoppages and much more. Such was his success that he was able to report to his mother that 'my training lasted barely four weeks. I am the first of my class to be sent to a field flying detachment.' In his case this proved to be at Chelm, to the southeast of Warsaw. On 20 July he described his life there in a letter to his mother:

> I am here with Mackenson's army attached to the Austrian 6th Corps.
>
> Now we are in a war of motion again. I fly almost daily over the enemy and bring back information. I reported the retreat of the Russians three days ago. It is a lot of fun, anyway, more than playing at being an ordnance officer. We live in tents. The houses are nearly all burnt down and those standing are so louse-infested that no one wants to go into them. I am especially happy to be able to play a part here, in the most important theatre of the war. In all probability, the decision whether we have a long or short war will be made here. I have already been working for fourteen days.

August von Mackensen, nicknamed the 'Last Hussar', who began the war as a 65-year-old general, successfully led the XVII Corps at Gumbinnen, Tannenberg and at the First Battle of the Masurian Lakes. In so doing he helped drive the invading Russians out of most of East Prussia, becoming a national hero in the process.

However, now fully mobilised the Russian Armies sought alternative targets and by April 1915 had conquered much of western Galicia and were advancing towards Hungary. In response to this fast-developing situation, the German Chief of Staff, Erich von Falkenhayn, agreed to form a joint Austro-German army, under a German commander, to attack the Russian flank and bring their advance to a halt. After much discussion the Austrian High Command agreed to Mackensen's appointment as supreme commander to lead this coalition force.

Hans von Seeckt, who became his Chief of Staff, later described Mackensen as an 'amiable hands-on commander with the instincts of a hunter'.

Led by such a man and with an overwhelming advantage of artillery, this joint force soon smashed through the Russian lines between Gorlice and Tarnow and continued eastwards, gaining huge momentum in the process. The Russians were given no time to regroup or establish a new, stronger defensive line and were quickly driven back again, allowing the enemy to recapture Przemyśl and Lemberg, then retake most of eastern Galicia.

As a very small cog in a very large wheel, von Richthofen observed these battles from above, reporting their progress, learning his trade and a gradually becoming more aware of the fighting potential of aircraft. Did he think in terms of the greater glory and rewards that this form of warfare offered or did he simply wish to see more action? As a hunter, a professional soldier and a man who sought adventure, the challenges were only too obvious as were the chances of acquiring more decorations. But it seems to me that these were probably secondary considerations, 'the hunt' being his true pursuit – until he grew tired of the whole business, as most men did when battle fatigue set in.

In June 1915 the day-to-day excitement of being in the chase dominated his life and in his autobiography he captured, in an almost breathless way, the sense of exhilaration he felt as he went into airborne battle for the first time:

I was sent out to the only place where there was still a chance of a war of movement. Mackensen was advancing gloriously. He had broken through the Russian position at Gorlice, and I joined his Army when we were taking Rawa Ruska. I was sent to the celebrated 69th Squadron. Being a beginner I felt very foolish. My pilot was a 'big gun', Oberleutnant Zeumer ... Every day, morning and afternoon, I had to fly and to reconnoitre, and I have brought back valuable information many a time.

During June, July and August I remained with the Flying Service participating in Mackensen's advance from Gorlice to Brest-Litovsk. I had joined as an inexperienced observer and had not the slightest idea about anything ... For an observer it is important to find a pilot with a strong character ... we were told that Count von Holck will join us. Immediately I realised that this is the man for me.

As each of us makes our way in the world we are lucky if we find men or women who can, by setting a good example and through sympathetic tutoring, lead us into the future successfully. In Zeumer and Holck, von Richthofen found two such men and both influenced him in very positive ways in the months that followed.

Georg Zeumer, who was the son of a factory-owning family in Mikołów, Silesia, was 24 when the war broke out, by which time he had qualified as a pilot. He joined the German flying service in August and was soon posted to Feldflieger Abteilung 4 on the Western Front. So exemplary was his service that by November he had been awarded the Iron Cross and then the Knight's Cross of the Military Order of St Henry. His success as an aviator was even more surprising when considering that he had been suffering from tuberculosis for many years, for which there was no effective cure then. With the black humour that will always be found among young men in the services, he was soon nicknamed 'the lunger'. The terminal nature of his illness seems to have made Zeumer more daring or, perhaps as some thought, more reckless. In time, and in recognition of his gallantry in the air, he acquired another nickname 'the Black Cat'; an insignia that was then painted on the side of at least one aircraft.

A transfer east, to fly Albatros B.II two-seaters with Feldflieger Abteilung 69, followed and here he was soon paired with von Richthofen, although it was not a mutually exclusive arrangement. Manfred would occasionally fly with other men, including Carl Friedrich Erich von Holck, with whom he formed a more permanent partnership when Zeumer returned to Flanders that August.

Holck, who was born in Monterrey, Mexico, during April 1886, was the son of a wealthy diplomat. After school he chose to become a professional soldier and served initially with the 3rd Guards Uhlan Regiment as a Leutnant. Here his skills as a horseman were soon recognised, with success in the 1909 and 1910 Kaiser Prize events held at the Berlin-Karlshorst racecourse, as was his daring as a racing driver. When war broke out, and by now a Rittmeister (cavalry captain), Holck was serving with Dragoon Regiment No. 1915, but then transferred to the Air Service, where he become a pilot. By mid-summer he was operating with FFA 69 where he flew with von Richthofen for the first time. Of Holck, von Richthofen later wrote:

> A strange magic emanated from Holck's person. Wherever he moved, whether at court in Möndänen kneipen, on the street, in the salon or with the troops, at home or in the field, everywhere he casts a spell over people. This must have been due to the upright, natural, open and masculine nature of this rider and aviator.
>
> He was a pilot of rare ability and, most importantly, he was a class far above the enemy. We made many splendid reconnaissance flights together into Russia.

Of his many patrols with both pilots von Richthofen recorded very little in his memoirs or in correspondence with his parents, and yet this was an immensely important period in his life as an aviator. However, there is no indication that he was harbouring a wish to become a pilot just yet, although he may have been considering the possibility and even discussed it with Zeumer and Holck.

The one flight he does record in any detail was his last with Holck – a patrol that could so easily have ended in disaster with both men being killed or captured.

With the Russians retreating rapidly before the onslaught, destroying and pillaging anything in their way, German commanders needed regular progress reports to determine what the enemy were dong and where they were going. To exploit any opportunity that might arise, they needed as complete a picture as possible and Holck and von Richthofen were just one of the many crews sent out that day to gather this essential information.

Their mission meant flying 'in the direction of Brest-Litovsk' and 'over the burning city of Wicznice' where:

> A gigantic smoke cloud drifted up to 1800 metres, which prevented us from continuing our flight because we flew at an altitude of only 1300 metres ... For a moment Holck reflected ... I advised him to fly around the smoke cloud, which would have taken about five minutes. Holck did not intend to do this. On the contrary – the greater the danger, the more it attracted him. So, straight through. This nearly cost us dear. As soon as we had disappeared into the smoke the aeroplane began to reel ... I couldn't see a thing ... Suddenly the machine lost its balance and fell turning, round and round [as often happens when flying blind without the help of an artificial horizon to help maintain balance]. I managed to grasp a stay and hung onto it, otherwise I would have been thrown out.

> We fell down to an altitude of 450 metres over the burning town and suddenly dropped out of the smoke cloud … now we had had enough of it and intended to return … Five minutes later I heard Holck behind me exclaim 'the engine is giving out' and presently it stopped running completely … So we went lower and lower … just managed to glide over a forest and landed at an abandoned artillery position, which the evening before had still been in Russian hands.
>
> We jumped down and rushed into the forest where we might defend ourselves. When we reached the trees we stopped and I saw a soldier running towards our aircraft … I felt sure he was a Russian. When he came nearer Holck shouted with joy, for he was a Grenadier of the Prussian Guard.

Von Richthofen's reaction to these events is interesting. Early in the war it became common practice on reconnaissance missions for the pilot to defer to the observer, who had been trained in these duties. He also had the time to study closely what was going on below and then could decipher all he had seen at the end of a mission. The pilot's role was to get him there and back safely. In this situation it made sense for the observer to tell the pilot where to go and what to do. However, in this case Holck was a Rittmeister and so senior to von Richthofen in rank and seniority, which in action could make orders difficult to give and advice easy to ignore. Added to this, Holck was an impetuous man who seemed to relish facing danger, seemingly without thought of the consequences.

In a later war a saying became common currency amongst instructors and senior pilots, who, when faced with young men too eager to fly and fight, fell back on these well-worn words, 'There are old pilots, and there are bold pilots, but there are no old, bold pilots'. Or as Ronnie Hay, a wing leader and ace in the Second World War, put it succinctly:

Press-on types never learnt by experience and were too brave or, some thought, too foolhardy for their own good. At the first sign of the enemy they dashed off without considering the risks or the best tactics to employ in any given situation. Some survived for a time, but invariably they didn't last long, often going out in a blaze of glory killed by an enemy they did not see.

The cautious were ultimately the ones that lasted longest and achieved most. In many cases they avoided combat if the conditions were not in their favour. 'Sneak in and kill the bastards when they weren't looking' was how one of my more successful pilots put it when briefing new recruits, 'and only mix it when the odds are in your favour or the situation is desperate, in which case go hell for leather, with your wingman close by, and break off as soon as the risk has passed'. I couldn't have put it better and those who followed these golden rules were more likely to survive the longest and prosper.

The more self-disciplined and thoughtful von Richthofen would probably have agreed with this when considering the character of his dashing, gallant pilot. However, on this one occasion, and despite Holck's foolhardiness, they got away with it. So it may have been with a sense of relief when shortly afterwards Manfred was transferred to the West, where he would again be paired with Georg Zeumer, now serving with the Brieftauben-Ableitung-Ostende (BAO) operating in Belgium.

On his way there von Richthofen briefly paused at his home in Schweidnitz eager to see his family before taking up his new duties. By this stage of the war his father, though long retired from the army, had been reactivated and placed in command of the military hospital at Kattowitz in Silesia. He longed for a front-line posting, but such a thing was impossible bearing in mind his deafness, a condition he found increasingly irksome as he watched his sons so heavily engaged in the battle. However, during 1915 he was posted to Gnadenfrei Prisoner of War camp as its commandant, which may have been of some small consolation for being unable to fight.

Meanwhile Lothar, after a long period of illness, was on the Eastern Front with the 4th Dragoons. Always wishing to be close to the action, he nearly lost his life when his horse was shot from under him. But with autumn approaching, and perhaps seeing what his brother was achieving, he had made up his mind to transfer to the Air Service as well and would soon be on his way to begin training as an observer. Ilse was not to be left out of war work and soon volunteered for nursing duties, much to her mother's undoubted pride, and by 1915 was well into her training and caring for wounded soldiers at the same time. And last, but not least, there was Bolko, who was too young to fight but just old enough to become a cadet at Wahlstatt, which, unlike his eldest brother, he seems to have enjoyed.

With all her family involved in the war in some way or other, Kunigunde would have found some passing comfort in knowing that her eldest son was briefly away from the fighting. But the thought that he was heading west again, where well-publicised battles were raging, resulting in ever-growing casualty lists, would do little to remove the constant worry that Manfred or Lothar might soon be dead or crippled. Nevertheless, with her husband unexpectedly returning home on leave at the same time she could enjoy a brief moment of family life:

> On the 21st Manfred announced his arrival by telegram. At midnight we picked him up from the train – accompanied by his orderly, the faithful Menzke, who had been in his squadron since before the war. Manfred was in fine form, he beamed and related some of his experiences of the Front, each more interesting than the last. We listened intently ... Manfred made some good friends ... He learned a lot from Lt Zeumer. The two of them became one heart and soul, many times

flying the endless routes, camping under their aeroplane with the stars above them and confided in each other, as friends do, as to what life has in store for them.

Half the night passed with conversation and questions; this time with only a little sleep. All the images Manfred's stories conjured up then went through my dreams. But I had now learnt how flying can fascinate a daring young sort of man like Manfred, and not let go.

Manfred left again only too quickly. He was in a hurry to get to his 'Giant Battle Plane' unit at Ostend. Life here at home went its usual way. The many small duties, which have to be taken twice as seriously in these times, occupied us fully and kept us from brooding.

During von Richthofen's absence much had changed in the air over the Western Front, the Fokker monoplanes having established a clear ascendency over the enemy. And as men and machines inflicted heavy losses on the enemy the names of the leading fighter pilots became household names.

Immelmann and Boelcke were still there gradually increasing their list of victories, as were such men as Otto Parschau, the bespectacled Kurt Wintgens, Kurt von Crailsheim, Hans-Joachim Buddecke, Ernst von Althaus and Rudolph Berthold. Such was their success that by the end of January 1916 the monoplane fighters, now with a version built by Pfalz added, had been credited with some 120 enemy aircraft shot down. Perhaps more importantly, their presence had an effect on enemy morale out of all proportion to their actual number. So great was their concern that officers commanding the Royal Flying Corps expressed alarm at the apparent willingness of pilots to avoid combat and not pursue their missions successfully. As a result, they issued an instruction that long- and short-range reconnaissance patrols should have three escorts flying in close formation with them. If they and the escorts lost touch with each other then the reconnaissance aircraft must turn back. And so it went on, month after month, until British and French manufacturers began to produce fighter aircraft capable of taking on and defeating the German monoplanes.

While serving on the Eastern Front, then at Ostend, von Richthofen would have been aware of the way the Fokkers were changing the face of battle. But for the moment his focus rested on his duties as an observer with the BAO, which had only come into existence during November 1914 when formed at Gistel, a few miles inland from Ostend. As it did so, the call went out for pilots and observers to volunteer for what was an 'undescribed confidential assignment', but in fact involved bombing operations against the British, on either side of the Channel.

Very soon hangars and other buildings were being assembled and the first aircraft were arriving by night in an attempt to preserve the secrecy of what was going on. In addition, a wooden runway, that could be laid and removed very quickly, was produced in an attempt to make it an all-weather airfield. In an area prone to flooding this could prove a godsend. Accommodation needs were also carefully considered and so living quarters were provided on a train that every evening could be shunted from the airfield to a small station nearby and back the following morning.

By 31 December pilots and thirteen observers had been selected and were soon assembling at Gistel and were allowed to choose the machines they wished to fly. Some even brought aircraft with them, including Albatros B type machines that had become a familiar sight over the front by then.

On 22 January 1915 twelve planes took off to bomb Dunkirk in daylight on their first serious mission, but losses meant they soon turned to night attacks instead. These began shortly afterwards but met with limited success. A transfer to Verdun, then to the Eastern Front followed, under the command of Hauptmann Hermann Gustav Kastner-Kirdorf. With him in charge, the unit were soon being re-equipped with Aviatik type B aircraft armed with Parabellum MG08 machine guns for the observer to use. For a time, they flew from Allenstein, then in East Prussia. Their stay there was fairly brief and ended on 20 April 1915 shortly after Oblt Victor Carganico and his observer Oblt Oskar Knofe attacked an important railhead at Bialystok, north-east of Warsaw, with 70kg of bombs. Two days later the unit's aircraft were dismantled and placed on railway cars and with that the whole show moved south to Czyczyny near Krakow, on the Galician Front, and assisted a final push on Lemberg during June. A few days later, with its manpower severely reduced, it returned to Gistel, where brand new C-type aircraft awaited them, plus a few twin-engined AEG Gs.

By the time the unit returned to Belgium a new commanding officer, Hauptmann Ernst von Gersdorff, had been appointed and soon began preparing the BAO for the next phase of its operational life. In an attempt to build up its numbers he recalled Zeumer, and sought other suitable recruits to fill vacancies. It seems likely that von Richthofen's name was suggested by Zeumer and his transfer arranged.

By the time he arrived the BAO had received some of the much heavier, ungainly Gotha G.I bombers; a type von Richthofen probably referred, in his memoirs, as the 'Big Battle Machine'. And there has been some speculation that it was in a G.I that he first flew with Zeumer from Gistel. If so, it was not a type that held much appeal for the men destined to fly it.

The prototype first flew on 30 January 1915 and was powered by two 100hp Mercedes D.I engines, and armed with a 7.92mm machine guns, which the observer operated in the front of a nacelle-type arrangement that sat above the wings and fuselage. The crew sat in this exposed position, where the field of fire was fairly unrestricted, and were protected, as were the engines, by 200kg of chrome-nickel armour. But it was soon realised that the G.I was not as good as expected, lacked structural strength, was underpowered and dangerous to the crew should they crash land.

By the time that von Richthofen joined the BOA, Hans Burkhard, the manufacturer's chief engineer, had begun to refine the design and the first of the modified aircraft was completed in late July and pressed into service a few days later. This new version, powered by two 150 hp Benz Bz.III engines, was built in three batches of six before production ceased at the end of the year; the final group receiving the slightly more powerful 160hp Mercedes D.III engines, a second machine gun and nearly double the weight of armour protection. Unfortunately, these modifications failed to improve the performance appreciably or help endear the type to their crews. Nevertheless, their impressive size meant that they attracted press attention in Germany, with journalists eager to trumpet the apparent strength of the bomber force soon to be unleashed against the enemy.

In his memoirs von Richthofen described these early days with the BAO:

Zeumer met me at Brussels Station ... We were accommodated in a requisitioned hotel on the Ostend Shore and bathed every afternoon. Wrapped up in our many coloured bathing gowns we sat on the terraces of Ostend and drank our coffee in the afternoon.

It was also at this time he acquired a companion who would become an important part of his life:

The most beautiful being in all creation is my Danish hound 'Moritz'. I bought him in Ostend for five marks. I was allowed to select one from the litter and chose the prettiest. Zeumer bought another puppy and called him 'Max' [both puppies were named after the famous children's books written and illustrated by Wilhelm Busch. Both men would have been familiar with these famous stories from their childhood].

It became quite common on both sides of the lines for aircrew to acquire pets of all sorts. They reminded the fighting men of their homes and to some their unquestioning affection provided a warmth and a necessary distraction from the business of flying. In the many months ahead it is certain that Moritz fulfilled this important role in Manfred's life, not so Max who, sadly, was run over by a car and killed.

All the offensive actions the Germans participated in from Ostend and Gistel were not entirely one-sided affairs, as von Richthofen later reported:

> One day [thought to be 7th September] we suddenly heard bugles and were told that an English Naval Warship Squadron [commanded by Vice-Admiral Reginald Bacon, of the 'Dover Patrol' and consisting of four monitors carrying twelve-inch guns, plus an escort] was approaching ... We heard a whistling in the air, then a loud explosion as a shell hit that part of the beach where a little earlier we had been bathing. I have never rushed into the 'heroes' cellar' as quickly as I did at that moment.

And it was, perhaps, in response to this attack that the big Gothas, and other aircraft from the BOA, patrolled out over the sea, to help spot incoming raiders and attack them should the opportunity arise. On one occasion this nearly ended in disaster:

> We had gone far out to sea ... experimenting with a new steering gear which we were told would allow us to fly in a straight line with only a single engine working. When we were far out I saw beneath a vessel [a submarine, friend or foe he couldn't confirm] ... I drew Zeumer's attention to my discovery and we went lower in order to see more clearly ... We had with us a couple of bombs and I debated with myself whether I should drop them or not ... I suddenly noticed that water was gradually disappearing from out of the radiator and

drew my colleague's attention to it. He pulled a long face and hurried for home. However, we were twelve miles from the shore ... The motor began running more slowly and I was preparing myself for a sudden cold immersion. But lo and behold we got through! We reached shore and managed to land at our base. It is good to be lucky, otherwise we should certainly have drowned.

Having survived yet another near miss, von Richthofen ruminated on the risks he faced before describing shedding his first 'drop of blood for the Fatherland':

I have never been really hurt. At the critical moment I have probably bent my head or pulled in my chest. Often I have been surprised that someone has not hit me. Once a bullet went through my fur-lined boots. Another time a bullet went through my muffler. Yet another time one went along my arm through the fur and leather jacket, but (so far) I have never been touched.

Then on a bombing mission against the 'English' his luck changed, albeit in a fairly minor way:

We reached our objective and the first bomb fell. It is interesting to determine its effect – at least one likes to see it explode. Unfortunately, our aircraft had the ridiculous characteristic that one could not see the effect of the bomb because the view was obscured entirely by the wings ... Therefore, I signalled to Zeumer that he should turn a little to one side. While waving to him I forgot that the aircraft had two propellers that turned to the right and left of my seat ... and bang! my finger was caught. I was a little surprised when I discovered that my little finger had been damaged ... I quickly got rid of the rest of my bombs and we hurried home ... I had to sit quietly for seven days and was disbarred from flying.

On this occasion Zeumer and von Richthofen may have been flying an AEG G.II where both propellers were situated dangerously close to the cockpit, so presenting a constant danger for the unwary. By comparison, the clearance between the blades and the cockpit of the Gotha G.I was much greater. Either way, it is difficult to check the date of this incident, but milestones such as his 'first fight in the air' are more easily verified by referring to his autobiography.

The date 1 September 1915 is something of a red letter day in his rise to fame, signifying, as it did, his desire to shoot down enemy aeroplanes, not simply observe or bomb targets on the ground:

> We flew every day for five and six hours without ever seeing an Englishman. I became increasingly discouraged, but one bright morning we again went out to hunt. Suddenly I saw a Farman aeroplane reconnoitring without taking notice of us. My heart was beating hard when Zeumer flew towards it ... Before I knew what was happening we had rushed past each other. I had at most four shots while the Englishman was suddenly behind us firing into our 'shop window' like anything ... We turned and turned around one and other until the Englishman, much to our surprise, turned away and flew off. I was greatly disappointed and so was my pilot.
>
> Arriving home, we were both in a very bad mood. He blamed me for having shot badly, and I blamed him for not having brought me into a good firing position – in short, our aviation rapport, which was so splendid before, had suffered badly.
>
> Later the same day we went on the chase for a second time but again had no success. I was very disappointed ... I had always believed that a shot would cause the enemy to fall, but soon realised that an aircraft can stand a great deal of

punishment. I felt certain that I would never bring down an enemy aeroplane no matter how much shooting I did.

On these occasion the two men appear to have been flying a Gotha G.I again because von Richthofen refers to it as 'a capacious aeroplane ... the apple-barge'. This is a nickname that fits the G.I better than the AEGs, if so, its lack of power and manoeuvrability probably accounts for their lack of success. Their opponent that day, described as a Farman, may well have been a Vickers F.B.5 'Gunbus' pusher biplane that flew for the first time on 17 July 1914. By the summer of 1915 they equipped two RFC squadrons – numbers 2 and 11 – both of which would have been patrolling the northern part of the front line where the BOA aircraft were operating. They were designed as armed warplanes to seek out and destroy other aircraft. To do this they were powered by a single 100hp Gnome Monosoupape nine-cylinder rotary engine driving a two-bladed propeller and armed with a drum-fed Lewis gun operated by the observer in the front of the nacelle.

In September 1915 these two squadrons would have been particularly aggressive because the British Expeditionary Force (BEF) were preparing for their biggest offensive of the war so far at Loos. To help maintain secrecy and so save lives, they would be briefed to attack on sight any enemy observation aircraft trying to gather information that might reveal the BEF's plans. By this stage of their war both squadrons were rapidly gaining experience in air fighting and on 7 November an 11 Squadron pilot, Second Lieutenant Gilbert Insall, supported by Air Mechanic T.H. Donald, proved this when destroying a German Aviatik two-seater, an action. This, plus a record of courage and aggressive service in the air, led to Insall being awarded the Victoria Cross shortly afterwards.

Whether von Richthofen and Zeumer faced a Farman or a Vickers that day is immaterial, because whichever it was proved better at air fighting than their 'apple-barge'.

Their performance also revealed much about the problem all aircrew faced when entering combat for the first time. Even though both men had considerable experience by then, and von Richthofen was a good shot when hunting animals and birds, translating this skill to the air could prove difficult. This was a theme taken up by Johnnie Johnson, the highest-scoring RAF ace of the Second World War, in a conversation with the author at his home in Derbyshire during 1992. He began by repeating words he'd used when writing his book *Wing Leader*:

> The pilot who could hit curling down-wind pheasant, or a jinking head-on partridge, or kill a widgeon cleanly in a darkening sky had little trouble bringing his guns to bear against the ME 109s.

But he now added some words concerning the skills needed to get into a position to fire that nearly all newcomers, no matter how good a shot, lacked:

> When I wrote about the ability to shoot I didn't mention the variables that came into play in the air – height, speed, an aircraft's ability to turn inside an enemy, the ability to see everything that is going on all around you at all heights, achieving an element of surprise and much more – and how it can take time for any pilot no matter how good they were to acquire these flying skills.
>
> Some became wonderful pilots but couldn't shoot. Then there were some very rough-handling pilots who seemed able to knock them down with apparent ease, at minimal risk to themselves, taking their aircraft beyond safe limits at times. My first few times in action, during 1940, early 1941, made all this clear to me. Even though fairly experienced by then as a pilot and flying with a practised man, the speed with

which aircraft came and went, often in a blur, left me feeling out of my depth. The trouble was trying to get the aircraft, which was just a gun platform, into a position to fire before the blighters disappeared again. The danger was that you opened fire at too early, or at too long a range, allowed insufficient deflection to compensate for movement or just shot off your ammunition too quickly. All was fine if the other aircraft flew straight and level, but no experienced flier would do that in the combat zone.

The only things that mattered were constant practice and surviving while you learnt your trade. It was well into the summer of 1941 before this happened to me and then I began to knock down enemy fighters.

The parallel with von Richthofen is an interesting one. Both men were naturally talented hunters who understood how to stalk their prey and do so patiently. Yet each, when they tried to apply these skills to air fighting, discovered unforeseen difficulties. The problem was a simple one. When firing from a static position, no matter how fast the target was moving, they didn't have to worry about their own movement beyond creeping into a suitable firing position. In the air there was so much more to consider as both hunter and quarry constantly moved around at speed, with the added difficulty that the target could shoot back. Both men adapted, but it took time to refine these skills, with Johnson eventually proving to be an exceptional fighter pilot and leader, in the process. Of course, von Richthofen was for the moment only observing and only time would tell if he could succeed as a pilot.

For the time being he and Zeumer could only practise these new arts in the aircraft assigned to the BOA, which, on the whole, were unsuited to this form of warfare. But they persisted and soon began to reveal the instincts of fighter pilots, together and separately. In Zeumer's case this was achieved by flying a single Fokker monoplane attached to the unit following their transfer south to Rethel on the

Champagne front. With the British at Loos being forced to give up the fight and retrench, attacks by the French, before winter set in, became more vigorous. Here the German aircraft might be better employed in gathering information, but the transfer allowed von Richthofen to spend time honing his shooting skills, this time with a little more success.

Here the BOA were able to operate with a number of aircraft temporarily assigned to them from the Brieftauben-Abteilung Metz, with whom Oswald Boelcke was now serving. At this stage he had shot down a number of enemy aircraft and was on the way to becoming a celebrity. And it was while travelling south by train to Rethel that von Richthofen met him for the first time. It turned out to be a life-changing event for the younger man:

> In the dining car at the table next to me was a young, unimposing-looking leutnant. There was no need to take any notice of him except for the fact that he was the only man who had succeeded in shooting down hostile aircraft, not once but four times. His name has been mentioned in communiqués [and had begun to appear in newspapers and magazines, gradually making him a household name]. I thought much of him because of what he was achieving. Although I had tried hard I had not brought an enemy down up to that time.
>
> I wanted to find out how Leutnant Boelcke managed this business. So I asked him 'how to you do it?' He seemed amused and laughed, although I had asked him quite seriously. Then he replied that 'It is quite simple. I fly close to my man, aim well and then, of course, he goes down.' I shook my head and told him that I did the same, but my opponent, unfortunately, did not go down. The difference between us was he flew a Fokker and I a large aircraft.
>
> I took the trouble to get more closely acquainted with this nice, modest man, whom I desperately wanted to teach me this

business. We often played cards together, went for walks and I asked him many questions. Finally, I decided that I would also learn to fly a Fokker. Perhaps then my luck would improve. From then on my whole aim and ambition was focussed on learning to manipulate the stick myself ... Happily, I soon found an opportunity to learn piloting on an 'old box' in the Champagne.

To modern minds this open discussion about how to kill other men is difficult to comprehend because it seems to betray a callousness of spirit. One wonders whether they ever addressed the ethical issues involved in killing or being killed in their country's service. There is no sense of the moral dimension to what they were doing or any expressed horror. My maternal grandfather, who led a machine gun team during 1917–18, realised that he may have been responsible for many deaths. However, he treated the whole business as a repugnant but necessary evil committed at the height of battle when much depended on turning back a determined enemy. He was always aware that he was killing and maiming men such as himself and later declared that 'only the morally bankrupt regarded this unforgivably odious business as anything but an unspeakable act of barbarity. Doing one's duty in war is necessary, but it must not be thought a game or a pleasure.' By this definition von Richthofen's stated desire to be a successful fighter pilot and score victories betrays a certain cold-heartedness and lack of self-awareness that only hunters seem to possess. Only time and increasing battle fatigue seem to have dented his drive and his certainty.

Boelcke, by comparison, having 'completed seventy-six war flights since I have been with No. 62 at Douai', seems to have addressed these issues more fully by the time he and von Richthofen met. This may account for his mild humour and surprise at being asked 'how to do it?'. But Boelcke was a clever, perceptive man who saw the young man's eagerness to learn and while they served together, and his own star continued to rise, he continued to advise his 'disciple'. However, he appears to have played no direct part in his training as a pilot, in which Zeumer took a leading role, but first Manfred was to experience his first success in the air, as he believed it to be. Although often quoted as being in late September, it seems more likely to have been after 1 October when he was operating on the Champagne front. In his memoirs he recalled the event:

> I flew with (Oberleutnant Paul) von Osterroht, who had a smaller aircraft than the 'apple-barge'. About three miles behind the enemy lines we came across a Farman two-seater. He allowed us to approach him, and for the first time I saw an aerial opponent at close quarters. Osterroht flew with great skill, so I could easily fire at the enemy. Our opponent probably did not notice us, for only when I had trouble with my gun did he begin to shoot back at us.
>
> When my supply of 100 cartridges had been used I suddenly noticed the Farman going down in peculiar spirals. I followed him with my eyes and tapped Osterroht on the head to draw his attention. Our opponent fell and fell and finally crashed into a large crater. There he stood on his nose, the tail pointing to the sky. According to my map he had fallen three miles behind the front ... At the time no notice was taken of aeroplanes brought down in enemy territory, otherwise I should have one more aeroplane to my credit.

It must have been with a certain amount of frustration that he landed at Rethel, but at least he could be satisfied that his gunnery seemed to be improving. Did this success encourage him to press ahead with pilot training, urged on by Boelcke and Zeumer, or was it already in his mind awaiting a suitable moment to apply for place at flying school? Probably the latter, because by then he had realised that the opportunities for combat were greater as a pilot. In the meantime, he seems to have persuaded Zeumer to give him a few unofficial lessons, presumably in a smaller Albatros B type or similar. And so his short life as a pilot began, as did his spectacular rise to fame that, in a little over a year, would see him feted and fated.

Chapter 4

Fight for the Sky

Without the instinctive skills which Boelcke and Immelmann possessed, von Richthofen was slow to learn to fly, crashing on his first solo and only mastering the aircraft by sheer force of personality. Time and again he escaped death by a miracle before he managed to conquer the 'unruly' aeroplane ... Ultimately he became an excellent flyer, but whereas many other pilots flew with a kind of innocent courage, Richthofen flew with his brains and made his ability serve him.

Anthony Fokker, 1929

Fokker, who was soon to befriend von Richthofen, was able to observe the young officer, and all the other men who became 'aces', from close quarters on the ground and in the air. As a successful businessman and pilot he understood human nature and the skills necessary to make a good aviator. All this made his assessments of these men even more valuable.

He believed that von Richthofen was not a natural pilot but was one who took a while to 'get the feel of an aircraft', as Douglas Bader later described this condition to the author. Until he could overcome this problem he tended to 'blunder about, a danger to himself and others', as Bader added. So it was perhaps with some fear and trepidation that Georg Zeumer set about teaching von Richthofen some basic flying skills; though by then he probably realised that his pupil, in the words of Fokker, 'knew little or nothing about the technical side of aircraft ... except as it was necessary to know for his own safety and development'. However, in little more than a week of practice flying Zeumer allowed his observer to fly solo, presumably hoping that this might satisfy von Richthofen's immediate needs. Did he think the 'trainee' was up to it? We shall never know, but at least the demands of friendship had been met.

Manfred, in a very open and honest way, later described his first solo flight and in doing so made little effort to hide how clumsy his efforts were:

> There are some moments in one's life that strains one's nerves and my first solo flight was one of them.
>
> One evening Zeumer told me 'now go and fly yourself'. I must admit I felt like replying 'I am afraid', but this is something a man must never say when defending his country. So, like it or not, I swallowed my fear and got into the aircraft.
>
> Zeumer explained to me every movement to follow once more. I scarcely listened to his explanations, for I was firmly convinced that I should forget half of what he was telling me.
>
> I started off, the aircraft reached the prescribed speed and I couldn't help noticing that I was actually flying. I didn't feel nervous, but elated … I made a wide turn to the left, cut the engine exactly where I had been ordered to do so and prepared for what should happen next. Now came the most difficult part – the landing. I remembered exactly what I had to do. I acted automatically, but the aircraft moved quite differently from the way I expected. I lost my sense of balance and made some wrong movements and stood the aircraft on its nose and succeeded in turning my aeroplane into a battered 'school bus'.
>
> I was very disappointed, looked at the damage to the aircraft, which was not great, and then had to suffer other people's jokes.

Such a determined man was unlikely to be put off by a crash landing, particularly as he had walked away without injury. It was a feeling captured in the words of a naval pilot's song from the Second World War, 'they say in the Air Force a landing's okay if the pilot gets out and still walks away'. To be able to shrug off disasters and setbacks was essential for aircrew and this is what Manfred did now. In fact, it seems to have made him more determined to succeed, egged on, no doubt, by the echo of his comrades' laughter. And so he 'went with great passion at flying and suddenly I could handle the aircraft'.

No matter how much Zeumer taught him about flying, the German Air Force had by this time introduced a more formal flight training programme. This included three increasingly difficult exams, which all recruits had to pass if they were to be awarded their Pilot's Badge. Having grown in confidence as a pilot in such a short time, Manfred may have expected to literally fly through these exams, but this proved not to be the case.

In mid-October he undertook the first test locally under the critical eye of Hauptmann Rudolf von Thuna, the inspecting officer and a pre-war aviator of note. After he had observed von Richthofen flying a figure of eight several times, landing successfully at the end of each circuit, he found insufficient evidence of competence to pass him. Not deterred, Manfred practised more and sought re-examination. At the same time, perhaps realising that he needed more instruction, he submitted an application to train as a pilot at Fliegerschule (flight school).

In the meantime, the BAO had received a new 'Giant Aeroplane', as Manfred described it, but gave no further details. It is likely that it was, in fact, one of a new breed of heavy bomber, possibly of the Riesenflugzeug ('Giant Aircraft') type. These included the Zeppelin-Staaken VGO I and II, built under licence at the Gothaer Works in Berlin. The first of these appeared in 1915 and were designed to attack targets with a much larger payload than before, with Britain their likely target, although this role was eventually taken by the Gotha G.IV/V bombers of Kagohl 3 in early 1917.

If he had remained with the BAO it is likely that von Richthofen would have been involved in these operations, but in November his application for pilot training was approved and he was assigned to the Fliegerersatz-Abteilung at Döberitz, where he would again come under the critical eye of von Thuna.

Manfred wrote little about the training he was given or the content of the tests that followed. He simply recorded that:

> I went through my training with a dear fellow, Oberleutnant Bodo von Lyncker ... our aim was to fly Fokkers with a Fighting Squadron on the Western Front ... On Christmas day I passed my third examination. In connection with this I flew to Schwerin where the Fokker works are based, with my mechanic [though more likely to have been his orderly, Menzke] as passenger and from there we flew to Breslau, Schweidnitz and Luben before returning, to Berlin. During my tour I landed in lots of different places, visiting relatives and friends along the way.

For Kunigunde and Albrecht this visit proved to be a godsend, because they could celebrate Christmas with all four children present possibly for the last time, as she later recalled:

> Our wishes have been fulfilled. Once again I stood under the lit up tree with my four children. I sat at the piano and played 'Silent Night'. Manfred and Ilse (who had just qualified as a nurse) sang along splendidly with their beautiful clear voices ... I escorted each one to the table for the presentation of gifts. They had prepared small surprises in return ... There was laughter, joy and a happy time for us ... the blue fir tree was fragrant and shone with gentle light ... I watched the children thankful for these hours for which many German mothers would envy me.

In war such moments have to be treasured, for who knows what tomorrow may bring. With a return to the dangers of combat flying beckoning, and as a good son, it was important that Manfred took this opportunity to be with his family and reassure them that all was well. Yet when it was over he quickly returned to his duties, leaving a feeling of terrible uncertainty in his parents' minds. Both would have been fearful of what lay ahead for their sons on active service, especially now that Lothar, who had just completed training as an observer, was due to join Kasta 23 of Kampfgeschwader der Obersten Heeresleitung (Kagohl) 4 in the New Year.

They didn't have to look far to see the terrible losses being inflicted on Germany's young men, which Kunigunde continued to chronicle with ever-growing sadness. At the same time, perhaps spurred on by their sons, she may also have followed the exploits of the new fighter aces, whose number her eldest son might soon join. Manfred had spoken to her of Boelcke and now his face frequently adorned newspapers and gave her a taste of a life that would soon envelop her sons, and, by association, the whole family.

Boelcke's rise to fame had been rapid after his name began appearing in communiqués. Encouraged by the military authorities, journalists soon picked up the story of his and Immelmann's achievements and their deeds soon found a ready audience, ever eager for more stories. Very soon he was contacted by the Berlin Illustration Company keen to publish details of his life and produce 'Sanke' postcards to be sold to the public. As victory followed victory their propaganda value grew exponentially. But by late October Boelcke was growing so weary of the attention that he wrote in a letter:

> The Berlin Illustration Company will manage quite well without my photograph – I beg you not to send them one. I don't like all this publicity – I find quite enough articles in the papers about myself to be sick of it all. I am told an English paper lately announced that I had bolted to America before

the war because I could not pay my debts as a Leutnant and worked as a liftman in a New York hotel.

In recognition of their efforts in the field both Boelcke and Immelmann were awarded the Pour le Mérite in January 1916. This, as might be expected, only drew more attention to their exploits. Dinners with the King of Bavaria and Crown Prince soon followed, and much more, as the feting continued unabated. Their deeds also attracted the attention of 'poets' in Germany eager to celebrate their gallantry in a crude, school boyish way. A taste of this truly awful verse can be found in the regular work of a Professor Overbeck, writing under the name 'Gottlieb', in *Der Tag*:

Immelmann, the trusty flier,
Daily screws his plane up higher,
Boelcke, too, delights to roam,
In the clouds where he's at home.

Another foeman Boelcke scotches
And so his round half dozen notches;
'Oh,' thinks Immelmann, 'what tricks!'
And brings his total up to six.

It is little wonder that Boelcke was growing weary of this increasingly bizarre and, often, trivial attention he attracted as he fought for his country in a war of immense danger and violence. At this stage this may not have been the distraction it later became, because the air war was still set at a low key with many aircraft minimally armed and so unable to engage in combat. During 1916 this began to change as numbers on both sides built up and armaments improved. As a result, the strain on aircrew increased, taking a heavy toll of their health and well-being, with battle fatigue becoming an ever more concerning problem. Boelcke, with the added pressure of such great public attention, would, undoubtedly, have felt this stress more keenly and been unable to find the rest he needed to recover his poise and steadiness.

As von Richthofen returned to action he would have been aware of the public acclaim surrounding the aces. Did he wonder whether he might join their ranks in 1916 or be condemned to continue flying the more mundane observation aircraft he had become used to? Either way, he is unlikely to have foreseen how completely his life would change in so short a time. If he had been able to look into the future and seen what fame had in store for him, would the essentially reserved von Richthofen have chosen a different route? Or was fame his goal no matter what the price?

Naturally as a Junker and an officer he would have accepted that his country's needs came first, especially when the people had been told frequently that their cause was just and their country under attack by foreign powers. And to be awarded decorations for fighting was an acceptable ambition, signifying, as it did, unwavering service and courage under fire. As a professional soldier, with hopefully a long career in front of him, he would have seen these decorations as essential for promotion, but there was probably an element of vanity too. However, for most this was a passing phase, which experience of war, in Manfred's case, soon brought to an end, although the decorations continued to flow until the end of his life. For the moment though, as he returned to the front line as a pilot, fame and glory must have held some appeal, but equally so there must have been a desire to come through the war safely.

Having passed each stage of the pilot's training programme successfully there would have been a brief pause until his Pilot's Badge was awarded, then three months before being assigned to a squadron at the front. In the interim his movements are unclear, except for a flight home, with Lothar, on 2 February. However, it is unlikely that he returned to the BAO at Rethel, so he may simply have remained at Döberitz, flying when he could, as winter set in, hoping to enhance his flying skills before becoming operational. But with spring approaching the German Army was preparing for a 'big push' against the French forts at Verdun. Having been thwarted in 1914, when trying to take Paris, it was hoped that removing these obstacles would allow a war of movement to return and reopen their path to the French capital. Sadly, the German High Command had not learnt the lessons of 1915. Time and time again it had been shown that any advance against strongly held positions, protected by barbed wire, machine guns, concentrated artillery fire and more, was doomed to failure.

At Verdun the string of giant forts would make things even more difficult. When eventually these attacks, which began in February, were called off ten months later nearly 700,000 men had become casualties, with up to 250,000 of these believed dead. It was a butcher's bill that defied description and worse followed when French, British and Empire forces attacked across the Somme on 1 July. By November, when even the bullish, dogmatic Field Marshal Haig had had enough of the slaughter, all three armies had casualty lists of some 1.2 million men to contemplate that winter as they planned more of the same in 1917.

With this in mind, it is hardly surprising that troops and the general public, in each belligerent nation, were questioning the need to continue the war. But no dissenting voices could be tolerated for long and propaganda became an even more important tool in justifying the sacrifice. However, this torturing stalemate had one unexpected outcome for Germany, its army and its air arm.

Any military leader who presides over one disaster after another should not be allowed to continue. While the Somme might be considered a victory for the Germans, in so far as they held their ground, Verdun was an unmitigated and costly defeat. As a result, Erich von Falkenhayn, Chief of the Oberste Heeresleitung (OHL), came in for much criticism and a whispering campaign began that led to his removal from post. Hindenburg, who had proved so successful on the Eastern Front, led or aided by the dominating figure of

Ludendorff, was the obvious choice to replace him and in August this change took effect. With powerful friends and supporters lobbying on his behalf, Ludendorff was chosen to continue as Hindenburg's Chief of Staff, and Quartermaster General, before becoming the General of the Infantry.

Hindenburg took command of all the forces of the Central Powers, but it was Ludendorff who wielded true power and personally directed all that happened. And his control gradually spread into every aspect of life in the German war machine – military and civilian – with Hindenburg, in many ways, remaining a figurehead. So it is perhaps unsurprising that Ludendorff was quoted as saying that 'one thing was certain – the power must be in my hands'. By late 1916 this had become a reality, with the Kaiser, Hindenburg, Bethmann Hollweg, the Chancellor, and the Reichstag bending to his will, ever hoping that by giving him this power he might finally grasp an increasingly elusive victory.

His offices soon became the main centre of power in Germany and quickly began issuing orders and instructions, on a whole host of matters, to all parts of the Reich on a daily, even hourly basis. More frequent communiqués were despatched to a media ever eager for good news. And each day posters printed on yellow paper to make them more visible, appeared on billboards all around Germany trumpeting victories or acts of great gallantry, to supplement all that appeared in magazines and journals.

Ludendorff even met newspaper and newsreel editors to discuss what was happening, while applying the appropriate amount of 'spin' to each story. It was a technique that is very recognisable today, but then was a new phenomenon. Before long he became more celebrated and was even considered, by friend and foe, to be the 'Supreme War Lord' of Germany. As such, he was idolised by many and seen as the 'country's saviour'. It was an image that would be tarnished in time but between 1916 to 1918 his power was absolute and his influence and decisions appeared to go unchallenged.

Nevertheless, the German Constitution required that government be run by civil servants appointed by the Kaiser, not the military. For Ludendorff this was an unsatisfactory arrangement because it limited his power in directing the war as he thought fit. So, with the Kaiser's and Hindenburg's blessing, he volunteered his and the OHL's services in overseeing the war, the economy and industry. This was accepted, perhaps grudgingly by the Chancellor and the Reichstag, and soon such things as procurement, extraction of raw materials, control of labour and the production and distribution of food moved into his sphere of influence, placing him at the centre of all that happened.

Very quickly overly ambitious targets, under the grandiose title of the Hindenburg Programme, were set for military production. At the same time, Ludendorff actively participated in formulating economic policy and broader government strategies, not normally the domain of military men. He was later quoted as loudly pummelling the table with his fists at various meetings to gain acceptance of his ideas, even though men more senior to him in government were in attendance. And to further his influence he soon began to assign his staff officers to most government ministries, and through them kept tabs on what was happening. Armed with this information, he could press his demands and control output. Some later considered that his authority was so complete that he became a dictator in all but name.

Ludendorff, increasingly worried about declining morale, established a propaganda unit within his headquarters. Then he set in motion a mandatory programme of lectures for all troops, each containing a strongly patriotic message. The most important of these inferred that if the war was lost they would all 'become slaves of international capital'. The speakers then added a more sinister note aimed at silencing dissenting voices. The listeners were to 'ensure that a fight is kept up against all agitators, croakers, and weaklings'.

It was very clear that propaganda needs would feature high in Ludendorff's priorities. It was seen by him as the mortar that held the bricks together – illusionary perhaps, and ultimately self-defeating but real nonetheless in uniting a nation and pursuing victory. His only doubt would have been sustaining such an effort in a war of attrition where the Central Powers were constantly on the defensive, hoping 'to bleed their enemies white'. If events in 1914 and 1915 had shown the need for heroes and begun to exploit those who daily risked their lives, the years that followed would take this to a new level. Aviators clearly fulfilled this role better than most and so their exploitation grew rapidly more intense.

As spring arrived, and the Battle of Verdun was set on its bloody course, Manfred finally received the posting for which he had been waiting and to the Verdun front he went. Perhaps disappointingly, he wasn't destined to fly fighters just yet, but would return to observing and bombing duties.

By this stage of the war the Air Service was undergoing reorganisation as the number of aircraft grew and its workload increased. Two new combat wings were soon formed under the title of Kampfgeschwader der Obersten Heeresleitung (Kagohl). The BAO became Kagohl 1 and the unit at Metz Kagohl 2. To these were soon added three more Kampfgeschwader – Nos 3, 4 and 5, with each Kagohl being split into a number of sub-units known as Kampfstaffeln or Kasta, that initially contained six aircraft each. In due course, all these units reported to Hermann von der Lieth-Thomsen, who would be directly responsible to Ludendorff, when he took up his new command later that year. So it is little surprise that this service would have the highest profile and its successes given such wide coverage, but this was just the start.

It was in this atmosphere of change that von Richthofen returned to Metz in mid-March and soon found himself assigned to Kasta 8 of Kagohl 2, commanded by Victor Carganico, now a Hauptmann, based at an airfield near Landres, to the north-east of Verdun. On its strength at the time, and likely to have attracted Manfred's attention, were a small number of Fokker monoplanes. However, his arrival seems to have coincided with these aircraft being gathered together into two special fighter units, known as *Kampfeinsitzer Kommandos* (KEKs), leaving Kasta 8 as a two-seater squadron only. However, any disappointment he felt would be assuaged by the eventual allocation of a few more of these fighters to the Kastas as production rates improved. In the meantime, he flew the LVG C.II and then the faster Roland C.II Walfisch when these began to arrive at the front. Despite being quite cumbersome aircraft, by comparison to fighters, von Richthofen continued to seek combat in them with increasing success, as events in April proved:

> In the official communiqué of 26th April I achieved a citation for the first time, although I was not mentioned by name – only my accomplishment appeared. I had a machine gun which I had sited in the same way as found on Nieuport machines [if so it was positioned on the top wing and so fired outside the arc of the propeller]. People laughed at the way I had it fitted because the whole thing looked so primitive. Of course, I swore by this arrangement, and very soon I had the opportunity of assessing its value in practice.
>
> I encountered a hostile Nieuport aircraft apparently flown by a man who was also a beginner, for he acted very stupidly. When I flew towards him he flew away – apparently experiencing trouble with his gun. I had no idea how to tackle him, but thought, 'What will happen if I simply start shooting at him?.' So, I flew after him, approaching as close as possible and began firing a short series of bursts with my gun. The Nieuport reared up and turned over and over.
>
> At first my observer and I believed this was a ruse but the machine went lower and lower. Finally, my observer patted me on the head and called out, 'I congratulate you. He is falling.' As a matter of fact he fell into a forest behind Fort Douaumont and disappeared in the trees … behind enemy lines. I flew

home and merely reported that, 'I had an aerial fight and have shot down a Nieuport.' Next day I read of my action in the communiqué.

By this stage Georg Zeumer, who was also serving with Kagohl 2, although which Kasta is unclear, was regularly flying a Fokker and on 11 April shot down a French Nieuport Scout over Douaumont. But further successes eluded him and in June he had the bad luck to be shot down by a French fighter. Although only slightly injured in the crash, he broke his right thigh three days later when the car in which he was travelling had an accident in what Richthofen later described as 'quite stupid circumstances'. Following this incident Zeumer, already a consumptive, was now found to have developed diabetes as well, possibly revealed by blood tests carried out when his thigh did not heal properly. As a result of the accident, he was left with one leg shorter than the other, and had to use a walking stick. So it was hardly surprising that flying was out of the question for a time, though a man as determined as he had proved to be would soon find a way back.

Meanwhile, Erich von Holck was also flying monoplanes on the Western Front, but with far less luck than Zeumer; his headstrong attitude to combat undoubtedly being his undoing. Manfred witnessed his death on 30 April and later wrote:

> I noticed a Fokker attacking three Cauldron machines (over Fort Douaumont). Due to a strong wind from the west, that wasn't favourable to me, I could not reach the scene of action in time to help. The Fokker was driven over the town of Verdun in the course of the fight. I drew my observer's attention to the struggle ... We wondered whether it might be Boelcke ... Then I saw to my horror that the German machine had fallen back onto the defensive – the strength of the French having increased to at least ten. Their combined assaults forced the

German aircraft lower and lower to 550 metres while the pilot fought desperately. Suddenly he plunged into a small cloud which I thought might have saved him. When I arrived at the aerodrome I reported what I had seen and was told that it was Holck flying the Fokker and that he had dropped straight down, shot through the head. His death affected me deeply, for he was my model.

By now Manfred must have been growing fairly inured to the effects of violent death, after all it was a daily occurrence in the trenches and was becoming so in the air as well. But when a close friend is killed it still had the power to shock and sadden him. Slowly but surely the men he had known were gradually being killed and the sense of isolation, the lot of all survivors in war, must have been growing. Tim Hervey, who flew with 12 Squadron, 8 Squadron and finally Nieuport fighters of 60 Squadron, facing von Richthofen in the process, described this best when he wrote in a letter to the author:

At times our casualties were very high and new faces kept appearing in the Mess with gloomy regularity. Some only lasted a few days before 'going west'. In the beginning you made friends and then suffered a terrible sense of loss when they went. But experience soon toughened you up and dictated another approach. So, in an act of self-preservation, you maintained an air of polite indifference to what was happening around you. However, no matter how hard you tried this wasn't always possible and friendships still grew, especially amongst the veterans to whom you might cling as a drowning man does to a piece of wreckage. When they too were killed a heart could break with mental or physical collapse likely to follow. If a Commanding Officer was sensitive to such things and knew his men, then they might be rested before the lack of self-preservation this bred led to their deaths. In my own case

I was aware of this happening, after sixteen months of flying at the front, but was shot down and taken prisoner before fatigue had become too serious a problem. Others were not so lucky.

It seems to me, looking back, that the ones who survived longest were the wily old birds who were careful and cautious when attacking the enemy. They tended to commit themselves only when holding the advantages of surprise, height and speed – 'dive and zoom' was how we described this method at the time. It also helped if they were flight commanders who would have had their tails protected as they fought. Others in a flight survived as best they could and it was from amongst their number that most casualties arose. The great aces, if we must call them that, were a race apart. They seemed to live charmed lives whether flying alone, as Ball tended to do, or in groups, but the law of averages soon caught up with most of them as the air war grew in size and intensity.

In 1916 all von Richthofen could do was carry on as best he could, knowing full well that he would have to face even more losses. One of these might conceivably have been his brother Lothar who, having completed training, was now flying as an observer with Kasta 23 of Kagohl 4 at an airfield on the Verdun front. In July he would move further north to the Somme when the British offensive began there. Here, if anything, the fighting would be even more intense.

It is clear that Manfred confided his worries about the future with his mother, who later recorded:

Manfred wrote that 'in the long run, everybody gets it eventually'. These words do not leave me. He had plunged into the middle of dozens of air battles, but until now Providence had been merciful to him. On one occasion an enemy made him crash and another time he crawled forth (from the wreckage) completely unharmed after an accident on landing

> ... It is reassuring to me that Manfred and Lothar see each other now and then, and also stay in touch by telephone.

This was a theme he returned to again in another letter to his mother, suggesting that a sense of fatalism may well have run deep:

> In time death comes to us all – even Boelcke. The leader of Lothar's squadron did not return from a bombing flight. The day before, the leader of my old fighting squadron No. 1 was also shot down. He was Baron Ernst von Gersdorff, one of the most efficient commanders. I liked him very much [Gersdorff, a 38-year-old Hauptmann, was killed on 19 June 1916].

Did von Richthofen fear death? Probably not, because he had lived with its spectre for so long that he knew it could take him at any moment. Did he now feel its presence more intensely than before? With the loss of so many friends and comrades, with many more soon to follow, death had become his constant companion, affecting him deeply. However, he was nothing if not brave and determined to do his duty no matter what. He probably did not know of Shakespeare's play *Julius Caesar*, but one stanza stands out as describing the extent of his courage:

> The valiant never taste of death but once.
> Of all the wonders that I have yet heard,
> It seems to me most strange that men should fear;
> Seeing that death, a necessary end,
> Will come when it will ...

To protect himself from a growing sense of loss Manfred had few men he could turn to who weren't, themselves, facing the same daily ordeal. However, it seems likely that his ever-faithful and ever-present servant, Menzke, would have provided some stability and comfort.

And, when becoming a pilot, he acquired the services of Josef Holzaptel, who had served with the infantry before re-mustering as 'Workmeister'. He was subsequently assigned to von Richthofen, managing various duties, including, it seems, the maintenance of his aircraft and, like Menzke, remained with his leader until the end. Both he and Menzke remained his trusted companions in a unique relationship that could often exist between airmen and their ground support staff. Dave Millington, who served in such a role with the Fleet Air Arm, described what this meant in reality:

> I was attached to the same pilot for seventeen months. When around the ship the niceties of rank had to be observed, but in the hangar or on deck when flying all this was dropped. He was still 'sir', but we were made to feel their equals and did what we could to look after him and his aircraft. We took tremendous pride in doing this. We always had a sense of relief when we saw our aircraft in the circuit after an operation and I held my breath until he was down. We knew if he had been in action and quickly checked the machine over as it moved up the deck looking for any damage. As it came to a stop and as the wings folded we would jump up and see what state the pilot was in.
> On the 24th [January 1945] he just sat there, the front of his tunic covered in vomit and tears rolling down his cheeks. He couldn't move for a time, so we gently unstrapped him and waited for him to recover. He'd strafed an enemy airfield, been hit many times, including a bullet through his canopy, and seen a Corsair dive into the ground. The shock remained with him for a while and the CO came over to rouse him. We helped him down, but his legs barely supported him. Shortly afterwards he came round a bit and with the other pilots went to be debriefed, laughing and joking. Before the next op on the 29th he spent many hours with us going over the aircraft,

getting himself all oily and took a lot of time polishing the Corsair. This became a ritual before every op and lasted until we all went home a few months later. Over the months a very strong bond grew between us and together we existed in a kind of inner sanctum. I observed similar relationships developing between pilots and those who supported them on the ground.

Sadly, Holzaptel does not appear to have recorded his memories of his and Manfred's time together and Menzke's recollections were only briefly chronicled by Manfred's mother. If they had, more might have revealed about von Richthofen's state of mind as the pressure of combat flying and celebrity grew. One wonders whether he found some peace of mind, or even some respite, in the simple, undemanding relationship that existed between him and these two men, away from the many demands that threatened to engulf him each day?

Even though Manfred felt that 'in the long run, everybody gets it', this sense of fatalism does not seem to have blunted his desire to fly in combat. And finally, a Fokker was allocated to No. 8, which allowed him the chance to test his mettle in a fighter. It was an episode he recorded in his memoirs as though it marked a turning point in his life:

> From the beginning of my career as a pilot I had the sole ambition to fly in a single-seater aircraft. After canvassing my commanding officer for some time I at last was given permission to fly a Fokker. The rotating engine was a novelty and it was a strange feeling to be quite alone during a flight.
>
> This aircraft jointly belonged to a friend of mine (Leutnant Hans Reimann) and myself. Both he and I were afraid that the other would smash up the 'box'.

Reimann, who was the first to try the Fokker, proceeded over the lines and fought with a Nieuport Scout, which forced him down to a rough landing in no man's land. He hid in a shell hole until darkness fell and then made good his escape, returning to Kasta 8 the following day. Luckily, a replacement Fokker soon became available and it was von Richthofen's turn to take it up on patrol, an event he later recalled with some humour:

> A few days later I was given another Fokker. This time I felt a moral obligation to attend to its destruction myself! I was flying for the third time when the engine suddenly stopped working. I had to land right away in a field and, in a moment, this beautiful machine was converted into a mass of scrap metal. It was a miracle that I was not hurt.

This was an inauspicious start to his career as a fighter pilot, but one von Richthofen seems to have treated lightly, making a joke of the crash and laughing at himself in the process. Oddly enough he has often been portrayed as an austere, rather distant man who made few friends and lacked a sense of humour. Of course, he may have adopted such a mask as a means of protecting himself from the sense of loss that could soon swamp survivors, as Tim Hervey described. However, in von Richthofen's case I think this is only partially true and the general description of him being aloof, even cold, may well be wide of the mark. True, when becoming a commanding officer and taking responsibility for a large group of men, he would have to display these traits, but this is so of anyone who becomes a leader – the successful exercising of military discipline, in fact, demands it. But go beyond this and I believe you find a man of surprising warmth and generosity, who did indeed have a sense of humour and a sense of fun. This would not have been in evidence when flying in combat, which he treated with all the seriousness it deserved, but would emerge at other times, when there was less pressure. If this is true, the image of the cold, calculating soldier is incorrect. So where might the truth lie?

Kunigunde described her eldest son as 'quiet and tranquil', but also loving, honest, considerate, caring, patient, calm, 'always clear, orderly and prepared' and, undoubtedly, dutiful. He was also her confidant on many matters, demonstrating a maturity of thought that she found of immense help. To this end she wrote that, 'he could always understand the essence of difficult questions and give advice with a common sense that scarcely went with his youth'. And she also saw his bravery and fearlessness when faced with a challenge and a sense of fun when things didn't always go well. All this may well be true, but it is also a fact of life that a mother will inevitably describe her children in a generous way, especially after their death at an early age. Tragedy and grief will inevitably have this effect, so perhaps we have to look elsewhere for a broader view of Manfred's personality.

Hans-Georg von der Osten may have come closest to describing von Richthofen when he wrote of his late friend and commander:

> He had unbounded courage, which he matched with the stealth and patience of a great hunter. Not for him rushing in without thought of the consequences or the safety of those around him, for there was little point in throwing away lives unless the battle was so desperate as to require such a sacrifice. This certainly became the case in 1918 when we faced overwhelming odds.
>
> In the air his presence was commanding and in his little red machines we could all see him even in the midst of a battle, drawing courage from his presence and handling of the formation. At times he seemed to be everywhere, protecting us all. He couldn't alleviate all losses but he certainly ensured they were as few as possible. As soon as we landed his first concern was for our welfare and for any wounds to be quickly attended to. Some would still wish to fly even when patched up or exhausted, but the leader would not allow this, no matter how hard the pilot pressed him, until, that is, he was sure that

they had fully recovered. However, he never spared himself in this way as events in 1917 and 1918 proved.

When away from flying von Richthofen remained the leader, but did so in a calm and rational way, rarely if ever raising his voice. If he did, it was done so that he could quickly pull a person back into line before their behaviour required firmer action. He would exercise authority not as martinets, to whom the exercise of power is everything, but with measured authority calculated to make sure all ran smoothly.

He certainly had a sense of fun and enjoyed the occasional practical joke, even when he, or his pet dog, were the target. He laughed often and openly. I have seen the cine films taken by Anthony Fokker when visiting von Richthofen in late 1917 and they show the Rittmeister laughing and joking with his pilots, even acting for the camera in a humorous way. These films, although silent, capture the way he was day by day. Sadly, they do not record the sound of his pleasant voice. Although quite softly spoken it carried authority and made you listen to his wise words.

He was a strong and considerate man with whom you could talk on many issues, both professional and personal.

While respecting rank he did not allow himself to be sidelined by senior officers if he believed an issue to be of sufficient importance to his Jasta or Geschwader. Although at all times maintaining military etiquette he generally pursued an issue in such a way as to ensure that he made his point firmly and, more often than not, got his own way on such things as the way we fought, new equipment and much more. If he had lived he would surely have reached very senior rank, though whether he could have served Hitler is quite another issue.

Although he was of a high caste he carried no prejudices. If you were prepared to fight and die for your country, he accepted you for what you were no matter what your background or philosophies. Once you had earnt his praise he would always support you and place your needs first, whenever he could. In this he was quite unusual.

I liked him immensely and thought of him as a friend, despite our difference in rank. He was one of the most gallant men I have ever known.

To a certain extent much of von der Osten's words describe the man von Richthofen became in 1917 when fame had taken over his life. In mid-1916 this was still in the future when, for the moment, simply struggling with the monoplane fighter took up much of his time. However, all the basic ingredients of the character described here were in evidence, taking him forward, in Anthony Fokker's words, 'by sheer force of personality'.

By the time von Richthofen began his first tenuous attempts at flying a fighter, the tempo of war on the Western Front was growing more challenging, aided by new tactics being employed by the enemy and the arrival of some new, better aircraft. During February the tables began to turn with the arrival of first DH.2 pusher biplane fighters, fitted with forward-firing Lewis guns, which soon equipped seven squadrons. So armed the British pilots soon found themselves able to outmanoeuvre the Fokkers and gradually take a toll of their numbers.

A little later French-built Nieuport scouts also began appearing in ever greater numbers, swiftly adding to the Fokker's problems. Very quickly the initiative began to pass to the Allies, but science moved on and, as each side searched for new and better aircraft, the battle ebbed and flowed. As this happened the aces began to fall with gloomy regularity, including Immelmann, who died on 18 June. Nevertheless, in a war where a single battle could take the lives of hundreds of thousands of men the numbers lost in the air were paltry by comparison and other heroes soon came forward to fill the gaps.

For Manfred, the chances of joining this elite group appeared to be diminishing rapidly. With Reimann's help in destroying two monoplanes in such short order, with no more immediately forthcoming, both men had to be satisfied with going to war in two-seaters, this time to bolster the army on the Eastern Front. Here intelligence gathering gradually revealed that the Russians were massing for an attack, with the aim of drawing fire away from that summer's 'Big Push' on the Somme. With German forces in ever greater danger on two fronts, but weaker in the East, reinforcements were soon being despatched to counter the threat there. Increased reconnaissance was essential and the battle-hardened Kagohl 2 were soon on their way across Germany to provide this support.

After a four-day journey by train, Manfred arrived in north-western Ukraine and on 1 July began operations. However, it was a tour of duty destined to last only two months, brought to an end by the intervention of Oswald Boelcke himself. In the meantime, Manfred was fully involved in the new campaign:

> At last we arrived at Kovel where we remained accommodated in our railway carriages. There are many advantages in dwelling in a train. One is that we are always ready to travel and need not change our quarters. However, in the heat of the Russian summer a sleeping car is unbearable. Therefore, I agreed with my friends Gerstenberg and Franz Christian von Scheele to 'take quarters' in the forest nearby.

In Alfred Gerstenberg Manfred appears to have found a good friend, and they remained so until the end of his days. Born in April 1893, Alfred's life followed a similar path to von Richthofen's. After military school he joined the same Uhlan regiment, seeing service on the Eastern Front, where he was awarded the Iron Cross 1st and 2nd Class during 1914 for gallantry. However, his war was curtailed later that year when he was wounded and evacuated to Germany. On recovery he transferred to the Air Service at the same time as Manfred, suggesting that they may have discussed becoming airmen together.

For pilots and observers, the war in the East was very different in nature. Here the enemy air force they faced lacked the equipment or tenacious attitude of the French or British. But this war had its own perils, as Manfred well knew from his previous service there as an observer, and so careful preparation was necessary:

> One day our whole squadron set out to bomb Manjewieze, an important railway station twenty miles behind the lines ... this station was absolutely crammed with huge trains ... here was a target worth bombing.
>
> The aeroplanes were ready for starting. Every pilot tried his engine, for it is a dangerous thing to be forced to land against one's will on the wrong side of the front line. The Russians hate the fliers. If they catch a flying man they will certainly kill him ... The anti-aircraft guns used by them are sometimes quite good.

The attacks went on day by day with little way of knowing what damage they were doing. The daytime temperatures in the vastness of Ukraine during August can reach unbearable heights and so it proved to be that summer. There was little to do between raids except sit about trying to find whatever shade they could, anything unusual happening to relieve the boredom being greatly valued. A visit by Oswald Boelcke, by now a national hero, provided just the tonic they needed:

> In the evening the great man duly arrived [having been on tour in Turkey and Macedonia, seeing for himself how the aerial war was going there]. He imagined that he would now go to the Somme to organise a new fighting squadron [Jagdstaffel/ Jasta 2]. He had been authorised to choose men who seemed particularly well-qualified for this purpose.

I dared not ask him to be taken on ... Still the idea of fighting again on the Western Front appealed to me. There is nothing finer for a young cavalry officer than a chase in the air.

The next morning, he was to leave us [von Richthofen presumably having spent the night in an agony of indecision wishing he had said something that might have secured him the transfer he seems to have craved]. Quite early somebody knocked on my door and before me stood the great man with his Pour le Merite ... I had never imagined that he had come to look me up in order to ask me to become his pupil. I almost fell on his neck when he asked me whether I cared to go with him to the Somme. Three days later I was on a railway train travelling through the whole of Germany straight to my new squadron. At last my greatest wish was fulfilled.

When I left a good friend of mine called out after me, 'Don't come back without the Pour le Merite'.

As he journeyed westwards Manfred took time to visit Schweidnitz and see his mother, possibly for the last time, as she later recalled:

On 25th August, Manfred surprised us with a visit ... he was burnt brown by the Russian sun and in the best of humour, enthusiastically telling stories while we sat in the garden under the large chestnut tree. He described these scenes so vividly that you believed yourself there ... Manfred leans against the tree trunk. There is something joyful in his voice, 'Now, it's to be pursuit flying, Mama!'. The following day, Albrecht and Manfred went hunting in the Nonnenbusch. They shot 15 fowl. It is burning hot, every step on the street is an agony.

At this point Kunigunde describes how she was visited by a recently bereaved woman wearing mourning clothes and suffering in the heat. This clearly left her deeply depressed. Once the grief-stricken woman left, Kunigunde began to fret even more while her eldest son looked on:

> The woman has gone. We are alone. Manfred looks at me with his large eyes. 'Mama,' he says, 'Do not ever put yourself through such torment for me, promise me that.' These were his words. I looked at him astonished. Then he put his arm around me and laughed. A joyous, carefree laugh, which frightened away these disturbing thoughts.

As he passed through Germany the excitement over his posting would have dominated Manfred's thoughts, though undoubtedly subdued by the sight of his deeply worried mother. But the country he slowly traversed was in an ever-increasing state of turmoil. Such was the concern that many people were beginning to give voice to demands for peace negotiations to begin and bring to an end a war that had cost so many their lives. However, with Ludendorff dominating all around him, any such action seemed doomed to failure. Nevertheless, towards the end of the year, and led by liberal elements in the Reichstag, Germany and its allies publicly called for peace negotiations to begin, stating no specific conditions in advance beyond the need to retain some of the land they now occupied. And so feelers were sent out, perhaps more in hope than expectation of success, but at least with an intention of ending the conflict.

On the surface this appears to been a sensible step to take, but the politics behind it were complex and divisive. Chancellor Alfred von Bethmann Hollweg, the chief advocate of this initiative and never a great supporter of the war, thought time was not on Germany's side and a crushing defeat was inevitable if it continued. In this he was backed by the Social Democrats, the largest political party in the Reichstag.

At the same time, and desperate to break the military stalemate, Germany's military leaders sought approval to begin unrestricted submarine warfare, a course Bethmann Hollweg feared would bring the United States into the war on the Allied side. By pursuing a peace initiative, he believed that he might ease Germany's increasingly grave domestic and military position. If the Allies accepted Germany's peace offer, Bethmann Hollweg argued, unrestricted submarine warfare might be averted and negotiations could be based on the existing status quo, which heavily favoured Germany. If they refused, which was likely, the Allies would be responsible for prolonging the war, not Germany. This, it was hoped, would draw liberal and socialist elements together in supporting the war and might even encourage rapidly tiring forces to greater effort.

The Chancellor also believed that by publicising Germany's desire for peace it would highlight Allied intransigence, making it more likely that neutral countries, including the United States, would more readily accept the need for unrestricted submarine warfare. Finally, Bethmann Hollweg argued that a refusal by their enemies to negotiate a peace settlement would only spur anti-war movements in France and Russia to greater efforts, encouraging one or the other to sign a separate peace with the Central Powers. A naïve view perhaps, but, with Russia seemingly on a course for revolution and civil war, at least possible on the Eastern Front. But neither France or Britain, for that matter, would consider any peace agreement that did not see Germany evacuate the occupied areas. And their leaders had already formed the view that any settlement must see Germany admitting responsibility for causing the war, which would be impossible for them to accept.

So efforts to bring the war to an end, even when urged and supported by President Woodrow Wilson in Washington, came to nothing. In fact, this failure of diplomacy seemed to mark a worsening of the violence, with the towering figure of Ludendorff pulling all the strings on the German side.

In truth, any attempt to bring about peace in 1916 or 1917 stalled on the simple premise that the leaders of each belligerent nation found it safer to demand ever-greater efforts from their people than to admit that all their sacrifices had been in vain. As time went on, and the stakes grew higher, no player felt able to leave the game when outright victory remained a possibility. But as Germany continued along this path the difficulties faced by its people grew ever larger, probably greater than in France or Britain. With the Allies' ability to trade worldwide, sufficient food and raw material could be imported to stave off severe shortages and keep their war going. However, with the Royal Navy's blockade effectively strangling Germany's economy, famine remained a distinct possibility. And it was a problem that would only get worse as the third winter of the war approached.

The German economy was described at the time as 'managing to produce most of the industrial requirements of the war (often by creating new, "ersatz solutions" as they were called)', but at the same time its leaders 'failed to secure a sufficiency of food for all its needs'. With war on two fronts and supplies restricted, shortages at home and in the front lines became even more pronounced. With a particularly cold winter in 1916–17, these problems rapidly grew worse. The 'Turnip Winter', as it was called, was the result.

Poor weather led to a much smaller harvest than usual, with food supplies already shrunk by a third due to the blockade. In a near perfect storm of circumstances, the problem was exacerbated by the army appropriating agricultural horses for military service. Then there was the conscription of tens of thousands of farm workers, leaving only the old and infirm to work the land. And, finally, there was a shortage of fertilisers, much of which had been sent to Krupps for use in the production of explosives. As a result, many people had to survive on near starvation diets in which turnips were a mainstay.

Perhaps predicting the problems likely to be faced, the government brought in food rationing in mid-1916, under the control of the War Food Office. But with an ever-diminishing supply of foodstuffs, the daily diet was set at 1,560 calories, soon dropping to 1,000 calories per day that winter. This was a matter of the greatest importance because the Imperial Health Office had, for example, set a limit of

3,000 calories for adult working or fighting men. At the same time the government tried to set maximum food prices, in an effort to ensure that all could afford to eat. In practice severe price inflation crept in and when coupled to the shortages brought famine to many households.

The comparatively affluent von Richthofen family could not avoid these shortages, as Kunigunde gloomily reported. However, her husband's occasional hunting trips may have helped ease the problem slightly:

> Bread and meat ration cards were issued on 18th June. From now on there will be four pounds of bread per person each week, one pound of meat, one pound of potatoes and one pound of sugar per month. Semolina, barley and macaroni are nowhere to be found any more. There are rarely eggs, cheese or butter to buy. Running a household is now thoroughly unpleasant.

With morale seeming to reach rock bottom in late 1916, many in Germany might well have supported Bethmann Hollweg's bid for peace that year. But military ambition trumped all and as 1916 gave way to 1917 the need for good news of any sort became even more pressing; as did the need for heroes that the public could follow and whose example they might seek to emulate.

When he arrived on the Somme, in late August, Manfred could not have guessed what would soon befall him. If he had known, he may have recoiled in horror at the way his life would soon be taken over and exploited by commanders eager to keep the war going and secure victory, no matter what the cost.

Chapter 5

From Fledgling to Hawk

You must have wondered why I have not written before now. For the first time I sit at my table and take my pen in my hand. I have been kept continually busy. The last time I flew it was in a substitute aeroplane in which I could do little, and so got the worst in aerial combat. Yesterday my allocated 'crate' arrived, and just think, while test flying it, I saw an English squadron on our flank. I flew into it and shot one down. The occupants were an English officer and a Non-Commissioned Officer. I am very proud of my test flight. The shot down aircraft was naturally credited to me.

You know that my friend Schweinichen has fallen. I was going to visit him on the day he was killed, as he was right here in my vicinity [he was actually killed on 24 August while serving as a Leutnant with the 4th Guard Foot Regiment when Manfred was travelling west from Kovel].

Manfred writing to his mother on 18 September 1916

A sense of excitement is conveyed in these few short sentences, which is not surprising in the circumstances. Since his arrival at Jasta 2's base near Bertincourt, on the northern edge of the Somme battlefield, much had happened as he began to learn fighter tactics under the tutorship of the experienced, ever patient and perceptive Boelcke. During the summer this airfield, which was now only 8km from the front after the terribly slow advance made by the British and French armies, had been the home of several squadrons, including a Fokker Staffel. Because it was a well-established base, and the Somme front remained active as the British pushed towards Flers and High Wood, it was decided to establish Jasta 2 there.

In fact, its creation, was a significant step forward in the way fighter squadrons waged war. Ever aware of the changing face of aerial conflict, and prompted by a paper on the subject written by Boelcke himself, a conference had been held at Charleville on the eve of his departure to Turkey, attended by senior officers including Lieth-Thomsen. Its purpose was a simple one – to agree new tactics and ways in which the air force might be brought to battle more effectively. For example, operating fighters singly or occasionally in small groups would no longer suffice, especially when enemy formations had increased in size and strength. Earlier in 1916 the first step along this route had been taken with the creation of the *Kampfeinsitzer Kommando* units, which I described earlier. For a while this idea proved successful, but with the gradual erosion of the monoplane's superiority, a new and better solution was needed.

At Charleville Boelcke made a strong case for larger, better-equipped fighters and more numerous squadrons before as Lieth-Thomsen later recalled, before going on to emphasize that:

> It would not suffice to merely form a number of pilots into a company of single-seater fighters. On the contrary it was essential to train all members of the Staffel to co-operate by strict discipline and thus better organise aerial warfare ... Boelcke spent several days with my staff in order to collaborate with our experts in establishing the basic principles of scout flying and making preparations for the development of the air arm. The memorandum he wrote on the exploitation and development of the Jagdstaffels was an eloquent testimony to the clear-sighted view which enabled him to identify the significance of this weapon and foresee its possibilities.

After much discussion a target was set for thirty-seven new fighter squadrons being ready for service by the end of 1917, equipped with the latest fighters flown by specially selected and trained pilots. As a result, the first of these units, Jasta 1, led by Hauptmann Martin Zander, came into existence on 22 August, followed days later by Jasta 2, with Boelcke in command.

With the enemy pressing forward, Bertincourt was thought too close to the front for all but fighter squadrons, which had the ability to scramble and get away quickly in the event of attack. By doing so they were also in a position to intercept any Royal Flying Corps aircraft heading eastwards to bomb, observe or harry German forces on the ground. The airfield was well suited to this interception role. While the fighter pilots would often undertake standing patrols to ward of the enemy, much of the time they would sit by their aircraft while the sky above the trenches was scanned through range finders, telescopes and binoculars for approaching aircraft. In time, army observers, even closer to the lines, would phone through reports of enemy activity calling up support if needed. This meant that the fighters could be better directed and make best use of limited resources available to them.

Once established, these tactics became another 'string to the bow' for fighter squadrons to exploit as they fought an increasingly hostile enemy; and continued to be used, with refinements such as radar, for many decades to come. One only has to look at the way Fighter Command fought the Battle of Britain and the Luftwaffe defended the skies over Germany in the Second World War to see how these tactics continued to evolve.

In truth, Jasta 2's role, and that of the other new fighter squadrons, was primarily a defensive one, relying heavily on new more powerful fighters, with higher speeds and greater rate of climb, for success. The monoplanes lacked both these qualities and, with enemy aircraft getting better and more numerous, had become something of a liability, even when armed with two or even three machine guns. By the summer of 1916 more advanced aircraft were indeed reaching the front, led by the new Albatros D.I biplane fighter.

In many ways this was an innovative design for the time and had resulted from experimental work undertaken by the engineering trio of Thelen, Schubert and Gnädig. Following a series of successful proving flights, the aircraft was ordered by Idflieg in June 1916 and soon entered production, some of the first fifty built arriving at Bertincourt as autumn approached.

Experiments had shown that an aircraft such as this could be greatly strengthened if fitted with a semi-monocoque plywood fuselage. This also had the benefit of making it lighter than fabric-covered designs, and its flowing, sleek profile gave it good aerodynamic qualities, which helped increase speed, particularly in a dive. And with a choice of two motors – a Benz 150hp BZ.III or a Mercedes (Daimler) D.III 160hp six-cylinder, water-cooled, inline engine – the aircraft was ready for production. However, the second of these quickly gained favour because of its greater power, which allowed twin, fixed *Spandau* machine guns to be fitted without reducing the aircraft's overall performance.

Those who were soon flying the type in service found that its relatively high-wing loading could make it difficult to handle, but this was offset by its speed and armament, which, for a time, made them better than anything the enemy could put into the air. In Jasta 2's hands it soon proved its worth, as did the Albatros D.II and D.III that superseded it, though by the time the D.V appeared in July 1917 its superiority had waned considerably, as the enemy produced new and better aircraft.

No matter how confident the individual, being a new boy can be rather daunting, especially when you are being assessed in a very demanding role, facing rejection if falling short of expectations. Although von Richthofen had proved himself a capable pilot flying slow, ungainly two-seaters, stepping up to fly fighters, especially such a new and largely untried type, could present insurmountable problems for a newcomer, even with Boelcke's help. But he was not alone in feeling this way, because he was surrounded by a number of other men new to fighters. Hans Reimann had accompanied Manfred from Kovel; Erwin Bohme, at 37 perhaps too old to be a fighter pilot, came from Kasta 10; and then there were others such as Leutnants von Arnim and Gunther, accompanied by a large contingent of NCOs and men to support the ever-growing squadron.

As they began to assemble, so the first aircraft began to arrive. Vizefeldwebel Leopold Reimann, then with sister squadron Jasta 1, brought with him a single Albatros when posted to the new squadron and shortly afterwards two new Fokker D.III biplanes were flown in from 2nd Army's Air Park, one by Boelcke himself. And it was in one of these two aircraft that he forced down his twentieth victim on 2 September over Thiepval – a DH.2 flown by Captain Robert Wilson.

Slowly but surely Jasta 2 came together, with the less-experienced men such as von Richthofen beginning to absorb the valuable lessons that Boelcke had so recently learned himself in combat. Key to these tactics was the ability to fly as a cohesive group and the need to gain an advantage by using speed and height. Then there were such specific things as choosing when and where to attack and open fire (the closer the better), making use of the elements to screen your approach – out of the sun if possible – not turning away when attacked but responding aggressively, shooting carefully and economically and much more. It was a master class in tactics that von Richthofen soon absorbed, as would other fighter pilots then and in later generations. However, theory has to be turned into practice and for some this proved difficult even when flying superior aircraft, though not Manfred, as he later reported:

On the previous day we received our new aeroplanes, and the next day [17 September] Boelcke was to fly with us. We were all beginners, so everything he said to us was important and entirely true.

The 17th was a gloriously fine day, so it was to be expected that the English would be very active. Before we set off Boelcke repeated his instructions and for the first time we flew as a squadron ... We had just arrived at the front when we saw an enemy squadron proceeding towards Cambrai. Of course, Boelcke saw them first ... Soon we understood the situation, and we all endeavoured to follow Boelcke very closely.

We approached cautiously and positioned ourselves between the front and our opponents. If they wished to turn back, they had to pass us first ... They were seven in number and we were only five. All the Englishmen flew large bomb-carrying two-seaters and in a few seconds the 'dance' began.

Boelcke closed in on the first enemy machine, but did not shoot. I followed, with my comrades close by ... I did not think for long and took aim and fired as he shot back. We both missed and a struggle began. It was important for me to get on his tail ... Apparently he was no beginner, because he knew it would be the end if I got behind him. At this time I did not have the belief that 'he must fall' in these situations, but on this occasion I was just curious to see whether he would go down. There is a great difference between these two feelings. When you have shot down your first, second or third opponent then one begins to understand how it is done.

My enemy twisted and turned, flying in zigzag way. I am driven by a single thought, 'he must go down whatever happens'. At last, a favourable moment arrives when he has apparently lost sight of me. Instead of twisting and turning he flies straight and level. In a fraction of a second I am on his tail ... I fire a short burst ... I had flown so close I thought I might crash into him. Suddenly I yelled with excitement, the propeller had stopped turning and he was forced to land and it was impossible for him to reach his own lines. The aircraft was swinging from side to side. Probably something had happened to the pilot and the observer was no longer visible.

The Englishman landed close to the airfield of one of our squadrons. I was so excited that I landed also, in my eagerness I nearly smashed up my machine ... I rushed over and saw a lot of soldiers were running towards the enemy. When I arrived, I discovered that I had in fact shot the engine to pieces, and the pilot and observer were severely wounded. The observer died at once and the pilot while being taken to the nearest dressing station. I honoured the fallen enemy by placing a stone on their grave.

When I returned to base, Boelcke and my other comrades were already at breakfast ... I proudly reported that I had shot down an Englishman. All were elated, for I was not the only one who had been victorious.

These men had experienced a rite of passage as pilots and were quick to celebrate their success, and their survival. Although benefitting from the new Albatros, they were not fighting a defenceless enemy, but one that could fight back, in this case with the redoubtable F.E.2b. Although a pusher biplane, when handled by an experienced crew it could prove to be a difficult nut to crack. This was especially so with an observer able to use a Lewis machine gun with a wider arc of fire than the German fighter possessed. But under Boelcke's leadership Manfred pressed home his attack with great determination 'whatever happened' and triumphed, despite the risks involved.

Manfred, although grown used to killing as a hunter and the sight of death on the battlefield, was now faced with the rather more trying issue of killing men himself. However, there is a remoteness to air fighting that could often create the illusion that pilots were shooting at an aeroplane not a man, as many veterans later reported. The shock came when seeing their enemy close to during a battle, often when they were dying most horribly by bullet, flame or, in these early days of war before parachutes were available, simply falling from a doomed aircraft. Having landed beside his victim, von Richthofen now viewed the consequences of his own action. It is unlikely to have been a pleasant sight, especially with two men badly shot up and haemorrhaging blood. Even for a hardened soldier this could be a disturbing sight.

Von Richthofen doesn't seem to have been a cruel or uncaring man and was intelligent enough to know that the moral issues involved in killing in the name of king and country were not infinite ones. At some point the individual has to accept responsibility for the deaths their actions have caused. For Manfred this moment had arrived and although he dresses up his account with such words as 'elated', 'victorious' and 'proudly', the effect of these killings was probably a much more visceral experience than he cared to recall.

More importantly, those he killed, Captain Tom Rees and Lieutenant Lionel Morris of 11 Squadron, were not simply anonymous names to be recorded on a memorial stone, but men with lives and families who loved and relied upon them – as, in turn, did Kunigunde and Albrecht with their children. Such is the nature of war, but then to callously record these victims as 'victories' and then add them together to make 'scores' and 'aces' is a much darker issue to address. And yet pilots on both sides did the same; it wasn't just a German phenomenon, although they probably exploited it with greater energy and success than the British.

For the front-line pilots, obliged to kill and maim other men at close quarters, preserving one's sanity as they carried out such distasteful duties required something more than stoicism or indifference to survive. Some turned to drink and 'binges' in the mess to help them endure the strain, some bought pets, others turned to sex, while there were those who allowed a deep faith to cloak them and 'God's will' to direct their thoughts. Then there were a few like Albert Ball, who took up gardening and playing an instrument to help subdue dark thoughts, and others, like Edward Mannock, who allowed hatred of the enemy to govern their actions. But some didn't need any of these things, having little regard for the sanctity of life. These men tended to revel in war and the freedom it allowed them. Inevitably one is forced to consider whether von Richthofen, whose killing spree would go on for another twenty months and lead to many more deaths, was such a man or was there more to him than that? For example, did he simply maintain the cloak of being the great hunter as a means of calming increasingly deep misgivings about what he was obliged to do?

If there were indeed issues of conscience, he did much to disguise them, because very soon he adopted many of the trappings of the hunter. He would cut pieces of fabric from downed enemy aircraft or take other souvenir items – machine guns, an engine and so on – to adorn his quarters. Then he would order silver cups from a jeweller in Breslau or Berlin to celebrate each victory and so make light of the carnage he was inflicting. After all, it is one thing to kill an enemy in battle, no matter how unpleasant, because one is obliged to, it is quite another to celebrate those deaths in such a pitilessly cold way. In doing so was von Richthofen revealing himself simply as a killer, or was this a persona he adopted to help disguise his true feelings? As later events would show, it was probably the latter, but for the moment he had to witness the death of two men who had fallen under his guns.

My late grandfather summed up this dichotomy best when recalling an event that took place in May 1918. He and his Lewis Gun team were advancing over ground recently the scene of a German attack that had been turned back with heavy enemy casualties:

> It was the first time I had seen the results of machine gun fire close to. Before then we had been more concerned with harassing fire into back areas. This was very different because now we could see the dead and wounded brought down in

swathes. Many were wounded in their legs because we deliberately fired low to bring them down, but when hitting the ground were again shot but this time through their heads and chests, which did considerable damage.

We were soon moving forward amongst hundreds gathered together in a moaning mass; the living and dead piled up in front of the wire we had quickly erected overnight to hold them up. We were only doing our duty, but it was brutal and cruel nonetheless. I was sickened by the whole business and was greatly relieved to be invalided home a few days later with a flesh wound to my left leg. I had seen a great deal of action since arriving in France with the Post Office Rifles in March 1915, but this was the worst I had experienced. I was sickened by the part I had played in such a massacre. When I have nightmares about the war these are more often than not about that day in May 1918, and I had seen action at Loos, High Wood, Cambrai, Arras and Passchendaele by then so knew only too well the horrors of life in the trenches.

It is hard to imagine that Manfred did not have the same pangs of conscience on 17 September 1916, unless he was indeed a cold-blooded killer, which seems unlikely if his family and friends are to be believed. Either way, his life was soon too fully committed to the day-to-day business of flying and fighting to give these moral issues much thought. But they were there nonetheless and would continue to cast a shadow over him as his 'victories' and his fame grew. If he chose to hide his feelings by slipping on the mantle of hunter who can blame him, but the trophies he collected would act as a highly visible memorial to his success and eventually come to haunt him, as did the death of so many men. There is little wonder that some fighter pilots in both world wars described it as a 'game of blood' with, as Tim Hervey put it, 'no winners, only losers'.

Flushed with success, von Richthofen settled into the routine of flying the single-seaters and gaining experience. There would be many fruitless days as he did so. At the same time, he would look on in admiration, and perhaps some envy, as his hero went up almost daily to seek the enemy and, in so doing, rapidly extended his list of victories:

> This was a time when Boelcke's 'bag' of aircraft shot down increased from twenty to forty within two months. We beginners had not, at the time, his experience, and were satisfied when we did not get a hiding. It was a wonderful phase. Every time we went up we had a fight. Frequently we fought really big battles with forty to sixty English aircraft and unfortunately were often in the minority ... Sometimes they came down to a very low level and visited Boelcke in his quarters, at which they threw their bombs ... The spirit of our leader inspired all his pupils. We trusted him blindly.

Slowly but surely, as the Battle of the Somme drew to a close, and the pressure began to ease, the number of aircraft von Richthofen shot down grew, as did the number of silver cups and other trophies. Two went down to his guns on 23 and 30 September, then four more in October, but a tragedy lay in store that had serious consequences for the Jasta as a whole.

Following an enemy raid on Bertincourt it was decided to transfer Jasta 2 to Lagnicourt. At the time Boelcke was almost crippled by severe attacks of asthma. By rights he should been recovering in hospital, but he refused to leave his squadron, later writing that:

> I have to give my pilots some training. That is not so simple because they are all inspired with such fiery zeal that it is often difficult to put the brakes on them ... But until I get it into their heads that everything depends on sticking together through thick and thin and that it doesn't matter who actually

registers a victory as long as the Staffel wins ... I can talk myself silly, and sometimes I have to turn my heavy batteries on them ... But they take it very willingly.

However, on 28 October, and still in the throes of asthmatic attacks, this lack of co-ordination may have contributed to Boelke's death, as von Richthofen related:

We were flying with Boelke leading once more. The weather was gusty with many clouds.
From a long way away we saw two Englishmen in the air ... We were six ... The fight began in the usual way. Boelcke tackled one and I the other. I had to break away because a German machine got in my way. I looked around and noticed Boelcke getting on the tail of his victim 180 metres away from me ... Close to Boelcke flew a good friend of his (Erwin Bohme) ... both men were shooting and it was likely that the Englishman would fall at any moment. Suddenly I saw the two German machines make a wrong move. Immediately I thought, 'collision'. The two aircraft merely touched one another ... Boelcke drew away from his victim and descended in wide curves ... I noticed that part of his wing had broken off ... Now his aircraft was no longer controllable. It fell accompanied by his faithful friend.

Bohme, who also recorded his memories of this encounter before his death in combat on 29 November 1917, remembered these events a little differently:

We soon attacked some English machines we found flying over Flers; they were fast single seaters that defended themselves well ... We tried to force them down by barring their way, a manoeuvre we had practised successfully. Boelcke and I had

> just got one Englishman between us when another opponent, chased by von Richthofen, cut across our path. Boelcke and I dodged him, but for a moment our wings prevented us from seeing one another.
>
> How can I describe my feelings from the moment when Boelcke suddenly loomed up a few metres away on my right. He put his machine down and I pulled mine up, but we touched as we passed and we both fell earthwards. It was only just the faintest of touches, but the terrific speed made it a violent impact ... I only had a bit of my undercarriage ripped away, but the extreme tip of his left wing was torn away.

Bohme managed to control his aircraft, but Boelcke's upper wing broke away, causing him to crash. Shocked by the part he'd played in his leader's death, he landed heavily. His already damaged undercarriage collapsed and the aircraft came to rest upside down, its pilot unhurt. In the days and weeks that followed he was racked by guilt and could not be consoled, though, ultimately, no blame could be attached to him. Collisions during combat, when many aircraft are twisting and turning in close proximity to each other, were a fairly common occurrence and this was just another sad example of this happening.

Fate decreed that Boelcke did not survive, but by the end of October he was a very tired man whose physical state had been seriously undermined by illness. Earlier in the year concern for his safety had led him to be taken off operational flying. In anger he had written that:

> The Crown Prince would not let me fly again under any circumstances ... One of my fellow officers gave me a wise lecture to the effect that I was no longer a private man who could play with his life at will but the property of the German nation, which still expected much of me ... It was a direct order from the Emperor ... I was to sit in a glass case in Charleville.

However, the service was so hard pressed during August that getting men of his calibre back into the air again was essential and, in any case, he was willing to go, after a brief rest. It is impossible to say whether battle fatigue contributed to his death, but it may have done so. By October he had endured a great deal and had probably reached the end of his tether.

Fischer, his servant, was a witness to Boelcke's gradual decline and probably came closest to describing his condition at this time:

> My captain kept growing thinner and more serious. The superhuman burden of seven take-offs a day for fights and the worries about his Staffel weighed him down. General von Bülow wanted to send him on leave because he was overworked, but he would not go. 'I am needed here,' he said. He was always cheerful when he came back from a victory with the Staffel, but otherwise was often in a very depressed mood in the last few days.

In his case, and despite Boelcke's propaganda value, senior commanders seemed prepared to rest him permanently. However, his sense of duty to Kaiser, country and the men of Jasta 2, overrode considerations of his health and safety until it was too late. So personal choice trumped more practical considerations and Boelcke went to his death and the public mourned in a way not often seen before, exposing an obvious shortcoming in the cult of celebrity so cleverly exploited as a morale booster. When Immelmann died in the summer, flaws in this strategy were first revealed, now Boelcke's death marked a significant escalation. A living hero was one thing, a dead one quite another. But the German High Command, now with the ruthless Ludendorff in control, was committed to this policy and would pursue it no matter what the cost. And with this, new heroes were quickly sought for promotion and exploitation.

Standing in stark contrast to Boelcke's increasing tiredness and melancholia at this time, von Richthofen displayed a less troubled attitude to the war, if letters to his mother accurately reflect his state of mind at this time:

> A wing broke off and he plunged into the ground. His skull was fractured in the impact, so he was dead at once. It affected us all deeply, as if one of our favourite brothers had been taken. At his funeral, I carried the pillow with his medals. In six weeks we have had six dead and one wounded: two have lost their nerve.
>
> I shot down my seventh yesterday, after I had previously accounted for the sixth. Up to now my nerves have not suffered all the ills that have affected the others.

It is interesting how aware Manfred is of the way stress can depress the spirit of the fighting man. As a result, he seems to be looking inwards to see how deeply it might be affecting him. And in confessing his worries to his mother he found a confiding rock to cling to as the war became ever more desperate. She in turn had only her journal in which to confide her increasingly sad thoughts:

> These days I go around fairly depressed, perhaps it is because I have so many sorrows, like all the people I meet. I find the faces have changed – one doesn't find a 'peace face' any longer ... In most faces there is a certain hurried absent-mindedness. Malnutrition makes itself clear and the condition of the nerves is no longer good.
>
> At the front unspeakable things have been done. It is as Manfred once wrote, 'There is not so much iron as there are iron men out here'. But the pre-eminence of war's machinery, money and food is overpowering. I can no longer believe in a victory, as much as I revolt against such a thought. It will be well less than a stalemate ... How wonderful it would be if the war now came to an end.

Manfred had the war to distract him, his mother had nothing but gnawing worries to fill her days. In the event both showed courage, stoicism and fortitude in the face of these horrors, as did millions of others on both sides of the line. They may have questioned the legitimacy of continuing the war, but they still did their duty as best they could. In Manfred's case it had an added dimension because he would soon take on the mantle so bravely worn by Boelcke. Being selected to carry his medals at the funeral, almost as chief mourner, probably indicated that Boelcke's crown had now passed to the apprentice.

One wonders whether von Richthofen, whose fighting spirit was second to none, and who had begun to demonstrate leadership qualities, was deliberately chosen to fulfil this role? If so, it was a very astute move on a number of levels. He was an ace, who seemed likely to go on to even greater success, if he survived. He was a nobleman with some charisma who cut an attractive figure. He was a seemingly fearless fighter determined to pursue his country's cause no matter what the consequences. All in all, he was ideal material for Ludendorff's public relations team to knead into shape.

Consciously or unconsciously, von Richthofen was soon drawn into this world, as his score and reputation grew. One can only assume that he did not realise where this path would take him or understand the added stress he would have to bear as a result. It may also have been the case that the propaganda department little knew the monster they were creating. As the war went from bad to worse, and the privations increased exponentially, a man such as von Richthofen was valued 'above rubies'. Albeit, one that might be killed at any moment, destroying the hopes and dreams of many in the process.

With the loss of Boelcke, and many other pilots in the first few weeks of its existence, Jasta 2's personnel were changing constantly. Very quickly Stefan Kirmaier was promoted to Oberleutnant and placed in command, successfully leading the squadron until killed in November having brought down eleven enemy aircraft. His going left a gap that was temporarily filled by the Jasta's non-flying chief administrative officer, Oberleutnant Karl-Heinrich Bodenschatz, a man who would soon become an important figure in Manfred's life. While this happened it was necessary for a senior pilot to oversee operational matters and, it seems, von Richthofen fulfilled this role until a permanent replacement was found. This proved to be Oberleutnant Franz Walz, a pre-war aviator who, when flying two-seater reconnaissance aircraft, had been credited with six victories. Having just overseen the creation of Jasta 19, he was thought to be a sound replacement for Kirmaier. However, he seems to have lacked the fighting spirit of his two predecessors or von Richthofen for that matter.

At this stage it is important to introduce Bodenschatz, who was born during December 1890 at Rehau, Bavaria. Like von Richthofen he was a pre-war soldier who, in 1910, enlisted in the 8th Bavarian Infantry Regiment and was a cadet at the War Academy in Metz until 1912. Following Germany's entry into the war he saw active service on the Western Front. After being wounded four times, and possibly becoming unfit for front-line service, he was transferred to the German Air Force as adjutant to Jasta 2, arriving in the immediate aftermath of Boelcke's death. Although an administrator, he soon developed a keen awareness of the needs of the young pilots and ran matters on the ground in a firm, but understanding way. In this role he soon began to forge a strong bond with von Richthofen and, later on, Hermann Goring.

While these changes were taking place, von Richthofen continued to fly and fight, increasing the number of enemy aircraft he brought down. With winter fast approaching, opportunities became fewer and fewer as the Western Front grew quieter.

If the accumulation of medals was von Richthofen's aim, the award of the Order of the House of Hohenzollern may have assuaged this need for a time, but it fell short of Germany's ultimate award, the

Pour le Mérite. When told of this, Kunigunde allowed her maternal feelings, and a slight sense of injustice, to come to the fore:

> He (Manfred) shot down his seventh and eighth opponents [on 3 and 9 November, apparently killing three men as he did so]. When Boelcke shot down his eighth, he was awarded the Pour le Merite.

With the pace of war changing rapidly, the number of men able to claim a large number of 'victories' rose quickly. In response, the High Command took the decision to set the bar much higher for fighter pilots when qualifying for this most prestigious of awards at something closer to sixteen or more enemy aircraft destroyed.

Manfred does not appear to have commented on this change or expressed any displeasure he may have felt at receiving a less-prestigious award. However, it is possible that Kunigunde's words reflected the frustration her son felt and then conveyed to her during a brief period of leave following his eighth success, which she wrote about later:

> At dawn (on the 14th) Manfred arrived. He looked slim and well. And what things he has experienced. All the whole day he had such stories to tell. Boelcke's death affected him very deeply and he praised the man's inner simplicity and perfect self-control, plus the friendly steadiness of his character, which did not allow any sense of favouritism (I felt that Boelcke and Manfred shared many of these characteristics). Certainly he had not been inclined to show the slightest preference to one side or the other: he was the fulcrum, the mid-point.
>
> Manfred then described his own battles ... For him these are the last relics of an old chivalry found in a contest

where man is pitted against man. He doesn't think much of aerobatics. 'This is only something to catch the eye,' he believes. He usually flies at 5000 metres and only opens fire when at 30 metres. But he believes that one does not need to be a marksman. He then referred to Boelcke, with whom he went hunting a few times. Boelcke didn't hit a thing, yet in the air he always hit his target. They both agreed that the heart makes the fighter pilot.

Lately the enemy have appeared in greater numbers. Manfred shot down his eight from a squadron of 40 to 50 bombers. Often their own wings are riddled with enemy bullets. At first, these incidents were carefully considered, but now no one pays much attention to them. Many miracles happen in the air.

The next day we all went to Trebnig, where my brother's daughter was getting married ... We were all happy and Manfred was made much of. Yet on the night of the wedding, he left again.

Manfred returned to the Western Front and was very quickly in action again, suggesting that he might have flown one of Jasta 2's aircraft across Germany to visit his family family, a sign, perhaps, of his growing status and importance to the air service. However, with November producing exceptionally wet and cloudy weather, the opportunities for combat diminished and it would be four days before von Richthofen increased his 'score'. This time he triumphed over another F.E.2 in an encounter he later described in cold, simplistic terms in his combat report:

20 November 1916.
FE2b No. 4848.
18 Squadron.
Engine No. 295 WD 1359.
Guns: 3085; 1365. 16

15 hours above Grandcourt.

Vickers two seater, fallen near Grandcourt. Aeroplane could not be secured as under fire. Occupants: One killed – Lt George Doughty (the observer), Lt Gilbert Stall (the pilot), seriously wounded, prisoner.

Together with four planes I attacked a Vickers two seater type above the clouds at 2,500 metres altitude. After 300 shots adversary broke through the clouds pursued by me. Near Grandcourt I shot him down

Weather: Low clouds, strong winds and showers.

For a natural marksman to expend 300 rounds of ammunition von Richthofen was either having a bad day or the Matlock born, 25 year old Hall (not Stall as recorded in von Richthofen's report) handled his aircraft so well that Manfred couldn't take advantage of his aircraft's superior performance. Nevertheless, the British crew still put up a good fight before von Richthofen's gunfire finally took effect and they were forced down. The 21 year old, Edinburgh born Doughty, who occupied the observer's vulnerable seat at the front of the nacelle, quickly succumbed to his wounds, while Hall struggled on for a few more days in hospital at Cambrai before dying on the 30th. They were clearly brave men, but even an indomitable fighting spirit wasn't enough when flying such an unwieldy two-seater. However, three days later Manfred met a British 'ace' who would be more than a match for him. It was an event of such importance that it drew even more attention to von Richthofen and further promoted his name.

In his memoirs von Richthofen simply wrote 'Major Hawker' before describing this noteworthy day:

I was extremely proud when I was informed that the aviator I had brought down on 23rd November 1916 was the English Immelmann. In view of the nature of the battle it was clear to me that I had fought a flying ace.

Lanoe Hawker, a 25-year-old Englishman, was worthy of this praise, having become a well-established fighter ace and been awarded the Victoria Cross. Such was his reputation that word of his gallantry and accomplishments had soon spread to the German side of the lines. In the circumstances, it is little wonder that von Richthofen felt moved to call him the English Immelmann.

Born the son of a naval officer in Longparish, Hampshire, during December 1890, he was expected to join the Royal Navy, but found the course at Dartmouth too much for his apparently weak constitution. Stil determined to follow a military career, he transferred to the Royal Military Academy at Woolwich, where he was gazetted as an officer with the Royal Engineers in 1911. It was here that a fascination with flying took hold and two years later he was awarded the Royal Aero Club Aviators Certificate. In due course, he sought a transfer to the Royal Flying Corps and was posted to No. 6 Squadron, which was destined to reach the Western Front in October 1914. Initially the squadron was equipped with Farman biplanes, but then converted to the rather more advanced B.E.2Cs. From the beginning he showed great bravery and took part in many operations, later on as a flight commander. The most daring of these – a bombing raid against the Zeppelin sheds at Gontrode on 19 April 1915 – resulted in the award of the Distinguished Service Order and produced many headlines in Britain, where Zeppelin attacks on the mainland were causing great concern to the public.

Within days Hawker and No. 6 were embroiled in the Second Battle of Ypres, which ran from 22 April to 25 May 1915. Early on his aircraft was hit by ground fire and he was severely wounded in the foot. Nevertheless, he refused to remain in hospital and, after being patched up, returned to the squadron to resume flying again. However, he could only remain operational if he were carried to and from his aircraft each day. As soon as the worst of the fighting was over he finally agreed to take leave and allow his injury time to heal properly. Nevertheless, by June he was back in the air again and soon shooting down enemy aircraft.

On 25 July he was patrolling over Passchendaele in a Bristol Scout and attacked three German aircraft in quick succession. Into the first of these he emptied a complete drum of ammunition from his Lewis machine gun and watched as it span away out of control. The second 'was driven to the ground damaged', while the third he attacked, an Albatros C.I, burst into flames and crashed, killing its pilot, Oberleutnant Uebelacker, and observer, Hauptmann Roser. For this day's work Hawker was awarded the Victoria Cross for 'most conspicuous gallantry and very great ability'.

When Hawker was finally posted back to England in late 1915 for a rest he could claim at least seven victories in combat – one captured, three destroyed, one seen to go down 'out of control' and one 'forced to land'. With such a record of success he soon became the first British fighter pilot whose deeds reached a wider audience. Although there appears to have been no deliberate collaboration between newspaper editors and the War Office to promote Hawker's name, details slipped out nonetheless and his heroism was widely celebrated.

In early 1916 Hawker was promoted to major and placed in command of the RFC's first fighter squadron – No. 24, based at Hounslow Heath, equipped with the Airco DH.2 pusher biplane, armed with a single Lewis gun. In February they crossed to France and set up base at Bertangles, in the Somme area, to support the coming offensive on that front.

As commanding officer, Hawker should have obeyed a RFC dictate, introduced in the early summer, to stop men in his position flying operationally. However, he chose at times to ignore this order and continued to fly on patrols, as always showing great fighting spirit. But as the year wore on the enemy began introducing more advanced fighters, making life more difficult for the RFC. Faced with these new aircraft, DH.2 pilots soon found themselves severely disadvantaged and before casualties rose to an unacceptable level needed something more potent to fly in combat. It was at this crucial moment that Hawker met von Richthofen over the Somme. In many ways it was a contest of equals, which the young German later described very briefly in his combat report:

DH 2 No. 5964.
24 Squadron.
1500 hrs south of Bapaume.
With two other aeroplanes I attacked a Vickers one-seater at 3,000 metres altitude. After a long turning fight of three to five minutes, I had forced my adversary down to 500 metres. He now tried to escape me by flying towards the front line. I pursued and brought him down with 900 shots.
    Weather – Fine all day.

An official report has to be brief and concise, but to truly understand the reality of that day's event requires something more. However, in its immediate aftermath Manfred's mind was probably full of many blurred images, fleetingly registering as the battle ebbed and flowed. Such was the drama that all he could recall, in a letter to his mother, was that Hawker 'defended himself desperately and gave me the hardest fight I have had up to now'. In the months that followed he undoubtedly considered the combat and eventually tried to set his memories down on paper in a more cogent way:

I noticed three Englishmen ... I felt strongly inclined to fight ... I was flying at a lower altitude and waited until one of the enemy aircraft tried to drop on me. A little later one came 'sailing along' and wanted to tackle me from behind. After firing five shots he had to break away, as I swerved into a tight turn. He tried to catch me up from behind, as I tried to get on his tail. So we circled round and round each other like madmen at a height of 3,000 metres.

First we turned twenty times to the left, and then thirty times to the right, each trying to get behind and above the other. I soon realised I was not fighting a beginner and had not the slightest intention of breaking away. He was flying in a 'box' that could turn superbly. However, my 'packing case' was better at climbing than his and I, at last, succeeded in getting above and behind my English waltzing partner.

When we were down to about 1800 metres, without having achieved anything in particular, my opponent should have realised that it was the time to leave. The wind was in my favour and was driving us further over our side of the lines. But this gallant man was full of courage and when we were down to 900 metres he cheerfully waved to me as if to say 'Well, how do you do?'

The circles we made around each other were now so small that their diameter was probably no more than 75 to 90 metres ... I looked down into his aircraft and could see every movement of his head. If he had not been wearing a helmet I would have been able to see the expressions he was making.

He was a good sportsman but by and by things became a little too hot for him. He had to decide whether to land on German ground or fly back to the English lines. He tried the latter, after trying in vain to escape me by looping and such manoeuvres ... He went down to 90 metres and tried to escape by flying a zig-zag course ... This was my most advantageous moment. I followed him at a height of 75 to 45 metres, firing all the time, but my guns jammed and nearly robbed me of my success.

However, my opponent crashed, having been shot through the head, 45 metres inside our lines. His machine gun was dug out of the ground and now graces the entrance of my dwelling.

Hawker was buried in a rapidly dug grave alongside his crashed aircraft, but being so close to the front line meant that he didn't lie undisturbed for long – his grave disappearing, a victim of constant artillery fire. Yet memorials to his life remain, not least of all in von Richthofen's autobiography. And to this can be added a significant number of press reports and front pages dedicated to his life and accomplishments. These, most notably, were carried in the populist newspapers – the *Sketch*, *Mirror*, *Express* and *Mail* – which between them generated sales of nearly 4 million copies each day. Over on the other side, the German press were also quick to pick up the story, although in this case the headlines emphasized the part played by von Richthofen.

As this was happening, the German film industry had begun producing newsreels and films that could, within days, be screened in local cinemas across the country. Short sequences showing German heroes, especially the aviators, soon appeared with Immelmann and Boelcke's faces becoming ever more familiar to the paying public. Even Kunigunde was drawn to this new medium, especially when it involved Manfred:

> We all went to the cinema to see the film of Boelcke's funeral. Manfred carried the cushion with the medals. He was clearly recognizable ... After dinner, my sister and the relatives went to the cinema again where the film of Boelcke's funeral was still being shown. They had the film shown quite slowly; they were very interested, and in this way I was able to enjoy an odd reunion with Manfred.

As his fame spread and cameras were given greater access to the squadrons, more films appeared, with von Richthofen clearly becoming the star of the show. The moment was his and fame beckoned, urged on by forces he little understood as the media exploited his growing accomplishments. With so much happening in the background, he might have been forgiven if he'd lost focus as his reputation continued to grow, but as Christmas approached he continued to fight with a single-minded determination. In so doing, he destroyed two more DH.2s on 11 and 19 December, then sent down two F.E.2bs on 20th and 27th, raising his score to fifteen confirmed 'victories' and putting him even closer to the award of the Pour le Mérite.

As casualties mounted in Jasta Boelcke (as Jasta 2 became during the last few weeks of 1916, in honour of its famous leader), new recruits were urgently required. On 21 November Werner Voss, a recently commissioned officer, who was awarded his Pilot's Badge on 28 May 1916, arrived from Kasta 20, where he had been flying 'large battle aeroplanes' over the Somme then, it seems, on the Bulgarian front. It is unclear how or why he ended up as a fighter pilot, though it is safe to assume that he may have requested a transfer or was chosen for these duties having shown himself to be promising single-seater material. As things turned out, this proved to be a wise choice and a close friendship, tinged with rivalry, soon developed between the 19-year-old and von Richthofen, which both men seemed to enjoy.

It did not take Voss long to show his mettle. On 27 November he brought down two British aircraft – a Nieuport 17 of 60 Squadron and an F.E.2b from No. 18. For a newly minted fighter pilot, this was a remarkable achievement, but one he didn't repeat for several weeks. A move to Pronville on 19 December allowed Jasta Boelcke to take advantage of the winter weather, which restricted combat missions, but two days later Voss shot down a B.E.2d from 7 Squadron. In the months that followed he flourished as fighter pilot and his score rose rapidly.

Manfred spent Christmas that year with Jasta 2, being joined there by his father and brother for the celebrations. In a letter to his mother on the 28th he described this brief pause in the action:

> Papa and Lothar both joined me on Christmas Eve. It was a memorable day. Christmas in the field was indeed more fun than you in the homeland might think. Our celebrations consisted of a Christmas tree and a very good meal. The next day, Lothar made his first solo flight. A comparable event will be his first victory. Yesterday I shot down my 15th Englishman ...

Albrecht, now apparently based near Lille, would soon become a regular visitor to the airfields from which both sons flew. It is hard to say whether this would have been good or bad for a worried parent. But he clearly felt proud of both his sons and may even have lived vicariously through them, having been denied front-line service himself. However, being so close to the action came with many risks, not least of all seeing his boys die in action. He would also find himself swept up in the PR bandwagon that would soon surround both sons and feature in many press photos and several films that appeared to great acclaim in 1917–18. But celebrity is a double-edged sword because the camera does not discriminate between joy and grief, only seek a good story. Both these extreme emotions, and much else besides, are recorded without sympathy or mercy, as he would soon find out to his cost.

Meanwhile, Lothar, who seemed destined to live in his brother's shadow, was soon to receive his Pilot's Badge, having made a name for himself flying as an observer with Kasta 23. Such was his success that in December he was, according to Kunigunde, presented with the Iron Cross 1st Class by von Hoeppner himself. Yet any sense of accomplishment Lothar may have felt was soon eclipsed by Manfred, who was promoted to command Jasta 11 on 15 January and, a day later, received word that he had been awarded the Pour le Mérite by the Kaiser.

His promotion to Jastaführer probably came as no surprise to those around him, bearing in mind his fighting record and the leadership skills he had begun to demonstrate in the weeks since

'Dulce et decorum est, pro patria mori' was a belief drummed into young men in Germany, Britain and France before the Great War, as was 'learn to obey that you might lead' for prospective officers. As a Prussian Junker and son of an officer, Manfred von Richthofen (top left) was taught these concepts from childhood, each lesson being reinforced by attendance at the (Royal Prussian) Military Academy at Gross-Lichterfelde near Berlin (top right and below). (Charles Donald/Author)

In 1912 Manfred was commissioned and joined a Uhlan Regiment (above) with which he went to war, but it was a conflict that would have little use for cavalry. Instead, after a few months of service, he found himself in trenches on the Western Front. It is little wonder that he saw flying as a means of escape to a more glorious war first as an observer, then as a pilot. (Below) A scene common to von Richthofen in 1915, on the Eastern and Western Fronts – a German two-seater observes all movement below. (Author)

Von Richthofen (far left) when an observer with the Brieftauben-Abteilung Ostende (BAO) and having survived his first war wound, inflicted to his right hand when he caught it in one of his aircraft's two propellers. (Charles Donald)

Having qualified as a pilot in early 1916, Manfred's first efforts at flying a single seater Fokker E III monoplane fighter were far from successful, one flight ending in a smashed aircraft, as shown here. Judging by the state of the monoplane von Richthofen was lucky to walk away with barely a scratch. (Charles Donald)

Pupil and apprentice. By late 1916 Oswald Boelke (above left) was a national hero, albeit a very tired one as this photo reveals. When ordered to form a new fighter squadron, Jasta 2 equipped with Albatros D I and D II fighters, he chose, amongst others, von Richthofen to join him (above right, still eager and fresh-faced after two years of war – shown here when serving as a pilot with Kasta 8). (Charles Donald/Author)

Von Richthofen poses beside an Albatros D II of Jasta 2 in the Autumn of 1916 and joins a group of fellow pilots gathered around Boelke and his aeroplane after a mission. (P J Carisella)

Some of the men who would shape von Richtohen's rise to fame and oversee his unconscious elevation to a legend of very great potency; one that even crossed national boundaries. (Opposite top left) Walter Nicolai, General Ludendorff's spymaster and propagandist extraordinaire. (Opposite top right) George von Ompteda, (Opposite below – left to right) Peter Lampel and Kurt Tucholsky. (This page top row – left to right) George Wegener, then Erich von Salzmann, flanked by Manfred and his brother, Lothar and, to the right, the photographer Nicola Perscheid. By 1916 all these noteworthy men, and others, were employed and directed by Ludendorff and Nocolai, to promote Germany's new hero and regularly report and illustrate von Richthofen's life and achievements. (Charles Donald/Author)

Roucourt April/May 1917, where von Richthofen's Jasta 11 were based for a time during the Battle of Arras, became a regular destination for VIPs and reporters eager to be seen with this new hero as his 'score' climbed to 50 or more. Here Ernst von Hoeppner, the air services' Kommandierender General der Luftstreitkräfte (Kogenluft) is introduced to his pilots by von Richthofen (here the general is seen shaking hands with Lothar von Richthofen). (Charles Donald)

Away from the propagandists determined to milk the von Richthofen story for all its worth, and amidst the constant stream of visitors, the more trying business of flying, fighting, killing and dying went on. (Above) Von Richthofen and Kurt Wolff enjoying a moment of fun before setting off on a visit both jammed into the rear cockpit of a two-seater. (Below) Here Albatros DIlls of Jasta 11, one believed to be flown by von Richthofen, take off on another patrol. (P J Carisella/ Author)

The reality and the fantasy. (Above left) Manfred poses with one of his injured pilots, thought to be his good friend Karl-Emil Schafer, and Moritz, whose presence in many photographs and films reflects his importance to von Richthofen – a rock in a stormy sea. (Above right) One of many heroic portraits that appeared in 1917/18 as artists clamoured or were commissioned to capture a likeness of the great man (on this occasion drawn by Adolf Schorling). (To the right) By May 1917 von Richthofen was headline news with his photo gracing the covers of many newspapers and journals. (Charles Donald/Author)

When von Richthofen departed on a well earnt leave at the beginning of May 1917 he was immediately caught up in a swirl of publicity that celebrated his status as a national hero. He met the Kaiser, Hindenburg and Ludendorff before moving on to meetings with von Heoppner and Lieth-Thomson (left) amongst others. He then flew to a more informal meeting with Kaiserin Augusta Victoria (below) at Bad Homberg. Wherever he went for the next few weeks crowds followed him. (Author)

Above, below left and below right: The cameras even pursued von Richthofen to hospital and then his home after receiving a severe head wound on 6 July 1917. There would be little or no peace to allow him time to recover, which for such an injury might have taken many months or years. In reality, the combined effects of the wound and his increasing battle fatigue undoubtedly contributed to his death in April 1918. (Author)

Although still very ill and grounded, if his doctor's instructions had been adhered to, von Richthofen still chose to return to combat in August 1917. However, he suffered as a result returning from each mission feeling sick and dizzy. He put this to one side and continued 'scoring' albeit at a much slower rate than before. Here he poses with Algernon Bird of 46 Squadron, whose Sopwith Pup he forced down on 3 September and with Anthony Fokker and fellow pilots as they examine Bird's wrecked aeroplane. (Author)

Reports suggest that von Richthofen, as his fame grew, found life in Germany increasingly difficult and longed to be with his men at the Front when away on other duties. A 'Band of Brothers' could offer shared understanding and solace, but also increase the sense of loss and loneliness when death claimed those around him. But still, despite depression, fatigue and insomnia he could, at times, still look relaxed for the camera. (Author)

During 1918 he was assigned a new Fokker Triplane, No. 425/17 (above) or so it is believed, which was soon painted red overall. He would die in this aircraft and its remains (below) would be souvenired by the Allied troops in the area at the time, who would also take many of his personal possessions and the clothes he was wearing. By this stage he was probably almost as well known on the British side of the lines as in his homeland such was the fame that propaganda generated (Charles Donald)

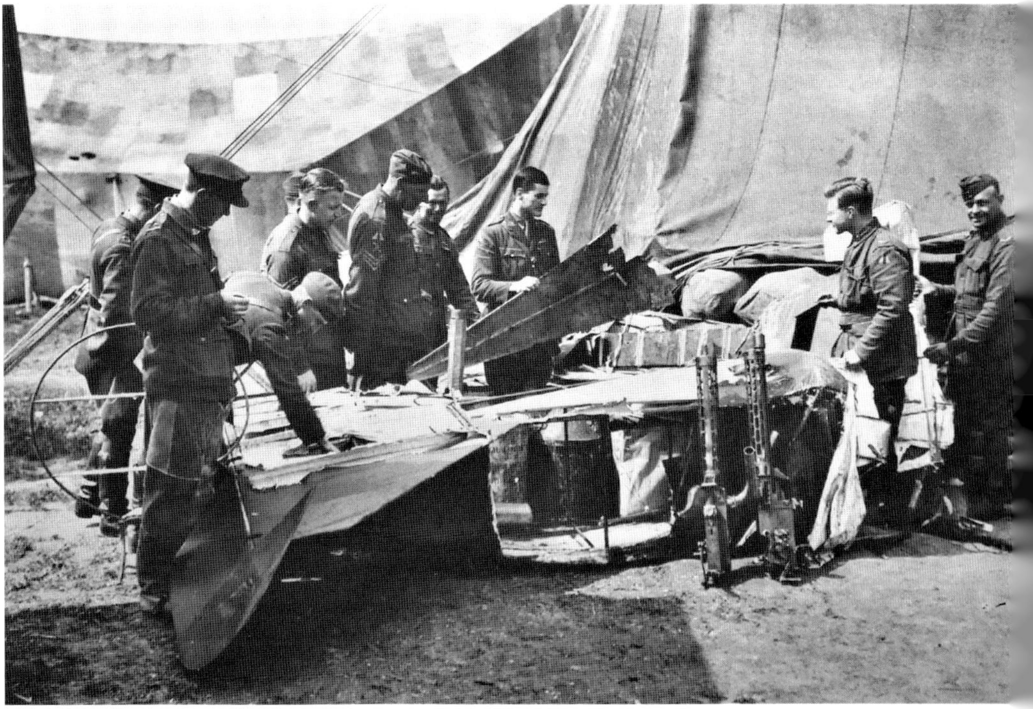

 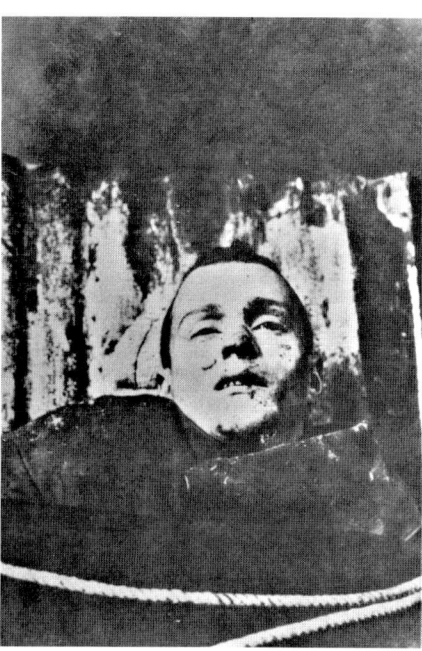

To be revered by friends is one thing, to be honoured by an enemy in such a bloody war is almost beyond belief. And yet there it was. (Above) In death Manfred became an object of great interest to be examined and photographed as shown here (Jack Moses/Charles Donald). With so many Allied troops dying daily and simply left unburied or given a slight covering of earth in the nearest shell-hole, to give a full military funeral to an enemy responsible for the deaths of so many comrades is quite remarkable (below). And his demise made headlines in Britain, France, the USA, Australia and Canada, as well as Germany (Overleaf). (Author)

THE YPRES BATTLE: GOOD DAY FOR THE ALLIES
DAILY SKETCH.
THE PREMIER PICTURE PAPER.

No. 2,851. LONDON, TUESDAY, APRIL 30, 1918. ONE PENNY.

THE FUNERAL OF VON RICHTHOFEN.

---

5. Mai 1918
Nr. 18
27. Jahrgang

Berliner
Illustrirte Zeitung
Verlag Ullstein & Co, Berlin SW 68

Einzelpreis einschließlich Teuerungszuschlag
15 Pfg.
oder 24 Heller

Ueber Richthofens Grab.

Boelcke's and Kirmaier's deaths. In the words of Douglas Bader, von Richthofen would have been seen as 'press-on merchant' by comrades and leaders alike – a man eager for battle and for victory, but with the skill to lead and shape other men along the way. But to be truly successful in such a role he required broader leadership skills to meet all the needs of an active service unit, as Mike Tritton, a wing leader in 1944–45, remembered:

> To manage one or more squadrons successfully you had to be a politician, a diplomat, a teacher, welfare worker, engineer and clerk. Basically a 'jack of all trades'. Leading in the air, with all its perils, at least meant you could escape for a brief moment a sea of paperwork and the demands of all those who supported the squadron and do what you had been trained to do.
>
> Everything you did as leader was essential to the smooth running of the wing or squadron. Key amongst these were 'ground' duties to ensure that sufficient aircraft and fit pilots were available for each operation, which in the front line might soon prove impossible to achieve as high rates of attrition reduced numbers and exhaustion set in. There had to be sufficient spares to meet maintenance needs and suitably trained men, of many trades, available to do the work. This was not always possible in the front line where the supply organisation was often stretched to the limit by many competing demands. To keep going was often a matter of begging, borrowing or stealing anything you could lay your hands on, which was a time-consuming, frustrating business, requiring endless amounts of paperwork and much scurrying about.
>
> Perhaps the most difficult duty was coping with a group of young pilots, many of whom were barely out of school, who had been asked to do something very difficult, if not impossible, over a long period of active service – or until killed, wounded or their spirit broke. The tough ones lasted longer but all

would eventually fall victim to a deep-rooted fatigue. Trying to spot which ones needed to be rested, and when, proved to be very a difficult at times, especially when our leaders were urging even greater efforts. As a result, many is the time that good men died because they were exhausted and became uncaring of their own safety. As leader, you tended to ignore these things in yourself, which could prove very costly in the long run. However, your sense of responsibility to others, and being constantly busy ensuring their wellbeing, could carry you through some very difficult times. But even so you had your limit and woe betide those who chanced their luck for too long.

Von Richthofen, although still a fledgling in these matters, seems to have had a natural understanding of some of these issues and even before promotion to Jastaführer had begun to understand the political nature of the role he was taking on. The late A.E. Ferko, in his well-written and well-researched book *Richthofen*, provided a graphic example of this:

Richthofen's front line experience told him what was required of a fighter aeroplane. The following attests to this.

Oblt Wilhelm Siegert [Inspector of Flying Troops] wrote that on 22nd December 1916 a conference made up of Germany's most experienced fighter pilots was convened at Headquarters, Kofl 1, Cambrai. The purpose of the meeting was to air the views of those present as to the way future fighter development should proceed. The majority wanted the two-gunned 120 hp Halberstadt D.V. Only one pilot pleaded for a 150 hp machine – the relatively unknown Ltn von Richthofen [with which, as we have seen, he'd already enjoyed considerable success]. Perhaps unknown to the assembled pilots, the Albatros Company, with the co-operation and support of Idllieg, had proceeded with the development of their model D.III ... By spring 1917 the D.III was largely responsible for aerial superiority over the Western Front and delivery of them could not move ahead fast enough.

On this issue von Richthofen wouldn't be swayed, stood his ground and, as a result Albatros fighters remained the mainstay of the Jastas until better aircraft began to appear. It may also be the case that this determination to get what he wanted, coupled to his outstanding war record, impressed von Hoeppner. So when considering who should lead each squadron in the rapidly expanding fighter arm his name would have been high on the general's list. Perhaps the issue of publicity and propaganda also played a part in this decision; if so it was a choice that would pay unexpected dividends in the months to come.

In reality the task he inherited when taking over Jasta 11 might have proved too much even for an experienced leader, let alone von Richthofen. For the situation that awaited him at La Brayelle near Douai was hardly a satisfactory one.

Formed in October 1916, it had been placed in the hands of the experienced 27-year-old Oblt Rudolf Emil Lang, who hailed from Munich and trained as an aviator during 1914. According to his personnel records, various postings followed during which he seems to have flown two-seater reconnaissance aircraft. All this changed in December 1915 when he was posted to FFA 6b as an *Eindeckerflieger*. In May he then transferred to Artillerie-Fliegerabteilung 103b in the same capacity, but remained there for only two months until placed in command of Kampfstaffel 31b. With such a wealth of experience he must have been seen as a wise choice to lead Jasta 11, but in practice he seems to have found this a difficult task to complete successfully.

Some reports suggest that he was ill-suited to commanding a fighter squadron, lacked the skill to train his men as Boelcke had done and lacked a true fighting spirit, so leaving his pilots leaderless where it mattered most – in the air. True or not, by Christmas the Jasta had claimed only one victory, by Lt Konstantin Krefft, which had not been confirmed. They were floundering and their lack of success undoubtedly attracted criticism and scrutiny. However, the whole fighter arm was still in its infancy and had few talented pilots and leaders available to populate all the Jastas being created. So, while they learnt their trade, there were some serious shortcomings to deal with. All in all, it was a difficult balancing act, that quickly benefited von Richthofen at the cost of Lang, who was transferred to Jasta 28 to try again. In due course, they too would dispense with his services, leaving him free to return to reconnaissance work for which he seems to have been ideally suited.

It remained to be seen if von Richthofen could do any better, but he began his command in a positive way by flying a new Albatros D.III from Pronville to La Brayelle, suggesting that a strong new leader, suitably armed, had arrived. Up to then the Jasta seems to have made do with Halberstadt D.II and D.Vs and a few Albatros D.Is, which may have contributed to their conspicuous lack of success. Over the next few weeks this would all change as von Richthofen led his pilots to glory and with this his legend began to grow, allowing Ludendorff's masters of propaganda to begin their work in earnest.

Chapter 6

In the Devil's Iron Grip

In his biography of Lawrence of Arabia, a man whose rise to fame in the Great War mirrored von Richthofen's own emerging status as a celebrity, Michael Yardley coined the phrase 'Backing into the limelight'. The theme of grudging acquiescence is relevant in both cases. Neither sought public attention, but in achieving so much, and displaying great courage and fortitude along the way, their chances of remaining in obscurity soon disappeared. In a war of such terrible slaughter and little movement, men such as Lawrence and von Richthofen were seen as rising above the senseless carnage into cleaner air where fading illusions might be sustained for a time. It was a hopeless task, but in a world gone mad clinging to any wreckage was essential for survival. And here lies the essence of von Richthofen's appeal; a fascination carefully managed by a media in thrall to Ludendorff and his entourage, yet ultimately damaging to the hero they proclaimed.

In early 1917, having established himself as Hindenburg's second in command, but in reality the Supreme War Lord who pulled many important strings, Ludendorff expressed his concern about the state of mind of Germany's civilian population, fearing that revolution might soon break out, later recalling in his memoirs that:

> The spirit of the people at home rendered some action imperative. We have the best prospects of winning the war, but it was not over and what we have won must be kept. We are still a long way from that. The popular state of mind (at

home and in the Army) jeopardized everything ... This is now becoming a burning issue.

In accordance with a proposal submitted to me by Nicolai, General Headquarters arranged for patriotic instruction to begin in the Field Army. But this is only a poor substitute for the work of enlightening public opinion at home.

Nicolai, a man of unfailing industry and devotion, is responsible for the military direction of the press and the cognate duty of watching and fostering the morale of the Army and the people at home ... The military censorship of the Press is another of Nicolai and his subordinates' duties ... Another great branch of his work consists of the Secret Intelligence Service, prevention of spying, supervision of post, telegraph and telephone services, and the adoption of measures against industrial spying and sabotage.

By 1917 Walter Nicolai, then a major, wielded power considerably greater than his rank would usually allow and in this role was instrumental in promoting von Richthofen to the status of national hero. For this reason alone, Nicolai, a man who seemed able to move through the shadowy worlds of espionage and propaganda with great skill, is worthy of closer scrutiny.

He was born on 1 August 1873 to a Prussian Army captain and his wife in Braunschweig. With such a background it was perhaps inevitable that he would follow a military career. Shortly after attending the War Academy in Berlin he was appointed to the intelligence services, having displayed talent for such work. In so doing he became a Russian specialist, could speak the language fluently and often visited that country in the course of his duties.

In 1906, Nicolai was transferred to Abteilung IIIb where, among other things, he controlled the East Prussian news station based in Königsberg. Here he soon created a major centre for espionage against the Russian Empire and, in 1913, became the Abteilung's head. As such he was well-positioned to lead and dominate all secret service activities during the war. One of his most high-profile activities was the recruitment of Mata Hari as Agent H21, whose case officer, Major Rodell, worked directly to Nicolai. Then in 1917 he was complicit in the plan to allow Lenin free passage across Germany to Russia. Here the German aim was a simple one. This well-known political agitator, who was living in Paris at the time, would, it was hoped, incite revolution and help bring an end to the Tsarist regime. This, in turn, might end the war in the east and release the forces tied down there to boost numbers on the Western Front and so achieve a favourable decision there.

As the war went on Nicolai acquired more power and influence, both of which he exercised with considerable dexterity and cunning. So it is hardly surprising that Ludendorff came to value him highly and trusted him with many other issues including the question of propaganda. With a growing concern that the civilian population might soon rebel against the war, the scene was set for this arch propagandist to intensify the crucial battle for hearts and minds. At the same moment von Richthofen stepped into the limelight, a ready-made hero whose image could be used to the full.

As only a very hazy account appears to exist concerning Nicolai's propaganda work seems to exist, hardly surprising when considering the man's character and the secret nature of his duties, the way he undertook this task has had to be slowly pieced together from many sources. First and foremost, the messages he decided to impart had to have some basis in fact and conveyed, or appeared to convey, the truth.

From the beginning of the war each side had tried to highlight the rightfulness of their own cause. In so doing they emphasised the awfulness of the enemy – peddling tales of atrocities and much more besides. This had been successful for a time in Germany, but, with so many men dying or returning home crippled this approach was no longer as effective as it had once been, especially with severe food shortages and deprivation eating into public morale. Outrage is difficult to sustain on an empty stomach, especially where little prospect of a speedy victory exists.

So Nicolai took a different course – one based on personal responsibility, the rightfulness of the German cause, loyalty to the Kaiser and the glamour of heroes sacrificing all for their country. There would still be an emphasis on the brutality of the British in blockading German ports, for example, but this was a message played down because it highlighted the shortages too much and Germany's own unrestricted U-boat war. Better to stress that the country was coping despite enemy action and things might get better if only it continued the struggle.

However, understanding the message is quite different to conveying it in a way that has maximum effect. In a country governed entirely by the military, it seemed unlikely that anyone except those in uniform would be allowed to manage this task. Certainly, the Reichstag, which now had elements displaying strong anti-war feelings, and making their views felt in public, could not be trusted to do so. As a result, it fell to Nicolai and his representatives to find ways of creating and transmitting these messages in a strong, positive way, using censorship to ensure their missives were handled benevolently by publishers and their editors. Today we call this 'spinning a story' but then, as now, the end result was just the same.

With the military determined to maintain total control of this process, it was important that professional writers, imbued with these ideas and standards, be employed. Very cleverly the army looked to its own ranks for these skills. With millions of men in uniform, it didn't take long to find five suitable candidates who displayed these qualities – Georg von Ompteda, Erich von Salzmann, Peter Lampel, Georg Wegener and Kurt Tucholsky. By early 1917, as von Richthofen's rise to fame began, these five noted writers had begun this task in earnest, eager to find stories that might inspire a jaded population – at home and in the trenches. Here it helped that being in uniform gave them easy access to the battlefields, where they could meet and observe the men whose actions might provide strong, inspiring stories. So, it is of little wonder that they soon found their way to Jasta 2, then Jasta 11 and its remarkable young leader, in the process becoming frequent essayists on his activities and those of his men.

Inevitably, one asks the question why these five men were chosen to fill such important roles in Ludendorff's propaganda machine? The answer can be found in a brief review of their lives up to that time.

Von Ompteda, who was born in Munich in 1863, was probably the most famous of the five. Like Albrecht von Richthofen, he decided to make a career in the army, and like him had to retire prematurely from the service during 1892, in his case following a fall from a horse. It seems that writing had always interested him and he was already a published author when forced to give up a military life. So, with his family's support, he became a freelance writer living in Berlin, Dresden and Munich, soon adopting the pseudonym Georg Egestorff. Gradually his reputation grew as a writer, translator of Guy de Maupassant and poet and by 1913 he had published some twenty-one works of fiction and poetry. It seems that he also wrote widely as a journalist, which then, as now, is an important way for authors to make their names as well as supplement a less than regular income.

Again like Albrecht von Richthofen, the coming of war saw him seek re-entry into the Army. However, his age and medical condition precluded active service at the front, but not in support areas and it was here that he moved into Nicolai's area of activity, retaining the rank of Rittmeister. Here his skills as a writer, observer of military matters and his many contacts in the press ensured that his involvement in propaganda issues grew rapidly. He soon became a frequent visitor to front-line fighter squadrons, most particularly von Richthofen's. It was an association that quickly resulted in many press reports and the active promotion of Manfred as a vision of the Teutonic warrior personified.

Erich von Salzmann was born in Stettin during 1876 and as the son of a Prussian general it was natural that he would follow his father into the army. He was commissioned as a Leutnant in 1894, then saw service in China as part of the international force sent to crush the Boxer Rebellion. Service in German South-West Africa as an Oberleutnant followed, and here he found himself caught up in a conflict with the Herero tribe. During one skirmish he was seriously wounded and evacuated to Germany for treatment, resulting in one leg being left 5cm shorter than the other. So, like Albrecht and Ompteda, he was discharged as being unfit for further service.

Having commenced a career as an author with the publication of *Im Sattel durch Zentralasian: 6000 Kilometer in 176 Tagen* in 1903, when still in the army, it seemed only natural for him to become an author full-time. Another book followed in 1905, describing his adventures in Africa, and this led him into journalism, where the pay was undoubtedly better.

By 1908 he had become an occasional correspondent for the August-Scheri Publishing House in Berlin, and had begun to write about life in Japan, China and then South America, where he was living at the time. When war broke out, he returned to Germany and, despite his disability, managed to have his commission reactivated and was appointed to command the 2nd Battery of the Reserve-Feldartillerie-Regiment No. 46. But his front-line service was not destined to last long. During an action in Flanders on 15 January 1915, a shell splinter penetrated his head, partially blinding him and ending his fighting career for good. Undeterred, he returned to writing and journalism and soon found a position as war correspondent with *Vossische-Zeitung*, the liberal newspaper published in Berlin.

He soon gained access to troops in the front line and commanders in the rear areas, which gave his work greater authenticity. He also felt less inhibited by the rigid Prussian conformity he met and so his work was more open than it might otherwise have been. This was something that suited his publishers, especially when questioning the conduct of the war. It was in this role that he found his way to Jasta 11 during the spring of 1917 to investigate and write about an emerging new hero and the men he commanded. As a worldly wise man with a deep understanding of human nature, Salzmann soon befriended Manfred and, more significantly, gained his trust.

The appointment of Karl Friedrich Wilhelm Georg Wegener to the army's headquarters in Spa as a war correspondent came with an already established connection with Manfred.

Born in May 1863, the son of a pastor, he shone academically and studied geography, history, literature and religion at Heidelberg, Leipzig, Berlin and Marburg. After completing his doctorate, he set off to explore the world, with China and the Far East proving of particular interest to him. He then wrote many vivid accounts describing his travels, making a name for himself in the process as an author and geographer. In many ways he was following in the footsteps of one of Manfred's relatives, the 1833-born explorer, Ferdinand von Richthofen. Moving in the same circles, Wegener seems to have befriended Ferdinand, who died in 1903, though to what extent is unclear.

In 1910 Wegener, with his name in scientific circles assured, became a lecturer and professor at the Handelshochschule Berlin and then, in time, its rector. In 1914 he, like many men of his age, and too old to fight, sought some sort of war work. With his well-honed writing skills, links to journalism and friendship with Crown Prince Wilhelm established when they visited India together in 1910, doors were soon opened and he became a war correspondent attached to the High Command. Whether Nicolai was involved in his selection is unclear, but Wegener would soon become involved in the work of Abteilung IIIb, writing many articles on their behalf. In early 1917 he would also make the acquaintance of Ferdinand's now famous relative and begin a number of visits to Jasta 11, writing about all he observed there.

Peter Martin Lampel, being a much younger man than Ompteda, Salzmann and Wegener, having been born in 1894, took a slightly different path into the field of journalism and writing about the war. Having enlisted in 1914, he entered a period of education in Breslau before training as an aviator and seeing service with various bomber squadrons. Up to the beginning of the war any ambitions he had to be a writer were muted, but combat seems to have unleashed something within him and in 1917–18 two books appeared based on his war experiences: *Zeppelins in Attack* and *Bomber Pilots*. It was these works, some essays for *Der Flieger* among others, plus his frequent contact with fellow aviators, including von Richthofen, that seem to have brought him to Nicolai's attention.

The last of these influential men, Kurt Tucholsky, was in fact the editor of *Der Flieger* and in this capacity was already a regular commentator on flying matters in the German Army. He was born a German Jew on 9 January 1890 in Berlin and, from the earliest, writing became his passion. However, after successfully passing through school, he chose to study law, but despite this literature remained an obsession, so it is hardly unsurprising that when the time came to choose which path to follow, he favoured a writing and journalistic career. With his 1912 book, *Rheinsberg – a Picture Book for Lovers* he produced a story in which he adopted a rather fresh and comic tone, most unusual for that time, which brought him to the attention of a far wider audience for the first time and made his name. This was soon followed by a whole swathe of work, much of it about the arts and politics, and soon he was asked to take on editorial responsibility for *Die Schaubühne*, a weekly magazine about politics, art and the economy. But just as his career was blossoming the war came and all changed for him and millions of others. Although called to arms, he was, by his own admission, an unlikely soldier. He later wrote of his time in uniform:

> For three and a half years I dodged the war as much as I could – and I regret not having had the courage shown by the great Karl Liebknecht [socialist and anti-militarist] to say No and

refuse to serve in the military. Of this I am ashamed. I used many means to avoid being shot and avoid not having to shoot – not just once ... Many did just the same.

In his attitude to war he seems to have been the polar opposite to von Richthofen, who embraced duty and sacrifice as a matter of course. Nevertheless, Tucholsky did go, albeit reluctantly, to the Eastern Front in 1915, where he served as a 'munitions soldier', presumably moving ammunition to the front line or to artillery units in the back areas. Then, perhaps in recognition of his skill as an author by someone with a dry sense of humour, he was appointed company writer. In due course, he was transferred to the artillery and then the Pilot Academy at Alt-Autz in Courland as an administrator. Here his writing skills were recognised, and he was tasked with editing and publishing the field newspaper *Der Flieger*. It was a role he fulfilled with great skill, judging by his output, and this continued until 1918 when posted to Romania, where he saw out the war.

It is now difficult to determine whether *Der Flieger* was a Tucholsky brainchild or simply the creation of someone else that he then took over. Either way, it became his most important war work and served the ultimate aim of keeping him as far away from the front as possible. Whatever his motives, though, he still managed to produce a monthly newspaper of some merit that was widely read in the Air Service and more broadly by the general public. Much of its content, carefully choreographed by Nicolai, would find its way to the national papers and reach an even larger audience.

There is little doubt that everything about Manfred would make 'good copy'. This was something Ludendorff, Nicolai, von Ompteda, Salzmann, Lampel, Tucholsky and others would soon realise and a hero of almost godlike proportions was born, although this was unlikely to have been their aim.

In this they were aided by photographers, artists and publishers, each enlisted to help record the life of Germany's heroes, and von

Richthofen in particular. First among this group was Willi Sanke, who ran a business based in Berlin producing postcards. With the support of the High Command, he began manufacturing a substantial number of photo-postcards, all of which sold in huge quantities across Germany. In doing so, Sanke employed a number of photographers, such as Fritz Fischer, Nicola Perscheid, and Alfred Krauth, who all became famous in their own right and were familiar figures to the fighting men they met in Germany or at the front.

In an age where moving pictures were beginning to creep into daily lives, the presence of cameramen near the front was becoming commonplace and an accepted part of life. Soon this new media would reveal much about squadron life, and through these flickering images capture something of von Richthofen's personality. But the old arts still had a part to play in this modern world and soon portraiture was enlisted as a propaganda tool. For von Richthofen this meant occasional exposure to the work of such artists as Professor Arnold Busch, of the Breslau School of Art, Richard 'Fritz' Reusing, Theodor Rocholl, Adolf Schorling and Rudolf Bauer, the avant-garde artist and contributor to the art and literary magazines *Der Sturm* and *Jugend*. In many ways their work helped produce images more potent than simple photography could ever do. And during 1917 von Richthofen would sit for these men – on the Western Front and at home in Germany – regularly being exposed to their relentlessly uncompromising gaze and interpretation of his character. The results, though possibly uncomfortable at times, were revealing, nonetheless.

Much of this was in the future when von Richthofen took command of Jasta 11 and was faced with the task of turning a group of under-achieving pilots into a successful fighting force. And yet the basic material he inherited, and then added to, was quite promising. In due course two of them, Karl Allmenröder and Kurt Wolff, would become leading aces and Pour le Mérite holders, and two others he enlisted later on, Karl-Emil Schafer and his brother Lothar, would do likewise. Added to this there were a few others – Bockelmann, Esser, Mohnicke and Festner – who would also do well under von Richthofen's tutorship.

Nevertheless, Manfred could be ruthless in weeding out underachievers or those he felt did not share his fighting spirit. After a trial period, during which they were given every chance to prove themselves, men such as Sergeant Hans Howe were posted away when shown to be failing in some way or were clearly out of their depth. And yet others, such as Konstantin Krefft, he chose to retain despite an equal lack of success in the air, primarily because they displayed a fighting spirit or had other talents. In Krefft's case his engineering skills made him the ideal technical officer for the Jasta. In this role he soon flourished and remained with von Richthofen, then his successors, until the end of the war, ensuring that all aircraft in his care were kept in the best possible condition.

In a position such as his, some leaders become self-serving martinets who rule without thought of others except in the way they might promote their own careers. Von Richthofen wasn't built this way and thought only of the wider needs of the Air Service and the welfare of all his men. He could be a hard taskmaster and occasionally a stern one too, but he knew only too well that the battles they faced would be very difficult ones indeed. Only by being well trained, well led and operating as a unified group could they fight successfully and hope to survive until the end of the war.

Von Richthofen may also have been helped in his great endeavour by the arrival of more Albatros D.IIIs, which gradually replaced the less than satisfactory Halberstadts. Not only were they the best available, but their sleek looks held greater aesthetic appeal for the men destined to fly them. These things shouldn't matter, but they often do, especially to the young who are more likely to be image conscious. But to this touch of vanity von Richthofen soon added a flourish of his own – having his aircraft painted red overall. At a time when Nicolai and his image-makers were keenly propagating the hero cult, such a development was bound to be seized upon and exploited to the full, and so the image of *Der Rote Kampfflieger* was born.

Von Richthofen did not explain his reasons for adopting the colour red in his memoirs, but his mother recalled a conversation she had with him during a very brief, but emotional, leave in early February:

> It is still early, the house sleeps, the bitter cold makes it good to be in bed. I believe I hear a sound. I turn on the light; the clock shows seven in the morning. Then the door quickly opens and Manfred stands in front of my bed, fresh and happy, no trace of fatigue after the long night's journey. The blue star glitters at his throat – the Pour le Merite ... How did you get in? Was the garden gate open? No it wasn't, but it didn't matter. The Knight of the Pour le Merite climbed over the fence.
>
> Promptly, we appeared at breakfast for morning coffee. No war brew, please! A handful of coffee beans have been scraped together – saved up for a special occasion. That hour has now arrived.
>
> Manfred talked, we listened intently. The enemy calls his plane 'Le Petit Rouge' because he had painted it red. I found this frivolous, but he believed that 'one cannot make oneself invisible in the air, so at least ours recognize me'.
>
> Manfred produced a Berlin Zeitung with yesterday's date which he passes to us. It is reported that he has shot down his 19th opponent ... I cannot deny myself this question, that was perhaps imprudent. 'Why do you jeopardize your life in this way every day? Why do you do this?' He looks at me intently; great seriousness is written on his face. 'For the man in the trenches,' he simply says, 'I wish to lighten his heavy load by keeping enemy fliers away from him.'

I understood that night what made the character of the fighter pilot, and what enabled these young people, scarcely out of childhood, accomplish such deeds according to Death's design.

There may have been a touch of ego in his actions, but painting his aircraft in such a startling way did, in reality, make him more visible to his fellow pilots. In the confusion of battle seeing a greatly respected leader flying his red Albatros could reassure troubled, frightened men and provide a rallying point in all the disorder around which they could gather. The effect he had was almost talismanic and quickly became so to the enemy as well, as he soon discovered:

> I had the good fortune to shoot at a Vickers two seater [an F.E.2b on 24 January for his eighteenth confirmed victory, the seventeenth being claimed on the 23rd], which was peacefully photographing our artillery positions. My friend the photographer did not have the time to defend himself. They had to make haste to get down on to firm land as the aircraft began to give an indication of catching on fire ... (and) coming to earth it burst into flames.
>
> I felt pity for them and decided not to send them down, but merely compel them to land ... I had the feeling that my opponent was wounded, for he did not fire a single shot.
>
> When down to an altitude of about 500 metres engine trouble compelled me to land without manoeuvring. The result was very comical. My enemy with his burning aircraft landed smoothly, while I, his conqueror, came down beside him in the barbed wire of our trenches and overturned my machine.
>
> The two Englishmen [Lt John MacLennan and Captain Oscar Grieg of 25 Squadron, both of whom were wounded], who were rather surprised at my crash landing, greeted me

like sportsmen ... they could not understand why I landed so clumsily.

They were the first Englishmen I had brought down alive, consequently it gave me particular pleasure to talk to them. I asked them whether they had previously seen my machine in the air. One of them replied, 'Oh yes. I know your aircraft very well. We call it 'Le Petit Rouge'.

The fact that the red Albatros became so familiar to the enemy only a few days after von Richthofen had taken over Jasta 11 is quite remarkable. In such a short time it is possible, of course, but one wonders whether artistic licence may have coloured his memory. It probably happened, though not on the day he described, but later when his reputation was more firmly established on both sides of the line. Either way, this transformation had the desired effect on friend and foe alike. However, on the downside, it would soon give rise to an unwanted appellation to von Richthofen's name – Red Air Fighter, Red Baron and all the rest. So, the need for a good story, to prop up an ailing population, took on a life of its own, ensuring that a myth was created, which von Richthofen was forced to live with for the rest of his life. Soon images of his red Albatros appeared on posters, in newspapers, magazines, adverts and would soon adorn the cover of his memoirs when they appeared later in the year.

In early 1917 the first manifestations of his rising fame would have been hard to detect, but as the public's interest grew this quickly changed. Soon the communiqués issued daily by the High Command, which increasingly highlighted von Richthofen's ever growing number of successes – three more victories in February and ten in March – were seized upon and given prominence in newspapers.

From early in the spring of 1917, Ompteda, Salzmann and Wegener became frequent visitors to Jasta 11 in search of stories to feed the ever-growing demand for news about Germany's new hero. In doing so they produced absorbing eyewitness accounts of

Manfred's life and the constant battle for survival at the front. Of these the most interesting was written by Wegener during a visit to La Brayelle, having been commissioned by *Die Kolnische Zeitung*, a leading national newspaper at the time, to write an article on von Richthofen. Surprisingly it is remarkably free of propaganda, though occasionally it is a little banal and clichéd in its descriptions. In essence, though, it is a simple account of a typical day in Jasta 11's life.

Having been entertained by von Richthofen in his quarters Wegener briefly recounted what he saw there:

> [Richthofen's] room is decorated with trophies ... the colourful national insignias and other parts taken from aircraft he has shot down. From the ceiling hung a Gnome rotary engine modified into a chandelier ... over the door hangs the machine gun from his most dangerous opponent, the English Major Hawker ...

Aware of the significance of Wegener's mission, von Richthofen ensured that high-powered optical equipment had been set up so the journalist could closely observe any action over the front, as he and his men flew into combat:

> Every pilot has his own personal aircraft, in which he always flies ... giving it a special marking that allows his comrades to keep him in sight during combat ... One machine has white, red or some other colour stripes, another carries them diagonally or vertically ... From Richthofen's eyes shine the pride of the warrior knight, whose shield and helmet ornament are known and feared by his opponents. 'I make sure my flight sees me wherever I am'.
>
> One after the other they climb into their flying kit, which looked like a combination of a diver's suit and a Dutch fishing

outfit. And with their hands in their deep pockets, laughing and joking they wandered amongst the groundcrew preparing their aircraft for take-off or over to a large telescope to carefully scan the sky. Even Richthofen had already put on his flying gear and carefully searched the sky with his eyes.

All of a sudden a bell hanging nearby sounds the alarm. In a moment all the mechanics ran to their aircraft ... the pilots climbed into their seats, the propellers thundered and one after the other they lifted up and quickly climbed into the blue sky. The last one to leave was Richthofen's ...

The observers had spotted a formation of six R.E.8s from 59 Squadron, which the German pilots soon destroyed, one of them by von Richthofen himself. To Wegener back at the airfield the combat seemed undramatic at first until he saw an R.E.8 crashing in flames. This quickly brought home to him the reality of aerial warfare and the level of violence it engendered. A little later he watched as the Staffel returned:

Scarcely half an hour had passed and they were all back again. The pilots climbed out of their seats and stood amongst their well-wishing comrades laughing, proud and happy while they recounted in an animated way recent events ...

No one was injured. It looked as though it could have been a successful sporting event. But Richthofen's machine showed how little it was like that. An enemy machine-gun burst had hit his left lower wing and the fabric looked like it had been pulled back, for about a metre and a half, by the slashing motion of a large knife. And on the outer wooden shell close to the pilot's seat ran a second tear close to the cockpit showing how another bullet had come close to ending his life.

He influenced everybody, all of whom were obviously committed to their leader with a mixture of friendly camaraderie, great admiration and absolute obedience … As with Boelcke, Richthofen's effectiveness and value to us is not only his fighting technique, but the way he has, within his staffel, created a band of men whom he has filled with a Boelcke-type spirit, spurring them on to greater successes.

Von Salzmann was as equally impressed as Wegener when meeting von Richthofen for the first time that spring:

We were standing on a street in Douai when a small boneshaker of a car came rushing towards us. Two young officers got out and came over to me, one wore a short, undone fur coat, his hair all awry, of medium height and solid in build, and one said in a clipped, military voice, 'Richthofen'.

At the time he was just at the start of his stunning rise to fame, perhaps only one of many then. Despite this he caught my eye immediately … Richthofen possessed in abundance that inborn and appealing self-awareness and self-assurance which can never be learnt.

If any heads were turned by the attention of these influential writers, and their masters, these feelings had to be quickly put to one side before yet another operational patrol began. Although the Albatros D.III gave its pilots a huge advantage, the new biplane wasn't without its faults and von Richthofen had to display true leadership skills and take prompt action to see that any defects were quickly dealt with. It was here that his growing reputation proved very useful.

When intercepting MacLennan and Grieg on 24 January he was forced to land not by engine trouble, as recorded in his memoirs, but because 'one of my wings broke during the battle … It was only due to a miracle that I reached the ground without being killed. On the same day three new aeroplanes of Jasta Boelcke fell … It is possible that what happened to me happened to them.'

Armed with such graphic evidence, von Richthofen quickly expressed his concerns to those in authority. As a result, the D.IIIs were grounded by the Commanding General's staff on 27 January and temporarily replaced by Halberstadts. Suitably modified, the D.IIIs soon returned, but their reputation had been damaged and trust in these aircraft undoubtedly took time to be restored.

Perhaps of greater significance is the extent to which von Richthofen led from the front and trained his men so effectively in tactics that he ensured that they were well-equipped to fight and survive the coming battles. So successful was he that over the next twenty months they produced an outstanding return on his investment. On 23 April 1917 they claimed their 100th victory, the 200th on 17 August and by the end of the war the total had risen to 321, although it may have been higher than this. In the process twenty-one pilots were killed, nineteen more wounded and two captured. However, with a ratio of losses in battle of nearly one in ten over the enemy they were easily the most successful German fighter squadron of all.

It would be too easy to give von Richthofen all the credit for this success, because many other men were involved, but his influence cannot be denied or his value to the propagandists overstated. And soon many of his men would also be caught up in the PR maelstrom, including Lothar, who completed his training, 'evolving into a brilliant pilot', according to his brother. As a result, Manfred quickly secured his posting to Jasta 11, then based at La Brayelle, where he took up residence on 6 March. Such was his developing skill that before the month was out he had shot down his first enemy aircraft, an F.E.2b of 25 Squadron, east of Vimy. With major British offensives due to start that year, his arrival could not have been better timed.

If there was one month in the war that has come to represent the magnitude of von Richthofen's and Jasta 11's achievements, it is surely April 1917. February and March had seen the pilots begin to exercise the skills so carefully fostered by their leader and, with their improved DIIIs gradually began to take an ever increasing toll of enemy aircraft. April would see them rise to new heights, unconsciously aided by the Royal Flying Corps, whose aircraft, for the moment, hadn't kept pace with those being produced 'the German aero industry. A balance would soon be restored with the arrival of the S.E.5, Bristol Fighter and Sopwith Camel, but for the moment Jasta 11 was confronted by many slower, outdated and poorly armed machines. So, they 'made hay while the sun shone' and claimed eighty-nine of the 298 aircraft believed destroyed by the German Air Service during that month alone.

Despite their heavy losses, the Royal Flying Corps didn't back down. With a spring offensive due to start on the Vimy–Arras front on 8 April, followed by operations at Messines in June, Ypres a month later and Cambrai in November, the stakes were too high for this to happen. With so much going on, intelligence had to be gathered by whatever means possible, no matter what the cost or risks to air crew. 'Bloody April', as it was called, was the inevitable result. British commanders were only too aware of recent events, where they had been caught out by the Germans' sudden withdrawal to the Hindenburg defensive line. In great secrecy, and apparently without Allied knowledge, they had built an immensely strong set of defences, which ran for 40 miles or more from Arras south to Soissons. Then, in a clandestine way, and aided by its fighter pilots who drove off many intruders, they withdrew to this new line in March, applying a scorched earth policy to the land they gave up to the Allies.

This tactical withdrawal placed La Brayelle behind enemy lines, so forced Jasta 11 to shift their base to Roucourt, a few miles to the south-east of Douai, from where they could still easily reach the front line. Here they lived comfortably in a château adjoining the airfield, in the middle of which sat a small wood that provided some cover for the aircraft.

The battle that raged in the skies over Arras and Vimy that April was an uneven contest that just fell short of total annihilation because of the RFC's superiority in numbers, and the aggression and resilience shown by its airmen. Nevertheless it was a close-run thing, and cost far too many young airmen their lives. By now von Richthofen and his pilots were used to the battles and the bloodshed, but for the newcomer or the casual observer it could be a sobering experience to witness. In the excitement of the moment the thrill of the hunt would often blind participants to the horror and tragedy of what was happening. Then just occasionally an account emerges that puts these things in a true perspective. In this case it was written by Hans Schroder, an observer on the Eastern Front, who transferred to the Western Front and became an Air Defence Officer during 1917. One of his key tasks was to observe aerial combats taking place over the trenches and report their outcomes. It is true to say that he found this almost unbearable to watch at times and, in recording his thoughts, has given us a gruelling picture of day-to-day life during that bloody month:

My observation post at Werwicq was called La Montagne … I arrived there in glorious sunshine and received a friendly welcome from Leutnant Lasky, from whom I was to take over.

'You are right in the thick of things,' he pronounced as he stood beside his corporal at the telescope. 'Do you see that Staffel over there? It's Richthofen's. Have a look through the glass – the red machine is his. And over yonder by Kemmel are the English machines. There will be something to report in a moment.'

I could not take my eyes off the telescope. The two formations were heading for each other. But why did the foremost Englishman go into such a sudden turn, and why did his followers imitate him? 'Ah, now they've recognised the red machine!' exclaimed Lasky. The red aircraft shot ahead of the Staffel in pursuit of the fleeing foe, and Richthofen singled out the English aircraft on his extreme left. The Englishman dived hard to gain speed, but the Fokker (Albatros) tore after it with amazing determination. I saw the distance between them decrease ... 150 metres ... 100 now 80–50 metres apart, and at last both machine guns are hammering out their bullets.

A wing breaks away from the Englishman – a streak of flame from his machine – the fuel tank is ablaze. It rears up like a mortally wounded horse – the engine and propeller have ceased working. The machine looks like a burning piece of paper.

One dot and then another fall from the aircraft. They are the unlucky captives. I have them in focus; I can see them spin round and around with outstretched arms. I can almost see that their fingers are spread wide open on their hands, and so they whirl through the air from 3,000 metres up. I can see them until they hit the ground. Their broken bodies will be lying somewhere between the lines now.

Six engines hum over our heads as I take my startled eyes from the telescope – I look up – the red aircraft is right over La Montagne – its pilot waves to us. 'Simply marvellous!' says Lasky. 'But, good Lord, what's up with you?'

I am forced to sit down on a chair; I feel quite dizzy. 'Horrible!' I gasp. 'Well you'll have to get used to it. That's our daily job – our hourly job should I say.' ... I know I shall not stay here long!

For those delving into military history it is easy to become blasé about the nature of combat and take it as a matter of course that men die. It is easy to forget that it is a vicious, wholly unappealing business where registering success as a score and a competition raises many moral issues. Killing and maiming is only a joy for the psychopath. There may have been such men in the ranks of wartime pilots, but the vast majority were simply fighting for a cause in which they believed and conducted themselves accordingly. They may have become inured to the sights and sounds of death, but any human being possessing a degree of self-awareness and a conscience can only take so much slaughter before their minds, and sometimes their bodies, rebel.

Reaching this limit will vary according to personality, beliefs, the tenor of the war they are fighting and much more, but they will all still reach it at some point. And when this happens the thrill of the chase, a huntsmen's instincts or a desire for glory cannot sustain an individual indefinitely. Only the ability to endure and a strong sense of duty will count, and even these have their limits when battle fatigue sets in. By the end of April, during which von Richthofen downed another twenty-one enemy aircraft, including three on the 13th and four on the 29th, it seems more than likely that he was reaching this point and a distaste for the whole business had begun to set in.

In some quarters he may have been considered a calculating killer, but essentially his character was much gentler, caring and nuanced than this description suggests. Although a parent will tend to see their children in the best possible light and so be blind to their faults, Kunigunde von Richthofen was too clever and down to earth to do that. She clearly loved her children but saw them plain, being able to see both strengths and weaknesses in them. To this end the thoughts she recorded are invaluable in understanding Manfred and the issues that motivated and sustained him. In him she saw a man of great substance with many sides to his personality who would always do his best for country and family no matter what the cost. By the end of April the cost was growing ever larger and only likely to get worse as the extent of his fame became more apparent and increasingly necessary to exploit.

During April, Germany's actions finally resulted in the USA entering the war on the Allied side – unrestricted U-boat warfare being the trigger. With the Russian Empire tottering on the edge of revolution and defeat, leaving the Central Powers able to concentrate their forces more fully in the west, such an outcome was unfortunate, to say the least. But the USA was ill-prepared for such a war and it would take it time to amass and train a large enough force to be truly effective. Nevertheless, its declaration of war was a severe blow to morale in Germany that propaganda could do little to assuage, although the promotion of its heroes shone a bright light into the gloom.

Throughout the month press reports made much of Manfred's victories, each one producing adjective-strewn headlines. And as each story faded, fresh ones appeared to keep the heroic image in the public eye. Germany may not have been achieving much on the battlefield but defend ground, but in the air great victories could be proclaimed and so provide a necessary distraction from the ever-growing casualty lists. Each day Kunigunde would scan these reports, taking pride in Manfred and Lothar's deeds, but growing sadder as familiar names fell on the battlefield and the war news grew worse:

> We now find ourselves in a state of war with America … The enemy has lost 44 planes. Whole squadrons are said to be have been destroyed. Leutnants Voss and Berthold are mentioned. But what is this? Five of our pilots have not returned … Why is Manfred not mentioned? Prince Friedrich Karl of Prussia has died of internal bleeding … Oberleutnant Berr has fallen. Finally, Rittmeister [promoted to this rank in April having been advanced to Oberleutnant on the 23rd March] von Richthofen has shot down his 38th and 39th opponents … the dice falls again … Manfred wins his 44th aerial victory; a few days later, his total leaps to 50. He is in all the papers, on the lips of all people; flags wave over his name. Cities honour him and royalty telegraph … The enemy is totally bewildered and what they do in response is disgraceful. One day we read the headline: 'English Blood Money for a German Flier! [Information via WTB Berlin, 4 May] The English

have assembled an air squadron of volunteer fliers, said to be exclusively aimed at destroying our most successful fighter pilot, Rittmeister Freiherr von Richthofen, who has already shot down 52 enemy fliers. The pilot who succeeds in shooting down or capturing Richthofen will receive the Victoria Cross, a promotion, his own aeroplane as a gift, £500 sterling ... A cinema cameraman will fly with the English squadron, and will record the whole incident for use in British films.'

If this report proves to be true, then the cry of a whole world, whose sons bleed in the trenches for the prestige of their countries, must answer for it.

To say that propaganda had entered von Richthofen's life would be an understatement; it had invaded every aspect of his existence. And while the truth of his daily encounters with the enemy are based on fact, the purveyors of propaganda could not resist taking the story into the realms of fantasy in an attempt to inflame passions. It would seem that the German intelligence services had recorded that the RFC had equipped 56 Squadron with the latest British fighter, the S.E.5, and in April 1917 they were sent to France to try and combat the ever-growing threat of the Albatros D.IIIs. Among their number was Captain Albert Ball, the leading British ace at the time, whose presence gave the story added zest, especially when it was realised that 56 would be based at Vert Galant, north of Amiens, and within easy reach of the Arras front and Jasta 11.

It seems likely that this news was suitably spun by Nicolai and his team, exaggerated and then fed to the press as fact. While 56 Squadron clearly had an important role to play in restoring the aerial balance on the Western Front, the idea of a group of mercenaries being gathered together to kill von Richthofen is, to be frank, ludicrous. Simply flying and surviving in combat was difficult enough, let alone trying to eliminate a single man in a squadron, where many aircraft also bore traces of von Richthofen's red paint scheme; other pilots being aware of how vulnerable an all-red fighter made their leader.

However, the truth was not something *Wolffs Telegraphisches Bureau* (WTB) was overly concerned about. During the war it had become the main agency for the dissemination of all news across Germany. As the conflict progressed, strict censorship rules were applied by the powers that be and the WTB, because of its central role, found itself virtually under government control. As a result, all newspapers tended to reprint Wolff's news verbatim so as not to fall foul of these new regulations. However, in a country grown more used to press freedom these restrictions soon inspired many complaints about the way WTB conducted 'its' business, but by operating under government patronage meant that any disputes were quickly crushed.

With Ludendorff's promotion in 1916 the level of control exerted over WTB by him, and not Germany's government, grew ever stronger. He, through Nicolai, then started to fashion news reports in a favourable way. By doing this they hoped to reassure the population that the war was necessary, despite the losses and hardship. In addition, they would also play down the damage caused by the war, while highlighting the effects of enemy aggression and levels of their cruelty and brutality.

Nevertheless, the discontent continued to grow and newspaper editors and publishers complained frequently about Wolff's monopoly, the agency's almost total obedience to the High Command, the poor quality of its presentation and a lack of accuracy in the material it distributed. Even accusations of deception and misrepresentation were bandied about, but to no avail, and it was not until the war was nearing its end, when Germany was facing revolution, that other voices began to be heard and military control of the media began to lessen. Meanwhile, all their combined efforts were seemingly being directed to the promotion of one man, who, as April gave way to May, began a period of leave, which proved to be anything but a rest for Manfred.

By this time his reputation had spread across the lines to the Allied camp, where his activities began to feature in press reports in an unparalleled way. Inevitably, perhaps, someone so successful at downing your own aircraft and killing so many of your men is bound to become the subject of much speculation and, more surprisingly, grudging admiration. As he had guessed, and his fellow pilots feared, 'Le Petit Rouge' had indeed attracted great attention. For many RFC airmen, he had become a symbol of enemy superiority and a nightmarish sort of 'bogeyman' who would hasten them to their deaths.

It was part illusion, of course, but very dangerous to morale, nonetheless. Arthur Gould Lee, who served with 46 Squadron, flying Sopwith Pups then Camels during 1917, caught a flavour of this when he wrote in a letter that:

> When I joined the squadron in May, the reputation of von Richthofen was already so high that he had not only become a symbol of the superiority of German fighter aeroplanes and their pilots, but had also taken on the appearance of a super-slayer, invariably present in any combat involving Albatros fighters.
>
> Through British newspaper reports taken from German communiqués we knew he was piling up his list of victories over British aeroplanes with a speed that was appalling, though those who were flying against him knew that he found his victims largely amongst our obsolete and inefficient two-seaters.
>
> The prestige attached to his name became a significant factor in determining the morale of the RFC, from May to his death. To each young airman arriving at the Front, he was accepted as a 'bogeyman', who came to epitomise all the horrors and danger they would face. He had an all-pervading presence that served to keep his name constantly on our lips

in the Mess, and even experienced, seasoned pilots were not immune from the sense of menace his reputation created. To encounter a formation created no alarm, they might well be a group of indifferently led and mostly inexperienced pilots ... But if we spotted a flash of red paint we knew we must nerve ourselves for an almost inevitably lethal fight, with the odds stacked against us.

Our greatest fear was going down in flames and many is the night that such thoughts permeated our dreams, making us wake in a cold sweat and then finding sleep impossible. By his mere presence at the front, and the threat he posed, von Richthofen achieved the same effect. Later on I realised that this was a trick of the imagination, but in 1917/18 it created extreme tension and led to many sleepless nights.

Others too shared these feelings of facing a superman and letters and memoirs are littered with similar thoughts and feelings. These included Cecil Lewis of 56 Squadron, who wrote in a letter to the author that:

We were all aware of Richthofen's reputation and the sight of a red Albatros did cause us great concern. We were undaunted because we had Albert Ball with us and we were flying the new SE5s. Nevertheless, we still had a sense that we were fighting an inhuman monster who knew no fear and could strike at any time or place without pity. An illusion of course, but a potent one nonetheless.

Propaganda plays on fears, especially when the existence of an apparently invincible foe makes them seem more real. In this way von Richthofen's greatest achievement may have been something over which he had no control, but yet relied on his reputation as a fighter pilot to help instil. So it is unsurprising that the seemingly apocryphal tale of Ludendorff later commenting that his presence in France was alone worth three divisions soon found favour.

And yet he was no superman and when sent on leave in May he was probably in need of a long rest. However, first he had to make a number of duty calls, undoubtedly due to his growing status as a national hero. As things turned out, the flight to Germany seems to have been the most peaceful part of his leave and in his memoirs it is described almost as a dividing line in his life – before fame and after it had truly taken hold. He may have had hints of what awaited him at home, in his mailbag alone, but operational flying and leading Jasta 11 would have been too distracting for more to seep into his consciousness. Now, on returning home, the full force of his fame hit him and his words capture the sense of transition from one life to another:

His majesty had expressed a wish to meet me ... I had to make an appearance on the 2nd May. I should not have been able to fulfil this wish by taking a train. I therefore thought I would travel by air. I started the next morning (1st May), not in my single-seater 'Le Petit Rouge' but in a large, fat two-seater. The man who would do the flying was Lt Krefft, who was going on leave to recover his strength.

I started on my journey rather hastily and the only luggage I took with me was my toothbrush ... The route we took was via Namur, Liege, Aix la Chapelle and Cologne. It was lovely for once to be sailing through the air without any thoughts of the war. The weather was wonderful. We rarely have had such a perfect time.

Soon our captive balloons were lost to sight and the thunder of the Battle of Arras was only heard in the distance. Beneath us all was peace. We saw steamers on the river and fast trains on the railways. We easily overtook everything below ... The beautiful mountains of the Meuse were not recognisable as mountains. One could only trace them by their shadows, for the sun was right above us. We only knew they were there, and with a little imagination we could hide ourselves in the cool shade of that delightful country. We were both in high spirits. Before us was a long leave of absence. The weather was beautiful.

Our arrival at Cologne had been announced by telegram. People were looking out for us. On the previous day the newspapers had reported my fifty-second victory. One can only imagine what kind of a reception they had prepared for us.

In the afternoon we arrived at Headquarters ... First of all I met the General Commanding the Flying Services. Then, next morning the great moment when I would meet von Hindenburg and Ludendorff ... It is a strange feeling to be in the rooms where the fate of the world is decided [and his fate as well]. So I was quite glad when I was outside the Holiest of Holies again to lunch with His Majesty ... He congratulated me on my success and on my twenty-fifth birthday.

On the following day I was to take lunch with the Kaiserin and so I flew to Hamburg. In the evening I was again invited by General Field Marshal von Hindenburg (to dinner at Bad Kreuznach) ... Some days later I arrived in Schweidnitz. Although I reached there at seven o'clock in the morning, there was a large crowd waiting at the station. I was very warmly received. In the afternoon various demonstrations took place to honour me, amongst other things, by the local Boy Scouts. It became clear to me that the people at home took a vivid interest in their fighting soldiers.

After this flurry of activity, Manfred didn't go straight home but decided to delay this visit for a while and take the opportunity offered to go hunting for a few days. Clearly the need for fresh air and some privacy were paramount in his mind after months of combat, now with the added pressures of celebrity. However, he obviously felt a pang of conscience in doing so and wrote to his mother a few words of apology:

> Surely you are angry that I have been here in Germany for almost eight days without writing to you. I am in Freiburg hunting wood grouse and will stay here until the 14th. Then I must go to Berlin to look at some new aeroplanes ... then I will come to Schweidnitz. You must excuse me that it is so long.
>
> From Schweidnitz I will travel to Furst von Pless to shoot bison. Then towards the end of the month will tour other Fronts in the Balkans, and so forth. This will take three to four weeks. Meanwhile Lothar leads my Staffel.

From now on, wherever he went, crowds followed him eager to see their new hero and his leave gradually became an endless round of social events where he faced hordes of well-wishers. And the masters he served also wished to be seen with their prize exhibit; Ludendorff in particular. But von Richthofen's meeting with him proved to be a trying experience, as Kunigunde later recalled:

> Ludendorff made a strong impression with his concise, impartial manner. Manfred's opinion is that he is no man for idle chatter and goes all out [in asking von Richthofen brief business-like questions about aerial warfare and ignoring such pleasantries as enquiries about his health or congratulating him on his successes]. On the other hand, there is Hindenburg, on whose right Manfred sat at dinner. He asked in his good-natured, jovial way, 'Now tell me, Richthofen, were you also a cadet?' Manfred told him that he had begun his military career with the 2nd Company at Wahlstatt Room 6. Hindenburg replied, 'There, you see, I also began in Room 6.'

On the whole, I believe that Manfred was glad to leave the General Headquarters behind him. For him such receptions are no source of pleasure. He longs for the drone of a propeller, the chatter of machine guns, and the disciplined but clear life with his comrades out there ... He wanted to conquer each day anew, at the risk of his life – that was his nature.

It seems clear that Ludendorff, undoubtedly guided by Nicolai and his staff, was assessing von Richthofen – as a fighting man, his potential as a leader and someone whose image could be used to bolster a fading cause. He was, to all intent and purposes, being measured and evaluated by a man of quite ruthless intent who was eager to exploit any opportunity that might come his way. In the circumstances, it is hardly surprising that von Richthofen was relieved to be out of his presence and be gently stroked by the more socially polished Hindenburg. Yet despite their different approaches, both were astute, hard-nosed men, although many made the mistake of undervaluing Hindenburg and overstating the part played by the more aggressive, controlling and, some thought, highly strung Ludendorff. Nevertheless, together they made a truly remarkable pair with clear views on the way the war should be fought and the way it should be sold to the German people.

It seems more than likely that during von Richthofen's visit to headquarters Ludendorff's team proposed that he pen a brief memoir for publication that year. In fact, it has been inferred that the book was written as a direct result of an instruction issued by the 'Press and Intelligence' section of the *Luftstreitkräfte*. Either way, he felt compelled to obey and with a short period of leave beckoning had time, so it was felt, to begin work. Undoubtedly, he had been persuaded that his efforts would greatly benefit Germany's war effort and, at the same time, offer Manfred some financial reward. Ever aware of his family's struggle to survive on Albrecht's income, as a caring son he would do anything he could to ease the pressure on his mother and father, especially in the event of his death. With prices rising constantly, due to ever-increasing shortages, any extra income could be a godsend.

So a deal was struck with the publishers Ullstein Verlag of Berlin and Manfred began work in May when staying on the estate of Prince Hans Heinrich XV of Pless in Upper Silesia. With other commitments to distract him, progress was inevitably slow. However, by the time he returned to the Western Front on 14 June, and with the help of a shorthand typist, he had made good progress, allowing the draft to be passed to Erich von Salzmann for editing.

As a friend, Salzmann had gained Manfred's trust and been named in his contract with Ullstein as his representative in the production of these memoirs. In this case, it was his responsibility to screen von Richthofen's text and revise it wherever he saw fit. However, the extent of his editing is unclear and so there has long been a debate about which sections are his and which are von Richthofen's. And then, of course, there were Nicolai's censorship and intelligence departments that the manuscript passed through before publication could go ahead. This undoubtedly produced a number of additional amendments. Finally, towards the end of 1917 this cobbled together book was published and soon became a bestseller. Such was his fame on either side of the lines that a version entitled *The Red Battle Flyer*, translated by James Ellis Barker, a noted historian, journalist and homeopath, appeared in Britain and then the USA during 1918, selling well in both countries.

In such a bitter war an outcome such as this might be thought improbable, but courage and the ability to endure are universally admired qualities, even in an enemy. This seems to have transcended many other considerations, including responsibility for so many Allied deaths. It was a bi-product of their plans that neither Ludendorff or Nicolai could have anticipated. When an enemy honours your heroes some might think you had gone too far in demystifying a potent weapon, even one based on propaganda. Nevertheless, the die had been cast and the advantages and disadvantages of celebrity had to be absorbed, in Manfred's case with some discomfort, as his mother recorded:

> The whole city seemed mobilized. I knew how much Manfred hated to be feted. But it couldn't be helped so now he reluctantly played his part ... The wonderful weather on Sunday favoured the mass hike to our house. At times, the entire street was black with people. Everyone wanted to see him. We stayed in the garden all day as delegations came and went ... military bands blared ... I see Manfred occupying himself with the children – how they hang onto him, how it makes him happy to look into so many young faces glowing with enthusiasm.
>
> Only once did I see a wince cross his face – as one gentleman regretted that all two or three thousand school children could not be here to shake his hand ... In the evening we could stand no more ... When the onslaught did not slacken, I resorted to an extreme measure and let it be reported in a newspaper that he had departed. We then went away from here by car to Stanowitz, where Manfred was pleased to shoot a buck in its beautiful old hunting grounds. He longed for a few days' rest.
>
> As we entered the town we were surprised to notice preparations for a ceremonial reception. The inhabitants lined the streets, faces looked out of all the windows, the castle flew a flag, photographs were taken and children sang songs of welcome ... Manfred's face grew even more gloomy ... It is becoming even harder for him to be away from the Front and his Staffel – he longs to be with them.

If the crowds in Schweidnitz were overpowering, he faced the same or worse wherever he went during his leave and must have felt oppressed by its intensity. His thoughts may have mirrored those of other veterans I spoke to who had considered the juxtaposition between life at home and their lives in the front line. Johnnie Johnson probably best summed up this feeling in a letter to the author:

> When with a squadron the reality of living daily with the excitement of combat and courting death soon stripped bare all other considerations. You lived life with an intensity those who haven't experienced it could not understand. Being with a group of men of like mind all taking the same risks, living and dying in the process made the meaning of Shakespeare's 'Band of Brothers' only too clear. The penalty, of course, was that our band was quickly and frequently diminished and sorrow had to be packed away and ignored as much as possible. But it could soon return, nonetheless, and few could avoid the way combat and loss soon exposed you to increasing fatigue and war weariness.
>
> A good Commanding Officer would spot the signs of this condition approaching a critical point and take action if at all possible. However, the person themselves might be oblivious of the dangers and hide their fears and carry on, though unfit to do so. Many were lost, or so I believe, because of this. They became uncaring of their own safety or simply became very careless doing things that even a beginner knew to be foolhardy. Everyone had their limit and some, like Douglas Bader, could go on longer than most, but even he should have been rested long before he baled out over France and was captured during August 1941.

In von Richthofen's case his desire to return to Jasta 11 was heightened by news that his brother had been wounded on 13 May and would be sidelined until September, and Karl-Emil Schaffer had been killed in combat on 5 June. His friend and protégé, who had recently gone on to lead Jasta 28, was a great loss. So, Manfred felt compelled to break away from his other duties and attend the funeral. He also took this opportunity to return to Berlin to pursue a campaign close to his heart and press von Hoeppner and Lieth-Thomson, and probably anyone else who would listen, for new and better aircraft. Bearing in mind his own experiences with Albatros fighters, a rising number of incidents involving wing failure, especially with the new D.V model that began reaching the front in May, and the pressing need for new and better enemy aircraft, this was hardly surprising. But now he could use his new-found status as a national hero to influence events in a way that favored the fighting men and, potentially, the course of the war. During the meetings that followed he would undoubtedly have been briefed on operational changes soon to be made on the Western Front and been engaged by Nicolai and his team on the broader issue of public relations and his memoirs.

While he had been away it had become clear to the Air Service that both the British and French were gaining in strength with new aircraft arriving at the front. The Allies, with a combined industrial strength greater than Germany, could produce aircraft in greater numbers, so creating an imbalance they would find difficult if not impossible to overcome. To try and maintain a tactical advantage it was decided to group a number of Jastas together in a single mobile force, the first of these was to operate under the 4th Army's banner. In theory, this large formation could move, at a moment's notice, to any part of the front where the enemy were particularly active and there try and achieve temporary superiority. At the same time German reconnaissance aircraft would operate behind enemy lines, mostly without escorts, using their ability to climb high over the battlefield to avoid the RFC's fighters and do their jobs. As needs must, of course, but with such a large group of fighters sweeping the front it stood a chance of success, although this depended heavily on the quality of their aircraft, the pilots and the skill with which they were led.

There was also the question of the United States' entry into the war, and its effect on Germany's armed forces, to consider. By June the High Command were putting the final touches to their 'America' rearmament programme that defined how they intended meeting this new threat. Part of this programme focussed on the air arm, which, at the time, employed some 88,600 men and was equipped with 2,460 aircraft of all types, at the front and in reserve at home in Germany. The plan was to expand this force to something in excess of 114,000 men plus an additional forty fighter and sixteen reconnaissance and bombing squadrons by the end of 1917. It was an ambitious plan and one that depended very heavily on sufficient men of the right quality being found to fill many vacancies. And here the appalling haemorrhage of men in so many fruitless battles since 1914 came back to haunt the perpetrators of these huge losses. There was also the question of industry's ability to produce all these new aircraft to consider, especially with raw materials becoming scarcer as the blockade continued to strangle supply routes into Germany.

It was these changes and more that von Richthofen, and the other Jastaführers, would most certainly have been briefed on during May and June. This change may even have hastened his return to the front. Such a strong, clear-headed leader would wish to be there to ensure that his ideas were implemented in such a way as to make the new, enlarged formation a success. In this though, he faced a potential stumbling block in the form of Hauptmann Otto Bufe, who was the Kommandeur der Flieger (Kofl) of 4th Army, under whom von Richthofen would serve when Jasta 11 transferred over from the 6th Army front.

It was initially planned that Jasta 11 would be grouped together with Jastas 6, 7 and 26, operating under the command of Bufe. Before this took effect, though, the Jasta numbers changed and 11 would eventually be united with 4, 6 and 10 instead.

Like von Richthofen, Bufe was of Prussian birth and also a career officer, but the 33-year-old was an observer, not a pilot, who seems to have had little direct experience of life in a fighter squadron. All this might have been forgiven if he had been imbued with good tactical sense or had been prepared to be led by those, such as von Richthofen, who had these skills, but this appears not to have been the case. Very soon cracks began to appear and a clash of wills between von Richthofen and Bufe seemed inevitable. It was a case of an experienced fighter pilot and national hero just beginning to realise the power he possessed in determining the future course of aviation in war, and an equally well-established officer, but with far less experience in these matters. In the event there was only ever likely to be one winner, even though Bufe, as Kofl, exercised, as advisor to the army commander on aviation matters, control over day-to-day operations of all the squadrons operating in 4th Army's area. In addition, he was responsible for the supply of aircraft, personnel and general supplies, co-operation with the infantry and artillery plus all training. With this in mind, he could, if he so wished, have made life extremely difficult for von Richthofen.

It seems likely that once transferred to 4th Army von Richthofen would have sought out Bufe as the man who bore responsibility for the tactics he would soon be asked to implement. Having enjoyed a productive working relationship with Hauptmann Maximilian Sorg, Kofl of 6th Army, who had given him freedom to deploy his force as he saw fit, there would have been a natural expectation that a similar arrangement would be employed by Bufe. But it seems that a meeting between the two men, shortly after von Richthofen's return to action, set a disagreeable tone for the future. It may be that Bufe, who was known to be ambitious, chose this moment to try and exert authority over Jasta 11's leader. Instead, he found a man of equal rank and greater personal authority who would resent being dictated to by an 'armchair warrior', who, at best, might be considered ill-informed. If this is the case differences would quickly surface and, if unresolved, lead to difficulties between the two men and perhaps even some personal animosity.

The main disagreement between von Richthofen and Bufe seems to have been over the way the new formation would operate and Kofl's desire to maintain strict control over all they did. To do this Bufe tried to institute a timetable of standing patrols over the front undertaken by small groups of fighters in what were called *Sperrfluge* operations. These simply involved flying up and down on a set course creating the illusion of a defensive line to deter enemy patrols. Von Richthofen felt these were a waste of effort, believing that the tactics introduced by Boelcke still held good and should be applied equally to these new, larger groups, especially if their operations were guided by forward observers. It was a basic difference of opinion that became even more pronounced when Manfred was formally appointed commander of Jagdgeschwader 1, as it soon became known, on 25 June, a day after its creation was announced.

As a Jastaführer his views would have carried some weight, but as leader of JG1 his authority was even greater. It also helped his cause that the order signed by Lieth-Thomson creating JG1 included the words, 'The Geschwader is a closed unit. It is appointed for the purpose of fighting for and securing aerial superiority in crucial combat sectors.' To this von Hoeppner added, 'The Geschwader is a self-contained unit. Its duty is to achieve and maintain air superiority in sectors of the Front as directed', later injecting, 'In the person of Rittmeister von Richthofen it has a commander whose steel-hard determination in relentlessly pursuing the enemy will so infuse every member of the Geschwader.'

With this backing von Richthofen was virtually given carte blanche to operate as he thought fit and it probably helped that Crown Prince Rupprecht of Bavaria, who commanded the 2nd, 4th and 6th Armies at the time, added his own support in a telegram dated the 24th. In it he reiterated the point that JG1 was a 'closed unit', with its purpose being 'to win and secure dominance in the air'. All this would have given von Richthofen added muscle if he wished to challenge anything Bufe might care to introduce. However, it wasn't the end of the matter and the differences between the two men would continue to fester and resurface, with some venom, during July when the Rittmeister was on an enforced absence from the front.

For the moment though von Richthofen was fully involved in gathering together the four Jastas that formed JG1 on airfields at Marcke (Jastas 4 and 11), Marckebeeke (Jasta 10) and Bissegem (Jasta 6) and prepare them for operations. He also focussed on the need for good external communications with 'spotters' at the front and, internally, between the four Jastas. Karl Bodenschatz, who was appointed to be the Geschwader's adjutant on 1 July, described how this worked:

> A circular telephone links the four Staffeln so that when von Richthofen lifts his handset all are connected simultaneously. In this way he puts his four Staffeln into action when necessary and then at a very quick pace. The aircraft are lined up, the pilots fully dressed close by and the mechanics ready to swing the propellers at any moment. If a take-off order comes, the Staffel can get off the ground inside a minute.

While these changes were being introduced, von Richthofen took whatever opportunities he could to get airborne again. The pace of his victories in April had been staggeringly high and unlikely to be repeated now that the enemy was better equipped, but the draw of combat must have been very strong and further successes soon followed. On 18 June he destroyed an R.E.8 and its crew – Ralph Ellis, from Surbiton in Surrey, and Harold Barlow, who hailed from Cheshire. Then five days later he sent down a SPAD S.VII while flying Albatros D.V No. 1177/17, only partially painted red, a DH.4 on the 24th and a second DH.4 on the day his appointment to command JG1 was confirmed. And July began with one more success. On the 2nd he incinerated the crew of an R.E.8 from 53 Squadron near Deûlémont, according to his combat report.

For the casual observer it must have seemed that Manfred was simply taking up the reins from where he had left off on 29 April. But he was not the same man, or so it seems. His continuing, and possibly unnecessary, squabble with Otto Bufe over tactics may well have been a sign that the pressures he faced were, after nearly three years of active front-line service, taking their toll. And this wouldn't have been helped by the demands placed on him by the press and the constant loss of many men close to him, including his cousin Oskar von Schickfus, George Zeumer and, perhaps worst of all, Karl Allmenröder on 27 June. Each loss added to an already heavy burden and then there was the steady drip of casualties among the men he commanded to tax his mind.

In the Second World War psychologists coined the phrase 'over-identification with the men you lead in combat' when studying battle fatigue in officers commanding squadrons, wings or groups. In simple terms this means that a leader becomes overly concerned with the welfare and safety of his men to the exclusion of all other considerations, including the success of the operations delegated to them. It is the natural reaction of a good, compassionate man, who has grown tired of continually seeing lives lost, and is so consumed by an overpowering sense of responsibility for their deaths, that he then seeks to avoid more losses by whatever means possible. It is at this point that those in charge cease to lead effectively, or so military psychologists believed, leaving the men under them without the strong, all-seeing commander they needed to carry on. Once this condition had been identified, the US Army Air Force were usually quick to act and replace these tired officers with fresh, less-troubled men.

However, the opposite could also apply. Men who were once capable leaders became callous and uncaring of life as battle fatigue transfixed them, sacrificing those they led without a backwards glance in the belief that a mission demanded success at all costs. In war loss is inevitable, but a capable commander has to balance means and ends to ensure the sacrifice is warranted. When they cease to be aware of this their usefulness is over and they must go, or so psychologists then and now believe.

In truth, it is a complex issue that is difficult to judge with any certainty because what makes a good leader will vary according to who is considering the issue. For those commanding armies or air forces, who see a much bigger picture, success is essential no matter what the cost in lives. For the mass being sent into battle there must be a chance of survival to make the fight worthwhile and so they look to their battlefield leaders, who, more often than not, share the same risks and dangers, to ensure this is so. They are then in an almost impossible position and the dangers of over-identification creates an unbearable strain on the individual concerned. In July 1917 von Richthofen found himself in just such a position and the threat of war weariness, compounded by the curse of fame, was in danger of overcoming this steadfast, young man. And then his situation suddenly grew much worse on 6 July during a patrol over the front near Wervicq, just inside the Belgium border.

Chapter 7

Into the Void

There was a mighty battle taking place between Wervicq and Comines. Richthofen had pitted himself against eight FEs [from 20 Squadron], which were revolving around each other in pairs, being matched by eight Albatros of Richthofen's staffel. The tactics of the Englishmen were remarkable – each aircraft should not look after itself but cover its partner. Each one protected by the other from attack by their German opponents.

The battle lasted for a good quarter of an hour without any of our people getting an opportunity to get to grips with the enemy ... The Englishmen refused to be rushed, and their steadiness gave them superiority. Meanwhile our aircraft tried to break their formation ... They pirouetted and spiralled, but their manoeuvres exposed them to more risks than their opponents, who appeared invulnerable.

Then Richthofen's red aircraft suddenly turned on its nose and dived down out of the throng of combatants ... I kept my eye focussed on him. Nothing seemed to impede his downward rush – he was finished ... Then – two hundred metres above the ground – he caught the machine and flew straight towards me ... it landed and taxied. I looked through my Zeiss glasses and saw Richthofen climb out, stagger and fall ... I reached him as he lay with his head resting on his leather helmet, while a stream of blood trickled down from the back of his head. His eyes were closed and his face was as white as a sheet.

'Are you in pain?' I asked. 'I feel better now. I want to go to (the hospital) Courtrai at once.' ... Then the ambulance arrived and we laid him carefully on the stretcher and put him inside. I got in beside him ... I stayed with him while the doctors examined his wound [at Field Hospital 76] ... he was put under anaesthetic, the hair around the injury was shaved and the surgeon [Professor Doctor Paul Kraske, who was a cancer specialist] probed the wound carefully. Luckily it was not of a dangerous sort ... I went back to my post.

Lt Hans Schroder

Von Richthofen was indeed lucky to survive this encounter with the F.E.2bs of 20 Squadron, whose tactics of flying in a defensive circle made them difficult to break down, even with the undoubted skill of JG1's leader. Later on, when he had recovered he set down his memories of the day, hinting at the trauma it created – both physically and mentally:

We had flown for quite a while between Ypres and Armentieres without contacting the enemy. Then I saw a formation on the other side ... We had a favourable wind from the east and I watched them fly some distance behind lines. I cut off their retreat ... My opponent turned and accepted battle ... he flies towards me, and I hope I try to get on his tail and open fire. Suddenly, something strikes my head. For a moment my whole body is immobilised. My arms hang down limply by my side; my legs flop loosely beyond my control. Worst of all a nerve leading to my eyes had been paralysed and I am completely blind.

I feel my aircraft plummeting downwards ... Suddenly, it occurs to me that this is what it feels like to be shot down and die. Any moment I expected my wings to break off [as he had seen so often before when others went down]. I didn't lose my wits for a moment and soon recovered control over my arms and legs and could grip the controls again. Mechanically, I cut off the engine, but what good does it do? I can't fly without my sight. I forced my eyes open – tore off my goggles – but even then I couldn't see the sun. I was completely blind. The seconds seemed to pass in an eternity.

Occasionally, my aircraft caught itself, only to slip away again. At the beginning I was at a height of 3,500 metres and now I must have fallen at least 1,800 or 2,700 metres. I focussed all my energy and said to myself 'I must see – I must – I must see!' Whether this helped I do not know, but suddenly I could see black and white spots and slowly regained my eyesight. I looked at the sun – could stare straight into it without feeling the least pain. It seemed as though I were looking through thick black glass.

Again I controlled the machine and continued gliding down. Nothing but shell holes beneath me. A big forest came into sight and I realised that I was inside our lines ... I wanted to land immediately, for I didn't know how long I might remain conscious. I noticed that my strength was leaving me and everything was turning black again ... I landed my aircraft without any great difficulty, tearing down some telephone wires ... I tumbled out of the machine and could not rise again.

I had a good-sized hole in my head – a wound of about ten centimetres in length – the bare white skull bone lay exposed [and he was running a slightly raised temperature, which in the circumstance is not unusual].

By any standards Manfred was fortunate to be alive with such a severe wound to his head and it can only be guessed from where the bullet came. The obvious conclusion is that it came from one of 20 Squadron's Lewis guns. However, some later speculated that von Richthofen may simply have flown through the flight path of another German aircraft as it opened fire on the F.E.s. Either way, the result was the same and Manfred was badly wounded and likely to be away from the fighting for some time.

Following surgery Dr Kraske, as was always the case, prepared brief medical notes to aid the treatment of his patient. In them he tends to make light of the extent of von Richthofen's injuries. Being so close to the front line, his workload must have been extremely heavy with many of the men he treated being in a far worse condition than the young man before him on the 6th, so this is hardly surprising. Later that day he wrote that:

> The perforation is to the bone. The bone shows only superficial roughness. There is no other injury ... The entire wound was excised within healthy tissue [all dead tissue, bone debris and foreign bodies, material from his flying helmet, for example, being removed leaving only healthy tissue when suturing began]. Fairly strong bleeding. Several catgut sutures through the galea [fibrous tissue that covers the upper part of the skull], skin sutures with silk.

Nowadays, it is recognised that head injuries of this severity require a complex set of treatments. Although such a wound will eventually heal, following treatment, being hit so violently by a bullet at high velocity can have many side effects. Only now are these issues truly understood, but in 1917 they barely registered in the collective minds of the medical profession. However, there were a few who were beginning to recognise the size and the extent of the problem, mostly through the observation of men in their care.

A wound of this sort is now described as a traumatic brain injury (TBI) and is recognised as having potentially long-lasting effects. Even at the lower end of the scale the symptoms, now well established by case work, manifest themselves in physical, cognitive, social, emotional and behavioural ways. For example, some of the key effects noted by doctors over the years include headaches, dizziness, reduced spatial awareness, memory and concentration impairment, depression, paranoia, anxiety, seizures, difficulty sleeping, problems with eyesight, reduced motor skills and more. And each effect could last for months if not years, depending upon the nature of a person's way of life – physical and mental stresses, age, general health and so on.

So how severe was von Richthofen's wound and what problems may it have caused him in the months that followed? The first thing to note is the effect of a bullet moving at great speed hitting the bilateral parietal bone in his skull, especially as its path of travel caused damage to the bone's central fibrous joint, the sagittal suture, and the adjoining lambdoid and coronal sutures.

Although the impact created a non-penetrating wound, it still seems to have fractured the skull. Such was the force of the blow that it cleaved the skin open and splintered the exposed parietal bone. The shockwave set off would have been an extreme one, shaking the brain violently and doing untold damage in the process, temporary blindness being one outcome. This, in medical terms, was caused by:

> A compression of the vertebral artery within the transverse foramen of the neck. The vertebral artery gets stressed and then compressed, thereby shutting down blood flow from the vertebral artery into the brain. This in turn shuts down the blood supply to the occipital lobe which processes visual information in the brain. This lack of blood flow results in the temporary blindness.

Whether Manfred was hit by a bullet fired by a Lewis gun or a German 08/15 aircraft-mounted machine gun is immaterial as both had similar muzzle velocities (2,440 and 2,800 feet per second respectively) and ranges. Even at the end of their trajectory they could still penetrate flesh and bone with some force and bring death to the victim. It may have been von Richthofen's good fortune to have been struck by a bullet fired from a distance, so when it hit him it was moving more slowly. If it had come from closer range his skull may have been blown open, so a glancing blow could have quickly become a fatal one. Still, the force of the blow was sufficient to render him hors de combat and an uncontrolled descent could still have finished him off.

By tremendous good fortune he survived, but the consequences of his injury were far from clear as he lay in hospital having the wound on his head gradually closed and dressed. And the hard-pressed doctors who tended him would have had a limited range of treatments to explore beyond the physical repair of an open wound. Whatever happened, he was left to his own devices and could expect no help in treating the longer-term effects of his injury. Being a self-possessed man of great inner strength he undoubtedly tried to push these things to one side, but psychological wounds cannot easily be cured by willpower alone and the consequences of that day in July were unlikely to leave him for a long time. Being a commander and a front-line fighter pilot, daily courting death, was probably the worst environment in which to recover and would, perhaps, make the symptoms worse.

One thing is certain though, the physical effort involved in flying a fighter, even by the unrefined standards of aircraft in the Great War, could be extreme. First and foremost, there were the effects of G force or acceleration and the unavoidable application of Newton's law of universal gravitation. Inanimate objects are built to resist these effects up to a point, less so humans unless they are extremely healthy and are given some shielding in the form of protective clothing. Pilots may have been fit in 1914–18 but the G forces they had to tolerate when turning, diving and manoeuvring at speed could be extreme and often caused a man to pass out, albeit briefly.

At the time the concept of such forces existing was little understood, even to the extent that an American 'specialist' coined the phrase 'Fainting in the Air Syndrome' in an attempt to categorise a problem that many pilots found afflicting them. In time the effects of positive and negative gravitational pull were better understood and limits a pilot could tolerate established. However, in this war the development of aircraft had easily outpaced advances in aviation medicine. As a result, fliers often had to face positive G forces so strong that blood was driven away from the brain and immense downward pressures were exerted that forced the pilot deep into their seat, making movement difficult and creating a sensation of 'greying out'. Alternatively, some manoeuvres such as outside loops or flying upside down generated negative G. This forced too much blood into the brain, causing 'red outs', eyes to bulge from their sockets, and the heart to beat much faster and create a sense of mental confusion.

Although it was found that being exposed to positive G by itself did no lasting damage to a fit person, negative G was quite another matter. Here exposure was found to cause blood vessels in the eyes or brain to swell or burst under the increased pressure, resulting in degraded sight or even blindness. And often it was the swift change from positive to negative, which happened in combat, that exacerbated these problems, making a pilot's life most uncomfortable at best, and, at worst, very damaging. However, it was also found that some individuals, for physiological reasons that are not entirely clear, displayed a higher tolerance to the effects of G force. Von Richthofen, who was known to have a robust constitution, probably fell into this category. But even he would ultimately fall victim to its effects after too long an exposure to these forces. And post-July, having sustained a serious injury to the head, his ability to tolerate these effects would have been compromised and probably diminished his ability to function as a fighter pilot, at least for a time.

With such serious consequences for a fighter pilot, it is interesting to note the current advice given by various medical authorities on this issue:

Flying with a recent brain injury, even a mild one like a concussion, can be potentially dangerous. One of the main concerns with a concussion is the development of a brain haemorrhage, with G forces, changes in altitude, or atmospheric pressure likely to bring on or worsen these symptoms.

With a leader of von Richthofen's quality and determination, who was unlikely to allow poor health to deflect him away from doing his duty, a quick return to flying was inevitable. Today, it is true to say, he would be grounded until a rigorous set of tests – both physical and psychological – had deemed him fit to fly again in a combat aircraft. And he would be given no choice in the matter. In 1917 no such regime existed and the long-term effects of wounds such as this were barely understood. But G forces were only one of the stresses affecting those flying in the skies over the Western Front, each of them likely to cause damage to both mind and body when experienced on a daily basis.

First of all, there was respiratory hypoxia to cope with when flying above 2,000m. By 1917 advances in aircraft design meant that most battles took place well above that height, a fact confirmed by von Richthofen's own reports. In those where altitude is recorded he reports combats regularly taking place at altitudes rising from 2,500 to 5,500m.

Nowadays, it is accepted that even the fittest person will begin to suffer the effects of a diminished oxygen supply at 3,000m. At this height the pressure in the lungs becomes insufficient to allow the haemoglobin in the blood to be saturated to a healthy level and, very quickly, oxygen starvation sets in. Although medical records for this period are few and far between, later research has pointed to a range of side effects resulting from lack of oxygen when flying. These include crippling headaches at heights above 3,000 to 3,500m, reduced concentration, a degree of apathy setting in, over-confidence, development of irrational feelings, falling asleep, and being unaware that you have done so. Although all these conditions could spell danger for aircrew, it is the blood pressure issue that medical specialists tend to highlight as the most serious side effect, with the risk of a pulmonary oedema forming in otherwise healthy people at heights typically above 2,500m running a close second.

On the ground a fit young man is likely to register a blood pressure of below 120 over 80, but this is likely to rise to 200 by the time the same man, without an oxygen supply, reaches 2,000m. At this point the effects of oxygen starvation become apparent as disruption of cerebral circulation begins. If left unchecked this is likely to cause hypoxia, which occurs when oxygen is not present in sufficient quantity to maintain an adequate state of homeostasis. In this case a swelling of the brain can occur, which could lead to irreversible changes in nerve tissues and, at worst, a comatose state that will have an obvious result if a pilot remains unconscious.

Beyond the effects of G forces and oxygen starvation there are other issues to consider when assessing how flying in the open cockpit of a Great War fighter could damage the health of a pilot, or, as in von Richthofen's case, make a poor condition even worse. Of these, noise and vibration present an obvious danger. Once again it would be many decades before flight surgeons began to assess and appreciate the effects of these dual problems. Yet even into the 1960s and '70s service chiefs in many countries still continued to question the validity of claims of loss of hearing and other neurological problems due to excessive noise and vibration experienced when flying propeller-driven combat aircraft. Most of these claims came from Second World War aircrew, although gunners and tank crew were not far behind. But the medical evidence soon became too much even for many diehard leaders to ignore and the problem was finally addressed with greater candour. However, this was too late for Great War veterans, most of whom were dead by then, having suffered in silence and coped as best as they could with the problems their flying service had created.

For a pilot flying in 1917–18 the sounds of an engine, its exhaust, a propeller turning at high speed and the buffeting caused by slipstream, generated a decibel level of 120 to 130 dB. Medical authorities have long concluded that such an intensity of noise, even in short bursts, 'is harmful to our hearing, and can take less than a second of exposure to cause permanent hearing damage'. From this one can imagine the effect of living with this level of noise for three or four or more hours a day, with the only protection being a leather helmet, with side pieces, strapped under your chin and, possibly, cotton wool stuffed into your ears. But this solution, although reducing noise levels very slightly, had no effect on the levels of vibration a pilot had to absorb. In the *Principles and Practice of Aviation Medicine*, first published in 1939, H.G. Armstrong, Surgeon General of the USAF, concluded that:

> The importance of vibrations in aeroplanes is that they are annoying and produce discomfort and fatigue ... which probably originates from both physical and mental sources. It is known that vibrations with an amplitude of more than 0.008 inch cause a tensing of the musculature and an inability to relax. This results in muscular fatigue and an equal or greater amount of nervous fatigue ... This results in a continuous muscular and nervous tension in readiness for an anticipated loss of balance ... vibrations arouse this fear which can seriously undermine a pilot's ability to respond when danger beckons and causes damage to the body's nervous system if exposure continues for too long.

Although an appreciation of these issues was, at best, very vague during the Great War, some wise souls, when seeing a stream of pilots and observers passing through their hands displaying a range of unexpected symptoms, began to guess that something more was happening. One of these was Lt Col Dr Cyril Dudley Hely Corbett, of the Royal Army Medical Corps, who in late 1917 was placed in charge of a ward at the 24th General Hospital at Étaples specifically for aircrew. He gradually became aware that men were being referred to him by front-line squadrons having been diagnosed as 'stale' by commanding officers or medics in forward units. The condition was soon referred to as 'battle fatigue', although some saw it as 'scrimshanking' (shirking their duties), or lacking in moral fibre.

Corbett, who graduated from University College Oxford before attending St Thomas' Hospital in London, where he qualified as a doctor, published a ground-breaking paper in 1918 shortly before his death at the age of 36 from influenza, which hinted at the size of the problem, its causes and possible treatments. In it he wrote that:

> A man first notices that he is beginning to feel generally tired, and that he has lost some of his initial keenness. His sleep does not refresh him. He gets occasional headaches ... His sleep may be troubled with dreams of flying and fighting, and nightmares of all kinds (particularly of being shot down in flames). He may notice that he is getting irritable and cannot stand the society of his friends, but prefers to go off by himself and read. He probably feels quite fit and keen in the air, but has to force himself to go up. After landing, he may be shaky and feel utterly exhausted ... He may cease to take trouble about his flying or fighting tactics. Tired pilots have confessed to me that they have got into a frame of mind, when, if they meet an enemy machine, they feel that they must either turn tail or go for it recklessly; they cannot trouble to think about manoeuvring. I am not sure how many good pilots have not met their end from sheer carelessness. They become too tired to think.

The working environment of a pilot in the Great War was indeed a dangerous place to be even without the challenge of combat. And to the list of stresses and strains they were constantly bombarded with, could be added many other things, among them close contact with noxious fumes and substances. These included cod liver oil spraying back from rotary engines, exhaust fumes and toxic materials used in the manufacture of aircraft then, including dope applied to their fabric covering and some paints. Of these Toluene, in vapour form, is considered the most dangerous when exposure is a daily occurrence. At between 200 to 5,000 parts per million Dr Armstrong concluded that this 'will produce chronic poisoning which is characterised by anaemia and a diminution of clotting time with spontaneous haemorrhages and leukopenia'.

In addition, there was the relentless exposure to extremely cold temperatures at high altitudes, without effective protective clothing, to consider. Then there are the unpleasant effects of constantly changing atmospheric pressures that could adversely affect the middle ear, sinuses and the digestive system. At the time aircrew were simply advised to take deeps breaths to help them overcome these side effects, as well as oxygen starvation for that matter. And in many cases eyesight was also affected, with loss of peripheral vision and tunnel vision being cited regularly in medical reports as a result.

All in all, a pilot's mind and body were overstimulated and assaulted by a whole host of substances and extreme pressures, the effects of which were barely understood then and individually could be very damaging. En masse the effects were overpowering even to the most resilient of men, such as von Richthofen. In the circumstances all they could do was grit their teeth, do their duty, carry on and hope for the best. In Manfred's case he could allow the Prussian creed of service to one's Kaiser and country, which had been drilled into him since birth, to guide him and, hopefully, help restore his tiring body and spirit.

For the first few days of hospitalisation sedation would have kept von Richthofen in a drowsy state, allowing him a time to recover and to establish if there had been internal bleeding or slivers of bone detached from inside his skull, which might have penetrated the brain. While this happened there would have been further probing of the lesion to ensure all the debris and damaged flesh had indeed been removed. This would have been followed by more suturing that gradually drew the sides of the wound together and finally covered the bone. For obvious reasons, visitors would have been kept to a minimum, but not for long, and soon they would begin to arrive to see a pale and shaken young man.

When Manfred woke up on 7 July from a drug-induced sleep, essential in the circumstances, he would quickly have become aware of the problems he faced in regaining his health, made worse by the long-term effects of flying in combat. This had been going on for nearly eleven months by then with any breaks he had enjoyed being fairly brief or full of other commitments relating to his status as national hero. And before that he had hardly been resting, with front-line service stretching back almost continuously to August 1914. By any standards he had probably seen too much war and now needed a long rest. However, his value as a propaganda tool, let alone a leader of incomparable skill, was now so high that those with the power to judge these issues must have considered whether it was best to let him continue or be rested permanently. As things turned out, and despite his own poor state of health, von Richthofen made the decision himself and returned to JG1 during July, having barely begun his rehabilitation. Only time would tell if he was fit enough to continue serving in such a pressured environment – on the ground or in the air.

Very early in his recovery pictures were taken of him while resting in his sick bed, his head swathed in bandages, and then, when dressed in uniform, around the hospital's grounds, sometimes with his nurse, Katie Otersdorf, or father. Then finally, on the 20th, five days before he returned to duty, he was allowed or chose to visit Marckebeeke, accompanied by his father and Otersdorf, to be with his men for a few hours, there to be photographed sitting among them, though still looking the worse for wear. One can only think that this was part of a public relations exercise that could be played out when news of his injury became public. Although these pictures would offer reassurance to those concerned that he was fit and well, they actually captured a man still in deep shock, eyes glazed into a thousand-yard stare, with a haunted look common to those with head injuries or shell shock.

Anthony Fokker, who knew von Richthofen quite well by then, was an eyewitness to these events. He recorded that:

> The news of his fall was kept from the German public, which superstitiously regarded him as a superman, beyond death. It was less than a month before he was back in the air again, but never as his old self. Something had gone out of him ... Now he knew that death could reach out for him as the others, and this is no knowledge for an airman to live with, day and night.

Inevitably when the story reached the press and became headline news, the public's reaction was indeed a profound one, resulting in a flood of mail to the Geschwader and his home at Schweidnitz. However, by the time this happened he had returned to JG1, probably against the advice of medical staff, but motivated by a keen sense of duty. In any case, he could read for himself reports of what was happening at the front, as the Allies continued to push forward, and understood how hard-pressed his comrades were with Oberleutnant Kurt-Bertram von Doring acting as commander in his absence. In the circumstances it is unlikely that he would stay away for long at such a critical time, despite the state of his health.

Following his departure casualties had soon begun to rise, one of them being Manfred's young protégé and friend Kurt Wolff. During combat on 11 July he injured his left hand, landed safely and found himself at Field Hospital 76 being treated alongside his admired leader. Other were not so lucky. Vizefeldwedel Linus Patermann of Jasta 4 was killed on the 12th and four days later he was joined by Vizefeldwebel Fritz Krebs from Jasta 6, who was shot down northeast of Zonnebecke. Then on the 17th Leutnant Kruger of Jasta 4 was severely wounded, dying later that afternoon, and on the 26th Jasta 11 lost Otto Brauneck, who had been with von Richthofen since the heady days at Roucourt. Added to these fatalities, a number of men sustained wounds – Hans Klein on the 13th and Karl Meyer four days later – and one pilot, Ernst Clausnitzer, became a prisoner of war on the 16th.

With the situation at the front so fraught, this casualty rate might be thought acceptable if the enemy's losses were higher, but it still aroused in von Richthofen concern that his command was not being used properly and the successes did not outweigh the costs involved. In addition, a report written by von Doring on the 17th intimated that Hauptmann Bufe may have been using Manfred's absence to pursue his own agenda again as regards the tactics employed by fighter squadrons operating in 4th Army's sector. Where von Richthofen promoted a high degree of flexibility in deterring enemy action, Bufe still advocated a pre-planned flying programme that concentrated the four Jastas of JG1 in the air at the same time at varying altitudes, creating a 'barricade'. So a difference of opinion that had first arisen in June quickly reappeared and encouraged von Richthofen to flex his not inconsiderable political muscle, with career-changing consequences for the unfortunate Bufe.

All these debates quickly coalesced into a letter written by von Richthofen on the 18th to old friend and fellow pilot Fritz von Falkenhayn, who by then was one of Ernst von Hoeppner's staff officers at Headquarters. In addition, he was also the only son of Erich von Falkenhayn, Chief of the General Staff until August 1916, and through him could exercise even more power if he thought it necessary to do so. Von Richthofen must have been aware of this and chose to exploit Falkenhayn's friendship quite deliberately to get his way in this debate between two officers of comparatively junior rank.

The wording of von Richthofen's letter was provocative to say the least and possibly incautious. Passages of complaint, such as those below, litter his communication:

When an enemy aircraft has been shot down recently, it was only accomplished by the Jagdgeschwader. What are the other 12 Staffelns doing [there being 16 on 4th Army's front]? This is not due to individual pilots or Staffel leaders but lies elsewhere.

When I came to this Army Bufe said to me, 'It does not matter to me that enemy aircraft are shot down ... rather that your Jagdstaffel by its presence at the front will barricade the air!' This is an insanely great mistake, one could not make a bigger one ...

The other Jagdstaffeln are unhappy about it. The Jagdgeschwader is a thorn in his side ... So now he uses the opportunity of my being sick to issue idiotic orders to do with the way the Geschwader should operate, how take-off preparations should go etc, as if he was the Commander of the Geschwader.

I can assure you that it is no fun these days to be the leader of a Jagdstaffel in this Army. In the 6th Army, after all, I had the good Sorg, who had no grasp at all of the fighter tactics and the purpose of a Jagdstaffel. This Bufe is prejudiced in such a way that it is impossible to deal with him ... For the past three days the British have done what they want. They come over, fly wherever they want and completely dominate the air ... Almost none at all are shot down [not entirely true, because in the period from the 7th to the 18th, when Manfred wrote this letter, JG1 claimed approximately thirty-three aircraft and balloons destroyed, against three dead, three wounded and one a prisoner of war].

Interestingly though, the letter ended with words that he hoped might deflect any thought that the reader had that he may have lost his bearings or sense of reason as a result of his head wound. He wrote:

> This letter is not a result of overwrought nerves or the boredom that plagues me considerably as I lie here in bed. Also it is not a passing irritation or personal dislike of certain people. I only want to bring to your attention the conditions that prevail in this Army.

The fact that he mentioned this at all is particularly revealing, because it suggests that it was something that concerned him, otherwise why reveal it to a friend when there was no need to do so. This was especially so when writing a letter that could, in theory, have ended up on Ludendorff's desk and raised some unpleasant questions about his fitness for front-line service and his ability to continue as a leader. Perhaps, this was his subconscious wish, but such a prized individual wouldn't be let go that easily.

At face value Manfred was simply following a course of action he thought correct, based on his recent experiences and the failure elsewhere of the tactics Bufe championed, particularly over Verdun in 1916. Nevertheless, in some quarters Manfred's letter may have been seen as the gauche response of a young man, who only seven months earlier had simply been a fighter pilot, albeit a good one. To others his response may have been judged disproportionate to the scale of the problem involved and not the response of an experienced commander. Worse still, some may have realised that he was in the middle of an emotional crisis, brought on by fatigue and a serious, life-changing injury, which led him to over-identify with his men and behave in an apparently irrational or inappropriate way. The truth probably contains all these elements, but the end result was not an edifying one. This was especially so, as he had already been given operational freedom by Crown Prince Wilhelm to act as he thought fit with JG1. In effect, he could choose to ignore the local Kofl if he deemed it necessary without fear of disciplinary action or reprimand.

So an act of apparently truculent nature, though achieving his immediate goal, ultimately did him and JG1 no favours, because it was likely that he would be judged a difficult prima donna. In the event it might have been better if he had been sent on the extended leave that his prolonged front-line service and poor physical and mental state demanded. Instead he remained at the front, possibly because his propaganda value was too great to do otherwise. Nevertheless, he was undoubtedly a very sick man, as he would soon realise when taking to the air again. To quote T.E. Lawrence, who himself suffered from extreme battle fatigue, 'something in the works had broken', and would need time and rest to repair, but neither would be forthcoming as Germany battled against increasingly heavy odds, made worse by America's entry into the war.

In some ways a return to JG1 did offer him a way of deflecting the gathering gloom that beset him – comradeship, an understanding that comes from shared experience and an unquestioning sense of purpose would all draw him in, as it did other veterans. The simplicity of life at the front, without the burden of fame, probably seemed attractive and distracting, but the reality would have been entirely different. Leading four hard-pressed squadrons in a relentless struggle against an enemy growing ever stronger and more aggressive, in aircraft fast losing any advantage they had once enjoyed, was not for the faint-hearted or the injured, no matter how resolute they were. But return he did to face a myriad number of issues demanding his attention, although soon there would be one fewer. In August Bufe was transferred away from 4th Army to serve with the 8th Army on the Eastern Front, to be replaced by the experienced and, hopefully, more compliant, Hauptmann Hellmuth Willberg, late of 1st Army. Had von Richthofen's complaints played a part in these changes? Possibly, but Bufe may have been judged a poor performer by others anyway, so who can tell.

However, there was one part of his critical letter that was more defensible than the rest. In a single paragraph he very cuttingly assessed the quality of the aircraft in his command, and by association the rest of the German fighter service:

Our aircraft are, quite frankly, shockingly inferior to the British. The Sopwith Triplane and 200 hp SPAD, as well as the Sopwith Camel single seater play with our DVs. In addition to having better quality aircraft they have many more ... The people at home have not brought out any new machines for almost a year, only these lousy DVs, and have remained stuck with the Albatros D.IIIs in which I fought in the autumn of last year.

In this denunciation he was probably on safer ground than when criticising Bufe, but his words might have been more effective if couched in diplomatic terms and contained more reasoned, less-emotive arguments. But his men were at a great risk and in his overwrought condition an over-zealous, possibly ill-balanced response was probably all he could manage at the time. And the position, as regards fighters, was not helped by the arrival of the mediocre Pfalz D.III in August, which was hardly an improvement on the Albatros D.V. Yet as von Richthofen probably knew, Anthony Fokker was in the process of producing a promising new triplane and a biplane, which if successful could soon boost Germany's ailing fighter fleet. However, with production seemingly held up by an over-reliance on Albatros, whose managers seemed to have established a virtual monopoly on the supply of fighters, Fokker seems to have found it difficult to break through. Certainly on 14 July a contract for twenty triplanes was signed, but, though better than nothing, this was hardly likely to assuage von Richthofen's ever-growing anxiety over the aircraft his men were forced to fly.

Although returning to JG1 on 25 July, Manfred still had to visit hospital for further treatment to have more bone splinters removed. While this happened the wound would have had to be partially reopened, so prolonging recovery. If he was feeling able to fly again, which he did in August, he was quickly reminded of the poor state of his health. This was especially so on the 16th, when during a patrol with four of his men he claimed to have shot down a Nieuport 17 for his fifty-eighth victory.

On feeling the effects of G forces, noise and fumes, raised blood pressure, as his Albatros gained height, he experienced dizziness and felt himself to be in danger of fainting. Nevertheless, he persevered and stalked the enemy fighter to send it down to crash near the Houthulst Forest, north-east of Ypres. As he did so, a severe reaction set in and he felt so sick and dizzy that he quickly returned to base to recuperate. However, in his combat report he recorded that this was due to descending to 'about 50 metres behind him', where, 'I flew through a cloud of gas from the explosion so that, for a brief moment, I became ill.' In deflecting the cause of his early return from his head wound to the effects of gas he obviously hoped to deceive his commanders into believing he was fit to fly, when clearly he wasn't.

He was only partially successful in this because on the 18th a telegram arrived from von Hoeppner congratulating von Richthofen on his success, but adding:

> I expect he is cognizant of the responsibility of deploying his person, and that he will fly only if absolute necessity warrants it until he has overcome the last traces of his wound.

There could not have been a clearer admonishment of von Richthofen's behaviour and this wasn't Bufe or Willberg but a man of real authority who was unlikely to treat disobedience lightly no matter how famous the transgressor. The general, who seems to have been a compassionate man, would have taken this line as a matter of course, but he would also have been aware of Manfred's importance in helping boost the morale of people at home. He, and the High Command, could ill afford to lose such a potent symbol of courage and national prestige. It was a difficult balance to achieve. Without further victories his newsworthiness might decline, but death could be even more damaging. And then there was the man himself to consider, with his ever-diminishing reserves of energy and resilience.

Nevertheless, he did fly again and on 26 August shot down a SPAD VII from 19 Squadron, seeing it explode near the ground and killing its pilot, Coningsby Williams, a young man from Leicester. During the action, 'due to poor incendiary ammunition' the Albatros' pressure line, intake manifold and exhaust were damaged. As a result, the engine appears to have failed, forcing von Richthofen to glide eastwards towards his airfield, which presumably he reached without having to force land again. Interestingly, his combat report for this encounter elicited a stern reminder from 4th Army that the Order of 12 August [which it is believed effectively grounded von Richthofen] must be obeyed and, 'asks to be notified in case this point is not satisfactorily taken into account'.

Manfred's attitude seems to have been that a leader must lead on the ground and in the air, which in the circumstances may seem reckless. Nevertheless, he felt impelled to fly for duty's sake, but also, it has been suggested, by a misplaced sense of competition. There can be little doubt that he took pride in being the ace of aces, though was probably far less keen on the fame it attracted. For some time his position had gone unchallenged, but in his old friend Werner Voss there was a competitor who might soon take his crown. With von Richthofen sidelined and unable to fly regularly, the younger man had quickly closed the gap. By early June, when Voss began a well-earned period of leave, he had shot down thirty-four aircraft and it seemed likely that this number would quickly rise when he returned to duty.

As proof of their comradeship, Voss invited von Richthofen to spend part of a much-photographed leave with his family at Krefeld. Then Manfred, in recognition of his friend's success, presented him with an expensive silver cigarette case with one surface covered in Prussian blue coloured enamel, inlaid with his coat of arms. Although a close bond existed between the two men, it did not preclude a spirit of friendly competition existing between them and this proved to be the case.

In late July, Voss transferred to JG1, at von Richthofen's request, to command Jasta 10, a move forced on him by the rapidly deteriorating eyesight of its current leader, Ernst von Althaus. By the end of August the younger man's score had increased to thirty-eight and then quickly advanced to forty-eight during September, with many more successes predicted.

A desire to lead from the front, and help secure his position, undoubtedly urged Manfred to ignore any instruction he had been given that grounded him and fly again. In this case he may also have been encouraged to do so by the arrival of the first two Fokker Dr.I triplanes, accompanied by Fokker himself. He, in fact, oversaw several public displays with von Richthofen's and Werner Voss' assistance. In this they were supported by such dignitaries as the German Chancellor, Georg Michaelis, who had recently come to power, Ludendorff, General Sixt von Arnim and General Fritz von Lossberg. All of this was carefully choreographed and captured on cine film and in press photographs for home consumption. But in doing so the cameramen also captured a very tired-looking von Richthofen, with his wound still visible, clearly not the man he had been only three months earlier.

In an effort to promote the new triplane and secure Fokker much larger contracts, Manfred soon flew Dr.I number 102/17 operationally and two more victories in early September soon followed. The first was an R.E.8 on the 2nd, resulting in the death of its observer, Walter Kember, and a wounded and captured pilot, John Madge. Then, on the 3rd, he faced a tougher opponent in the form of Algernon Bird, a 46 Squadron pilot flying an outdated but still potent Sopwith Pup, to record his sixty-first victory. Many years later, in his 1927 diary, Bird recalled the battle that ensued that day:

The flight took off shortly after 6 am and having attained a height of about 4,200 metres proceeded to cross the lines to a point about 10 miles over on the German side and commenced the patrol. Normally on these occasions we were treated to a liberal dose of Archie (anti-aircraft gunfire), but on the morning in question everything appeared more than usually calm.

As far as my recollection goes we had covered our allotted beat once and had just turned to repeat the process when an enemy machine was seen some way below us and the flight commander indicated his intention of diving. I followed suit and by this time another enemy machine having appeared proceeded to attack him.

It thus became clear that we were involved in a scrap with a large number of the enemy. While chasing my particular opponent I took a glance over my shoulder to find myself being followed by two triplanes [the second of these was probably, Dr.I No. 103/17, which seems to have been allocated to Voss and he may have been flying it on this occasion] which I at once took to belong to an RNAS squadron with whom we occasionally cooperated. The next thing I knew was that I was under a fusillade from machine guns at very close quarters, my engine cut out and I got one under my right arm which momentarily knocked me out.

On recovering I found that I had got to do all I knew if I was going to stand a chance of reaching our lines. The two enemy triplanes were making wonderful shooting at me and my machine was being hit many times without number, the splinters flying from the small struts in front of the cockpit and from the instrument board. It was impossible to fly straight for more than a few moments at a time before they got their guns on me again and my progress towards our lines was very slow compared with the height I was losing for my engine was a passenger only.

It began to be quite obvious that I should not succeed in regaining our lines as I was now within a few hundred feet of the ground and looking for a place to put my machine down. I found a field in which a German fatigue party were digging trenches, in this I eventually landed hitting, I believe, a tree in the process: all this while my assailants had kept up a heavy fire whenever they could get their guns on me.

Upon my machine coming to a rest it looked as if the trench digging party were going to finish the work that their airmen had begun but fortunately for me an officer drove up in a horse and cart and took charge, taking me back to the HQ of a Kite Balloon section where I was searched, my flying kit removed and my wound dressed. This proved to be very slight.

Before being sent to a prisoner of war camp, Bird was filmed talking to von Richthofen, who with Fokker had visited the crash site to be seen inspecting the wreckage. All this was carefully packaged up for use as a newsreel to be shown in cinemas and so reinforce the legend of *'Der Rote Kampfflieger'*, as his soon to appear autobiography would call him. Whether this burst of action was too much for von Hoeppner and 4th Army is unclear but von Richthofen was despatched on prolonged leave three days later, leaving von Doring again in command.

Although his mother was probably eagerly awaiting his arrival, clearly worried about his safety, Manfred was slow to appear; an invitation from the Duke of Saxe-Coburg Gotha to stay at his lodge – Schloss Reinhardsbrunn – to hunt, proving too strong to be ignored. Here he remained for a while, perhaps finding the solitude comforting as well as restful. But in his absence on leave he lost two close friends – Kurt Wolff, when flying triplane No. 102/17, and, worst of all, Werner Voss in the second new triplane on the 23rd. The impact of these deaths on the slowly recovering Rittmeister are not hard to imagine and may be gauged from his brother's response to this news. At the time he was at home on convalescent leave, which allowed his mother to observe his reactions from close quarters. She recorded that:

> His lips grew hard; he sat that way the whole day, glanced at his book and stared out of the window at the dark trees in the garden. None of us said anything. No one dared to. We endeavoured, when conversation was absolutely necessary, to talk of something else ... Lothar did not speak, but it showed in his face. Twilight came, he did not want a light.

If Lothar felt these deaths so deeply, it would be quite remarkable if Manfred did not feel the same way too. The only difference was that the more outward-going Lothar was not ashamed to reveal his feelings, while his more introverted, reserved brother preferred, it seems, to keep his thoughts to himself, as far as he could. But as the Battle of Britain and naval fighter ace Jimmy Gardner recorded, 'the strong silent types broke as easily as the rest when the stress became too much and, if not taken off ops, usually broke more completely. Bravery has its limits and though it could vary from person to person, each man would eventually face an impenetrable void.'

After his brief hunting trip, Manfred arrived at Schweidnitz on the 17th by air in, according to his mother, 'the red plane ... which is now his own property'. He then brought it down on a landing strip 'filled with a crowd', which drew from his mother the brief observation that 'we had trouble, in spite of the barricades in reaching our house'. After a few months away she clearly wished to see him and reassure herself that he was coping with all he had to bare, but was shocked to discover how poor his condition was:

> Manfred's wound is deeper than I thought. With sadness I noticed that the hair on his head has grown thinner. It looks as though he has a bald head.

> To my horror, I found that his head wound is still far from healed. The bone still lies exposed. Every other day he goes to a local hospital to have the bandage changed. He looks ill and is irritable.

Such was her concern that during his leave she summoned up the courage to express her concerns and seek to influence his thoughts:

> We walked through the garden, and now I chose to speak words I had resolved to say. 'Have done with flying, Manfred!' [He replied:] 'Who should fight the war then, if we all thought that way? The soldiers in the trenches?' [I replied:] 'But the soldier gets relieved from time to time and goes to rest camps, while several times a day you fight dangerous duels at 5,000 metres.'
>
> Manfred became impatient. 'Would it please you if I moved to a place of safety now and rested on my laurels?'

There was, as she soon realised, no moving him, so all she could do was stand by, give him what support she could and watch his health decline. The effects of this became only too apparent to her when her son was called to greet the constantly gathering crowds at their front door:

> After lunch, Manfred had scarcely lain down – his head was particularly painful today – when another group appeared. My husband had to go upstairs to wake him. A few minutes later, he appeared at the front door. He was almost unfriendly. The ovation he received did not suit him and he wasn't able to hide his bad temper despite all eyes being fixed on him. I suggested that he be friendlier on the next occasion. Manfred stormed out in an almost brusque way, his eyes narrow and hard [saying]: 'If I fly over the trenches and the soldiers cheer

me and I look into their faces, grey from hunger, sleeplessness and battle – then I am glad ... that is my reward.'

The next day, he left for East Prussia, to find solitude in the huge game reserve there. Here he would find himself more quickly. Here the soul of the forest would speak to him.

If he did find some peace of mind in the forests of East Prussia its effects would have been fleeting at best and do little in the long term to offset the pressure he'd soon face on returning to the front. To make matters worse, he would have seen, during these few weeks of leave in Germany, a country in turmoil – as anti-war protests and strikes reached fever pitch, with starvation and malnutrition becoming a reality for many. All this would have been only too apparent to Manfred as he toured his once-confident, ambitious country.

Although Ludendorff and the General Staff had virtually seized control of government departments, banks, mines, heavy industry, farming and indeed almost every element of life in Germany, the shortages of food and raw material and frequent strikes undermined all their plans. Combatting the blockade was proving to be an impossible task and the terrible winter of 1916–17 had only intensified the problem. According to historian William H. MacNeill, this resulted in:

> Thousands of soup kitchens being opened to feed the hungry people, who grumbled that the farmers were keeping the food for themselves. Even the army had to cut the rations for soldiers. Morale of both civilians and soldiers continued to sink.
>
> The drafting of miners reduced the main energy source, coal. The textile factories producing Army uniforms, and warm clothing for civilians ran short. The device of using ersatz materials, such as paper and cardboard for cloth and leather, proved unsatisfactory. Soap was in short supply, as

was hot water. All the cities reduced tram services, cut back on street lighting, and closed down theatres and cabarets.

Increasingly the supply of food was limited to the staples of potatoes and bread, with the meat ration falling to 12 per cent of its peacetime level. Worst still, fish had become almost impossible to buy, along with cheese, butter, rice, cereals, eggs and lard. To make matters worse, the harvest of 1917 was so poor that the supply of potatoes again ran short, and a repeat of the previous year's 'turnip winter' loomed large. As the situation worsened so more and more people criticised their leaders and questioned the need to continue fighting. With this opposition growing in strength, even support for the monarchy, which had sustained many people, began to slip away. This was best summed up by the protesting cry, 'When Wilhelm stands in the crosshairs, or stands in line for potatoes then the war will end.' And very quickly an even more potent chant was added, 'Enough with the murder at the front, down with the war! We don't want to starve anymore.'

Such was the growing outcry that in July 1917 the Reichstag passed Matthias Erzberger's resolution that sought 'peace without annexations or indemnities, freedom of the seas and international arbitration'. This was a significant change from the peace bid of 1916, undoubtedly showing a growing realisation of Germany's dire position. Bethmann-Hollweg failed to suppress this initiative, which led to his removal and replacement by Ludendorff's man, Georg Michaelis. He, in turn, only lasted until October, although managing to kill off Erzberger's plan in the process.

Although Germany's position was growing ever worse, Ludendorff and his intelligence services would have known that the French Army had mutinied earlier in the year and their ability to take offensive action was, for the moment, greatly restricted. And in the Italian Army something similar had happened. At the same time, Russia was edging towards revolution, partly fostered by Nicolai's destabilising work, and might soon sue for peace. Only Britain and its empire still seemed full of fight despite the awful losses on the Somme and during the battles of 1917. But with American forces soon to boost Allied numbers in 1918 the enemy's fighting strength and industrial might could soon lead to the defeat of the Central Powers.

As 1917 came to an end, Hindenburg and Ludendorff would have been only too aware of time being against them. So the first few months of 1918 were the best and only time left to strike a crushing blow before the enemy became too powerful. This success, though, depended on Russia being defeated, so releasing a huge number of men for service on the Western Front. With this in mind, the German people watched, waited and braced for what Ludendorff called the 'Peace Offensive' in Flanders. Meanwhile, many in Germany pursued their protests and strikes, with millions being drawn into these disputes.

It was against this background that Ludendorff and Nicolai's propaganda effort was stepped up, in an effort to bring disruptive elements into line. The only trouble was that propaganda and censorship will only work for a time, but rarely has a continuing effect when day-to-day life reveals a greater, perhaps harsher truth. And in Germany in late 1917 and early 1918 the truth was very harsh indeed.

As the last winter of the war beckoned the situation had become so bad that official press releases and communiqués were deemed to be so manipulated and censored by the military as to be near worthless. The one exception to this seems to have been the air war and, in particular, stories about von Richthofen and the courage and selfless devotion he displayed each day. These seem to have transcended this growing cynicism and, for the moment at least, continued to appeal to the German public in a deeply emotive way. Even though propaganda was failing as an instrument of war, this prize asset continued to shine, but how long it would last and how long it could continue to be exploited remained to be seen. At this stage, Ludendorff, Nicolai, von Hoeppner and the rest should really have been asking, 'How long can he last and should we seek to preserve his life,' not how much he is worth to us in the front line?

As a sign of von Richthofen's changing attitude to the war, and the business of killing, it was following his victory over Algernon Bird during September that he ordered the last of his commemorative silver cups from jewellers in Germany. After this there would be no more. A shortage of precious metal has been cited as the reason for this, but it seems reasonable to suggest that he was growing tired of killing and collecting the physical manifestations of his hunting prowess, and was sickened by the whole business. Perhaps, it was another consequence of his head injury and the battle fatigue that seems to have afflicted him or, simply, there was a rejection of such a crude pursuit.

Chapter 8

Immortalised

Someone sent me a copy of the London Times. The newspaper carried a review of Der Rote Kampfflieger. I think it quite difficult to evaluate something from the other side during the war, although I come out quite well in the discussion. Consequently, if I should fall into English hands, the 'Lords' will surely treat me decently ... God save the King!

Manfred's return to the front on 23 October must have been undertaken with a mixture of emotions. Having observed the sorry state of affairs in Germany and JG1's activities, its successes and too many losses, a sense of sombre reality probably prevailed. Although it was now four months since he had been wounded, its effects would still have been apparent to him, as they were to his family and his fellow pilots. Hans von der Osten recalled:

We were pleased to welcome him back and while he seemed rested he no longer cut the robust figure of old. His spark had gone, to be replaced by a grim determination to do his duty. This was accompanied by greater concern for our welfare. While he accepted that we had to fight and face death, he sought to reduce the risks and would only let us fly if the conditions favoured us or it was absolutely necessary to do so. Although never a 'party man' he now withdrew to his quarters as soon as his duties allowed him to do so, keeping his hound close by at all times. He would often be seen walking across the fields with Moritz his sole company ... Periodically, he still attended hospital to have his head wound treated, so it was clearly still troubling him.

Any mention of old friends who had been lost clearly pained him, particularly the two most recently departed – Wolff and Voss. However, all of us found accepting the loss of friends increasingly difficult and by then we all tended to avoid close friendships. Did this help? I'm afraid not, because each loss still had the power to hurt you deeply. By 1918 the Rittmeister had faced death constantly for nearly four years and was clearly brooding badly on these issues. We all felt that such a gallant man should have been withdrawn from service in late 1917 before the inevitable happened. But his sense of duty wouldn't allow this to happen and his value seemed to be too great to the High Command for them to sanction his transfer to non-operational duties.

So, he returned to Flanders recognisably unfit to fly again and facing the last major Allied campaign of the year. Before this attack began at Cambrai, Manfred flew a number of times without suffering nausea or dizziness, though he may simply have ignored these symptoms to avoid a confrontation with von Hoeppner over his fitness to continue on operations. However, he did have one near miss. On the 30th he was flying with his brother when, according to JG1's War Diary they, 'made emergency landings at 9.50 am near Zilverberg, both uninjured. The Rittmeister's machine totally demolished, the other machine undamaged.'

During a patrol with Jasta 11, in cloudy and wet conditions, Manfred was alarmed to see his brother's triplane behaving in a strange way and feared it might have been breaking up. A day earlier another Dr.I, flown by Leutnant Heinrich Gontermann, Jasta 15's commander, appeared to have suffered a major structural failure during an aerobatic manoeuvre and plunged to earth severely injuring its pilot, who died the next day. Seeing his brother's triplane behave in a such a way must have made Manfred wonder if the same thing was happening to him. Luckily, Lothar switched off his engine and glided down to a safe landing, but, presumably being anxious about his brother's safety, Manfred followed him down and wrecked his aircraft in the process. Stress, it would seem, played a part in this crash, especially when he could so easily have achieved the same result by circling and awaiting to see a sign from his brother that all was well. For such an experienced pilot it was an elementary mistake, which, if things carried on this way might be repeated.

The next day Manfred witnessed another triplane, this time flown by Leutnant Gunther Pastor of Jasta 11, suffer the same fate as Gontermann, and possibly his brother, when shedding its top wing during a patrol. Pastor would have stood little chance of survival and died when his aircraft crashed north of Moorsele. One such accident might be put down to chance, but two or more required closer scrutiny. Very quickly von Richthofen and Krefft, his Technical Officer, examined all the triplanes on JG1's strength and, in the words of A.R. Weyl, in his book *Fokker: The Creative Years*, they found:

> Extensive evidence of bad workmanship. It was obvious that production of the wings had been rushed, and that such inspection as might have been carried out had been sketchy. When the crash investigation commission arrived from Adlershof, accompanied by a much-subdued Fokker, von Richthofen showed them his findings ... This immediately revealed an insecure connection between the auxiliary spar and the wing-tip ... the interior of the wing had been affected by moisture: all the plywood webs had warped ... After the investigation Oblt Hoff interviewed Fokker [on 4 November] and issued a stern warning that he would have to improve

his production methods ... Fokker's lame excuse – that his factory had worked day and night to expedite delivery of the first triplanes because von Richthofen wanted them urgently – was brushed aside ... Until new wings were fitted, all Dr.Is were grounded.

Although Fokker's excuse was 'brushed aside', it did hold some truth. Von Richthofen had, in his letter of 18 July, criticised Albatros for the poor standard of their fighters and exerted pressure on his commanders to get better aircraft to the front as quickly as possible. Then in September he had actively promoted the new triplane, and publicly supported Fokker in selling it to Ludendorff, von Hoeppner and Lossberg, which led to an increase in the number on order. So, some might say that he bore partial responsibility for its hurried entry into service, though he could bear no responsibility for the shoddy workmanship and poor quality control at Fokker's Schwerin works. As a result, the Air Service had to continue with the Albatros D.V and Pfalz D.III until problems with the Dr.Is had been corrected. In the meantime they faced a Royal Flying Corps growing ever stronger and now supporting the offensive at Cambrai with great energy, despite their losses.

On 20 November, the British used tanks in large numbers for the first time and quickly forced a way through the German lines. Church bells soon rang all over Britain, but the celebrations were premature. When sufficient reinforcements failed to appear, the Germans quickly mounted a counter-attack and within ten days had forced the enemy back, virtually to their starting off positions, and the usual stalemate ensued as winter set in.

To help counter the threat at Cambrai, JG1 were hastily transferred to 2nd Army's front, but were then hindered in what they could do by fog, rain, low, thick cloud and high winds. Nevertheless, they engaged the enemy when they could and on the 23rd sent down three of their number, including one by Manfred, a DH.5, and a

Bristol F.2b by his brother. Three days later he repeated this success when flying with Lothar and Leutnant Gusman, sending down a 41 Squadron S.E.5a 'in flames in the vicinity of the Steinbruch Forest'.

It was shortly before these two victories that Manfred's old friend, Erwin Bohme, now commanding Jasta Boelcke, also attached to 2nd Army, visited JG1. He later recalled the day in a letter to his fiancée, capturing a revealing picture of his old comrade in the process:

> Yesterday afternoon [the 18th] on the flight back from the Front, I stopped for a coffee at Richthofen's airfield – they always have the best cakes there. Richthofen is constantly spied on by artists who want to paint his likeness. Yesterday he said that he wanted to give up flying altogether and busy himself with self-portraiture, which is less dangerous and at least makes one famous just as quickly.

His seemingly light-hearted observation is interesting. It portrays a man clearly becoming extremely tired of his role as a celebrity. Nevertheless, he tolerates it all for his country, as he did the buzz of activity that constantly surrounded him as JG1's commander. All this was observed by Anthony Fokker from close quarters during his occasional visits to front-line squadrons:

> He had a great deal of executive work to attend to as well as his daily combat flights. Secretaries raced about, and orderlies came and went all day ... He was an excellent teacher, and young pilots who showed exceptional skill were sent to his staffel to get experience ... Richthofen would gather his officers together for a conference and a discussion of tactics. Occasionally he would censure pilots who were too aggressive, or too willing to pull away before a battle was over. He was, perhaps, not so much liked as admired, but the respect other pilots had for him was unbounded.

Proud though he was, the acclaim for his achievements gave him no particular pleasure. He was not interested in publicity, and though he received letters by the ton from all sorts of people, he cared little for fan mail. When he was around, parties were never wild, for the other pilots felt constrained in the presence of their chief.

With the attack against Cambrai fizzling out and winter setting in, all became quiet on the Western Front for a time. This allowed Manfred to focus on other duties, including test flying a new triplane produced by Pfalz at their Speyer works during December. He then returned to JG1 to be with his men for Christmas, where he was joined by his father, who must have been greatly relieved to see both sons alive after all the perils they had faced. He and Kunigunde had seen only too clearly the damage, both physical and mental, they had already endured and it took little imagination to realise that with each passing day their chances of survival grew slimmer. Being a soldier, Albrecht may have come to accept the inevitability of casualties and loss, but when it is your own children, fear and doubt is like a 'fox under your cloak', as Henry Willamson described it in his novel of the Great War, gnawing away at the very essence of your being. So, throughout these festive celebrations he may have seen a bleak future beckoning.

Wilhelm Reinhard, commander of Jasta 6 at the time, observed all this and later wrote that:

> It was a marvellous sight when Father Richthofen spent time with us and his sons ... Their outward appearance showed them to be old-time Prussian officers, their character and conduct was soldierly through and through ... He loved his sons equally in an openly and sincere manner. In a Silesian way, he was a bit reserved with strangers ... He never tried to stop his sons or advise them to be cautious ... He understood our flyers' talk and shared with us the joys and sorrows of fighter pilots.

As the festivities drew to a close, fresh duties soon drew Manfred to Germany and then the Eastern Front. All this meant that his list of victories did not grow for some weeks and until then his newsworthiness was fostered by newsreels, the appearance of his memoirs and a number of public appearances.

The first of these took place shortly after Christmas when he was ordered, with his brother, to attend the opening stages of peace talks with a Russian delegation at Brest-Litovsk, a place he had often flown over earlier in the war. The overthrow of Tsar Nicholas II in the spring of 1917 had seen the creation of a more liberal regime under the direction of Alexander Kerensky. However, Walter Nicolai's plotting and Vladimir Lenin's secretly manipulated return to Russia, coupled with mass strikes by workers and soldiers, saw the Kerensky government fall and the communists take over. Eager to end the war as soon as possible, Lenin agreed to an Armistice on 15 December. This set in motion peace negotiations, with Brest-Litovsk chosen as the venue for both sides to meet.

In a process such as this, each party involved usually contrives a show of strength, as a means of intimidating the opposition. So, the highly publicised von Richthofen brothers were included in a party glistening with senior officers decked out in their highly burnished gold braid and dress uniforms. But at Brest-Litovsk the German delegation, led by Crown Prince Leopold Supreme Commander of the German forces in the east, failed to realise that Russia's new leaders could not be bullied – the struggle for power in their own country being significantly more important than a continued war against Germany. So Manfred and Lothar, after being photographed at the station greeting the Russians and then attending the opening sessions, were released, escaping for a time to the Tsar's hunting lodge in the Bialowicz Forest to shoot stag before returning to Germany. When back in his homeland, Manfred did as he was requested and visited factories to, among other things, speak to striking workers. Seeing his country seemingly on the edge of revolution and its people facing famine must have made him realise, if he didn't know already, that everything he valued was turning to dust.

This was undoubtedly an issue he discussed with his mother on a brief period of leave early in January when Lothar was hospitalised, having suffered a ruptured eardrum, resulting in inflammation of the inner ear. She, having seen the critical shortages of food and a growing disenchantment with the country's leaders and the war, could be relied upon for honesty when expressing thoughts and opinions to her troubled son:

> We sat in my husband's study. Manfred says that he would now be sent more often to munition factories – to meet striking workers. When he arrived they all rushed towards him and he spoke to them. He made it clear to them just how important their work was … Then some went back to their machines, but, perhaps, not for long. In this respect he was rather pessimistic.
>
> Together we looked at photographs that Manfred had brought with him. A very fine photo showed a group of young flying officers. In the centre was Manfred … 'What has become of him?' I pointed to the first. 'Fallen.' I indicated the second. 'Also dead,' and his voice sounded harsh. 'Ask no further questions – they are all dead' …
>
> Go no further, said a voice within me. Someone stands before me, who is so near death, that it stares him in the face more than once a day – and he is your child – then be careful and tactful with every word … So one remains silent, appreciates the moment, and enjoys the presence of the each other.
>
> I found Manfred very changed … he was taciturn, aloof, almost unapproachable; every one of his words seemed to come from an unknown place. Why this change? The thought haunted me … I think he has seen death too often.

'Actually [he said], there really is no point in it anymore.' These were words of a troubled spirit and would not be dismissed [from my mind]. I closed my eyes, as if I wanted to rest, though, none of his actions escaped me. How hard his features had become ... Something painful lay around his eyes and brow. Was it a presentiment of the future – the serious outcome of the war he had feared throwing a long shadow over him? Or was it only an after-effect of the deep head wound he had suffered in the summer?

Certainly, he had never complained, but for a time it had stripped him of all his strength. He had looked different; very wretched and sensitive ... that was now past, but solemnity, reserve, dignity and an enigma had taken its place. I have never seen Manfred so. I did not know him this way.

The serious mood Manfred left behind remained with us in the house. Cares, thoughts, despondency – evil spirits ...

Kunigunde was clearly concerned about her son. She had always been aware of a certain fatalism in his character brought on by war, but this was different, as she clearly realised. Now the stresses and strains he bore, plus the lasting effects of his wounds, were pressing down on him, taking away his peace of mind. This was battle fatigue at its worst, bringing on a sense of despondency and melancholy, which must have made her wonder whether she would ever see him again. She saw, without any doubt, that he should retire from the fray, but also realised that his all-pervading sense of duty would not allow him to do so.

In later wars this was a condition better understood, though not always acted upon when the individual refused to comply. Bill Foster, a naval ace who fought in the Pacific in 1945, witnessed this at first hand and later described what he observed in his own commanding officer, Mike 'Gammy' Godson:

Towards the end of the first operation over Sakishima there had been a weariness in his behaviour. He was still in command, but when talking there were a number of pauses and sighs. He seemed to be distracted and stayed more in his cabin. The CO from 1841 Squadron, Richard Bigg-Wither, apparently one of his oldest friends, came on board and they spent a long time together. Afterwards this very concerned friend went to speak to Captain Eccles and a little while later the Chaplain and the doctor visited Gammy. I can only presume that he managed to convince them that all was well, when clearly it wasn't. With the benefit of hindsight, it is obvious that he should have been rested.

In this case a tragedy that could have been avoided was not and a fine man went to his death when losing the good sense he had displayed on numerous other occasions. And Bill witnessed the tragic consequences at first hand:

Despite our precautions the ground fire was intense and we hadn't managed to hit anything or drop our bombs. Once again we climbed away, but Gammy was determined to attack once more, this time by himself. We circled for a few minutes to let things settle down and he ordered me and the others to create a diversion whilst he went in. I argued briefly with him over the sense in committing ourselves to another attack when the enemy gunners were ready and waiting. But he wouldn't be swayed … Just before releasing his bombs he climbed steeply to a hundred feet or so and staggered as shells hit him. The aircraft carried on for a 100 yards downwards in a shallow dive, with a stream of flame coming from the starboard wing. With that he hit the ground, cartwheeled and exploded. There was no chance of survival.

In many interviews with veterans of both world wars similar incidents were often mentioned – a tired pilot becoming uncaring of their own safety, losing their bearings and their instinct for survival and failing to balance risk against outcome, occasionally with tragic consequences for themselves and their men. Often, as in Godson's case, it was avoidable, but a decision based on operational necessity and an individual's self-assessment often overrode more reflective considerations. However, getting the balance right in such situations, when the stakes are high, will always be difficult if not impossible. But a lot of exhausted young men died as a consequence of an assessment falling wide of the mark.

With so many brooding thoughts hanging over his head, a return to the Western Front and being with his men sharing the same risk may have offered Manfred some solace, but first there was a long-running issue to address, which JG1's War Diary simply recorded as: '19th January: Rittmeister Freihher von Richthofen ordered to Berlin-Adlershof until further notice.'

Perhaps stung by von Richthofen's criticisms of the poor standard of fighter aircraft in his letter of July 1917, and the canvassing that undoubtedly followed, reinforced by the Dr.I's recent wing failures, Idflieg decided to hold a series of fighter trials to test all possible candidates for future front-line service. It would be an event that would involve a number of fighter aces, including von Richthofen, who would be given the power to decide which of the competitors was best. A risky business, perhaps, but its inclusivity might help stem the criticism that had recently been bandied about so liberally. It also allowed each manufacturer to showcase their latest aircraft and seek to influence the pilots selected for the task by whatever means they had at their disposal.

On 20 January selected pilots and manufacturers, including Fokker, Albatros, Junker, DFW, Kondor, Pfalz and Roland, gathered together at Adlershof, with more than thirty new or modified types of aircraft at their disposal, for these trials to begin. From the beginning it was agreed that pilots had to choose two aircraft from the group, one with a Mercedes in-line engine and the other rotary powered. Complete standardisation was thought too restrictive because it limited operational flexibility and so finding more than one winner was thought necessary. What followed was a programme revealingly described by A.R. Weyl:

> The idea was admirable in theory, but the results on the whole were no more than moderately successful. This was because some of the notable pilots who flew the competing aircraft were in the pay of individual firms and consequently gave biased opinions in favour of the products of these firms ... Ultimately it became an open secret that certain officers in command of fighting formations received favours [through wining and dining on a massive scale, financial incentives and, it is rumoured, lures of a sexual nature] from certain firms for 'plugging' their products and denigrating those of their competitors.
> Among the laudable exceptions was Manfred von Richthofen, who set an example as a conscientious Prussian officer of absolute integrity. At the other end of the scale was Hermann Goring. Officers serving with or under him knew that he could be bought.

Perhaps warned by von Richthofen, Fokker prepared for these trials very carefully and presented nine different models for the pilots to consider, including the V.II biplane and two Dr.Is with more powerful engines. By 12 February all the testing and assessments were complete, the politics, prejudices and sponsored favouritisms played out and the business of contracts could be set in motion. For von Richthofen there was a clear winner in the Fokker V.11, with the Roland D.VIa as runner-up. While in the rotary engine class he thought the Fokker V.13, powered by a Siemens-Halske

SH.III engine, to be the 'best all round type … easy to fly, very manoeuvrable, and similar to the V.11,' according to Weyl.

With Manfred's all-important support assured, an order was soon negotiated with Fokker to build his new biplane in large numbers, with some eventually constructed under licence by Albatros. In April the first few D.VIIs, as they were soon designated, entered service and seven months later the total had risen to nearly 800. And very quickly their superiority became only too obvious to aircrew on the other side of the lines, though their chief advocate would not get the chance to enjoy this dominance or participate in two more fighter trials that would take place later in the year. Nevertheless, in all he did he had assured his fellow pilots of aircraft worthy of their sacrifices – it was an invaluable legacy.

Now fully engaged with the air war again, Manfred prepared to fly from Berlin to JG1, but on the way decided to 'buzz' the Academy at Wahlstatt, presumably at a pre-arranged time to please his youngest brother. Before departing he scribbled a brief letter to his mother making no mention of their recent conversation and apologised for not visiting Schweidnitz again while there had been an opportunity to do so. Perhaps he found the thought of another difficult conversation with his mother, so soon after the other, too much to bear and so postponed his visit until his future was more certain:

> It would have been so nice and I would have enjoyed it very much. I now think that I will not be back in Germany for a long time to come.
>
> Lothar should remain at home as long as possible. He is very careless with his ears and does nothing at all to take care of them … I want him to know that he shouldn't return before 1st March [three weeks before the German 'big push' was due to begin].

By mid-February he was back into his stride with the Geschwader, now receiving the modified triplanes, and heavily involved in preparations for the coming battle, code-named 'Michael'. Secrecy was essential with the build-up of men, the big guns, tanks and supplies being carried out, whenever possible, at night. With British reconnaissance aircraft operating in strength over the Somme, there was always a risk that they might spot the telltale signs of the coming offensive. So a strengthening of German fighter squadrons operating in the area was essential, with JG1 taking the lead.

In the weeks leading up to the battle the weather favoured the German Army, in so far as it was frequently foggy, with rain and clouds also helping to screen their preparations. Some flying was possible, but successes were rare until 11 March. There was a Bristol F.2b on 16 February, a 'French biplane' on 8 March and a Sopwith two days later. Yet in the process JG1 sustained an irritatingly high number of casualties – Leutnant Friedrich-Wilhelm Lubbert of Jasta 11 was wounded in battle with an S.E.5a on 17 February and two days later Lt Hans Klein, Staffelführer of Jasta 10, had his index finger severed by enemy fire. Then, on the 26th, Leutnant Stapenhorst was forced down and captured, Leutnants Mohnicke and Just were both wounded on 1 March and Leutnant Bahr was killed in action on 6 March. And then Leutnant Skauradzum and Sgt Beschow were wounded on the 8th and 10th respectively.

This was a balance sheet that must have worried von Richthofen considerably with a major offensive so close, especially as the War Diary reported a high number of encounters with the enemy on days when the weather was fairly good – thirty-six on 26 February, nineteen two days later, twenty-three on 5 March and so on. With so little happening, and perhaps as a concession to those who advised him 'to fly only when it was absolutely essential', Manfred passed time alone in his quarters brooding and writing a fighter pilots' manual – entitled *Meine Erfahrungen im Luftkampf.* In this he sought to update all the things he learned from Oswald Boelcke, adding new things he had discovered himself. All the guidance it contained was valid, but it was a laboured effort, almost clumsy in its writing style. Nevertheless, von Hoeppner was content to authorise its circulation among the fighter squadrons on 19 April in what would become Manfred's tactical legacy, even a requiem for his short life. Perhaps more importantly, for someone still suffering the ill-effects of a head wound and depression, it offered a brief distraction from the dark thoughts that seemed to be haunting him.

Tedium and lack of action, or even a sign of his poor mental health, seems to have sparked a series of disagreements between Manfred and 2nd Army's 39-year-old Kofl, Hauptmann Wilhelm Haehnelt. On face value it appears to have been a repeat of his disputes with Otto Bufe a few months earlier. Here again Manfred believed he was being ordered to conform to a master plan that he found too restrictive. So he rebelled, seeking to enlist the help of Fritz von Falkenhayn again. On this occasion his arguments fell on deaf ears and the Rittmeister had to conform to the grand strategy, though he would deviate from it on a day-to-day basis as the battle developed. Such a strong-willed man was unlikely to do otherwise, but on this occasion he, in Haehnelt, faced a fellow aviator, an experienced tactician and an equally well-connected man of substance, who even von Falkenhayn would have felt unable to challenge.

If he flew during these fallow weeks Manfred failed to add to his score. Then, finally on the 11th, with the arrival of better weather, JG1 had some success – two enemy aircraft were shot down, one by his brother, the other by Vizefeldwebel Scholtz during fourteen combats recorded that day. The 12th was even better with five enemy aircraft and two captive balloons destroyed without loss, one of them, a Bristol F.2b from 62 Squadron, forced down by Manfred, as his sixty-fourth victim, behind German lines where the crew were soon captured. Later on, as a mark of respect for the observer, Henry Sparks, who had put up a strong fight although badly wounded,

Manfred sent half a dozen cigars with his best wishes for a speedy recovery.

Sparks barely survived the encounter and was permanently disabled, but went on to marry twice, helped bring a daughter into the world and died during July 1940, in a north London hospital, aged 50. The pilot, Leonard Clutterbuck, did even better, reaching the age of 73 and long remembered his close brush with death. In 1927 he wrote an unsolicited tribute to his late conqueror and his fellow pilots:

> To my mind they (JG1) were undoubtedly the pick of the German airmen. Although their methods of attack were different from ours, they were no mean adversaries ... Richthofen handled his machine very cleverly, was an excellent shot, and was entirely fearless.

Manfred repeated this success on the 13th, shortly after his brother was seen to crash his triplane near Awoingt, where JG1 had moved at the end of February to be closer to the action. An early report claimed Lothar was dead, but this was soon amended to injured, though to what extent was unclear. However, to help clear things up a worried von Richthofen is reported to have flown to the scene to see for himself what had happened. This was undoubtedly out of concern for Lothar, but may also have been to see if structural failure had contributed to the crash. Reassured, he soon sent a telegram to his mother letting her know what had happened before the press did so, followed up with a calming letter, which was slow in arriving due to the forthcoming battle:

> Thank God he is doing well. I visit him daily. So, please, do not worry about anything.
>   His nasal bones have already healed, only the mandible has been cracked, but all his teeth have been saved. He has a large

gash over his right eye, but the eye itself has not been injured. Some blood vessels have burst on his right knee and the left leg from the calf muscle down, similarly there has been some bleeding.

Blood that he coughed up was not a result of any internal injury, rather it had been swallowed in the crash. He is in hospital in Cambrai and hopes to be up and about in fourteen days. He is very sorry that he cannot be with us now [with the offensive due to begin shortly].

Without the reassuring presence of his brother, Manfred would have found the pressure he had to absorb growing more difficult to bear. And all the time the demand for more news, to feed the public, propagandists and the press alike, did not abate. In fact, the appearance of *Der Rote Kampfflieger* only made the clamour grow louder, with VIPs and reporters visiting the front to meet and interview him. One cannot imagine a more trying existence for a fit person, let alone someone suffering war weariness and poor mental health.

There are a number of accounts of Manfred in early 1918 that probably reveal more than anything about his state of mind and the price he was paying for his bravery. But they also reveal his stoicism and gentle, self-deprecating humour. The first of these was recorded by von der Osten in a letter written in 1968:

During the winter as the evenings grew longer and flying was restricted by bad weather, we passed the long hours of waiting playing many a game of chess. This was suggested to us by visiting artists who had been directed to paint portraits of von Richthofen. I don't remember the name of the first one although it may have been Theodor Rochell, but the second one was Professor Reusing, a charming man, who had also painted my wife when she was a young girl. He came to us at Avesnes-le-Sec in January and stayed with us for ten days or so. We often played chess together. Reusing made many preparatory sketches of von Richthofen. In one he sat in his plane with his cap on his head. When the picture was finished, it was a water-colour, we said, 'This is not him. This is not Richthofen!' Then Reusing got out the photo he had taken at the same time and put it beside the sketch. We did indeed see that the cap actually did distort his face quite markedly. Then the next day Professor Reusing painted a nice portrait in oils, which he finished within seven hours. Later it was exhibited, with some of his other portraits of the Rittmeister, in Berlin at Schulte's art gallery [before being presented to his parents].

A little later, we were returning by car from Adlershof to Berlin when Richthofen suddenly said, 'Well, I will get out here at Schulte's and have a look at the pictures that Reusing has painted.' He was wearing an overcoat with a large collar which he kept pulled up against the cold winter air. This also acted like a disguise. He went in to the gallery and walked up to the painting that showed him in his plane and was captioned 'Rittmeister Freiherr von Richthofen.' An elderly gentleman came up and stood beside him. Richthofen said, 'I beg your pardon, but I am told I have some likeness to this painting!' The gentleman put on his spectacles, took a look at the picture, took a look at Richthofen, and finally said, 'I think you can forget that notion.' Ten minutes later, Richthofen joined us at the hotel, beaming with joy, and related the incident to me.

Celebrity has it limits and, perhaps, Manfred found this humorous incident strangely reassuring. Yet of greater interest is the strong sense of comradeship conveyed by von der Osten's words. Away from the battle each fighting man who recorded their memories seems to have found life in Germany increasingly difficult; those at home appearing to be out of step with their existence in the front line. Only with their comrades did they feel truly at home, despite the horrors they faced daily. So, it is of little wonder that von Richthofen preferred to remain with his men no matter what difficulties he faced and the trials that lay ahead.

The second account emerged following a conversation between Kunigunde and Manfred's ever faithful servant, Menzke:

> [I asked] is the Rittmeister not frightfully excited after an air battle? Not a bit, merely tired – he likes to take a short nap. Also he likes to flop on his bed in the afternoon for half an hour, with clothes and boots on. I then walk about on tiptoe, lay a blanket under his feet so the bed linen won't get dirty. I go out again, ever so quietly. I know that he isn't really asleep at all – he merely lies there thinking. I stand outside to make sure all is peaceful. If the other men are ever loud, I take my sign from under my arm, which reads 'QUIET', and hang it up. Herr Rittmeister has ordered it to be so, and if not obeyed he can get very bad-tempered.

As only a good servant can, Menzke revealed enough to let Manfred's mother know the pressures her son was facing and their consequences, without breaking the crucial bond of confidentiality that existed between him and his greatly respected leader. But there was undoubtedly a far darker side that he witnessed that was only revealed by Manfred himself in the weeks before his death, when alone in his quarters, trying to describe what he was feeling in writing:

> Hanging from the ceiling of my 'dugout' is a lamp I created as a conversation piece from the engine of an aircraft I shot down. I mounted small lamps in each cylinder and when I lie awake at night and let the light burn, Lord knows the chandelier looks wonderful and strange. When I lie this way, I have much to consider ... The battle now taking place on all fronts has become very grim – there is nothing left of the

'spirited, cheery war', as it was called in the beginning. Now we must fight against despair and arm ourselves so that the enemy cannot invade our country.

I am in wretched spirits after each aerial battle. This, no doubt, is an after-effect of my head wound. When I set foot on the ground after a flight, I go to my quarters and do not want to see anyone or hear anything. I think of this war as it really is, not as people at home imagine it, with a Hoorah! And a cheer. It is very serious and very grim.

Despite the severe stress he was under, his growing unease brought on by the war and the after-effects of his head wound, von Richthofen continued to do his duty. So professional and polished was his performance that many of his men, particularly the newcomers, seemed unaware of his crumbling mental state. They only saw a man who led effectively and set an example for them to follow.

Friedrich-Wilhelm Lübbert, who had joined Jasta 11 from Feldflieger Abteilung No. 18, later wrote:

My joy and pride were great when I received the news in December 1917 that Rittmeister von Richthofen had asked me to come to Jagdstaffel 11. So now I shall come into close personal contact with him, the role model of all German fighter pilots. Until then, I had only met him briefly at the memorial service of my brother who was with Jasta 11 when he died [Hans Georg Lübbert killed in action on 30 March 1917], and I only admired him as the famous pilot. Soon I would come to know and love all his wonderful human qualities. Richthofen was an aviator through and through. He became one of the most popular men in Germany. One would have thought that with such exposure to one of the most strenuous activities there is, and with the great popularity he enjoyed, there would be no room left for friendship and camaraderie.

The opposite was true. For his officers Richthofen was as good a leader as a comrade. He played field hockey with us when we weren't flying and oftentimes participated in our card games. We could approach him with every question and every concern and were sure to find sympathy and help.

Richthofen had no equal as a teacher ... I never met a teacher who could explain the theory and technique of aerial combat to me as well as he did. He was always ready to answer any questions asked. In fact, he liked it very much when his pilots were quite curious. He never got impatient, no matter how simple and foolish our questions were.

Richthofen was very clear on one point – he only accepted pilots in the Staffel who really achieved something. He observed beginners for a while and if he then concluded that the person concerned did not meet the standard he set for a fighter pilot, then he would be transferred to another unit. However, everyone was clear that Richthofen would only judge them on their performance as a fighter pilot and nothing else.

This was a theme picked up by Wilhelm Reinhard, who was von Richthofen's chosen successor to command JG1 should he be killed. As an experienced fighter pilot and leader himself, he could provide a more balanced view of the man he had flown with since June 1917:

He judged others not by their looks, but only by their actions.

He was a very determined man. Often he was first to arrive at the airfield and we showed up to the airfield after him feeling guilty. He also knew what he wanted from his superiors. If he recognised a thing as correct, he pushed it through firmly.

He was interested in everything, especially military matters. He liked to talk to infantrymen who had just come out of the trenches from the battle, and was told how they had fared and what they had seen of German and enemy aircraft. If he drove past artillery observation posts, he liked to get out and look at the battlefield from there with his glasses. His interest was not only in fighter pilots; he was also familiar with the worries and pains of the Fliegerabteilungen, the Infanterieflieger, Schlachtflieger and Artillerieflieger and liked to talk to these men about the interaction of the different types of aircraft. In short, he was not a specialist in fighter aviation alone; he was interested in the whole military field and was a born member of the general staff.

Richard Wenzl, who joined Jasta 11 in late March 1918 from Jasta 31, never forgot his first flight with von Richthofen, the pace of life in such a distinguished fighter squadron and the way his leader led his men, on the ground and in the air:

> I had almost always led others myself, and I knew how difficult it was to bring a Staffel to the enemy correctly, and above all to bring them up so that you had the advantage on your side and each individual had an advantage over his opponent. I was so delighted with the way Richthofen led. He throttled back his brilliant engine in such a way that you kept up with him easily and were hard put not to overshoot him.
>
> Later that day I watched as Richthofen and others attacked a Bristol Fighter, the Rittmeister firing from 50 metres, setting it aflame. Since Hans Joachim Wolff [who was killed on 19 May 1918], whom we called 'Wölfchen', had also been firing on the Bristol, Richthofen pulled back in his favour.
>
> Since we always had to be ready for take-off, we wore our flight suits all day long, at the most taking off our flying helmets for a short while. Richthofen had no sooner given the order to take off than he was already seated in his machine. You really had to become accustomed to this incredible speed. But it held much of our success. During decent weather, there

would be no less than five take-offs [per day]; but I had already made seven with them.

Richthofen, first and foremost, was a soldier, and, as a soldier, the fighter pilot was the ultimate for him. He subordinated everything else to this concept.

Nothing was too difficult and nothing too impossible if it meant something for his combat flying, for his Geschwader.

His work on the ground was no less important than his work in the air. No sooner had he returned from a flight than you would find him already at work in his hut. Nothing went on in the Geschwader that he did not know about. If it were a question of making quick work of something, then he climbed into his Triplane and took off. I will never forget how he flew to Army headquarters once during absolutely unbelievable weather, when it was necessary to take care of some important matter.

The Rittmeister didn't know the meaning of 'prima donna' moods, although he could have easily indulged in them. He held comradeship above everything else and openly cultivated it. After a flight, his men could do and were allowed to do whatever they wanted. He took part in many a joke and put up with a lot.

Wenzl then commented on a more controversial issue that had gained some currency in the popular press, namely that von Richthofen had been awarded victories that should have gone to others or were unconfirmed in the normal way:

The number of his victories probably exceeded one hundred. He claimed only those victories which were absolutely indisputable and confirmed. He immediately stepped aside if someone else had been firing at the same time. This can never be emphasized enough, contrary to other claims. If Richthofen had operated in the way that many now falsely claim, or was usual among our enemies, he would easily have achieved twice the number of victories. We, however, prefer to accept this German man in the modest greatness that suits him well.

Finally, we have the words of Hans-Joachim Wolff, who in writing to Lothar shortly after Manfred's death, could barely contain his emotions at losing his friend and leader:

> We all, even the youngest mechanic, grieve. We mourn the loss of a man who was everything to us, to whom we would have given anything. But unfortunately we were not granted the opportunity to prove our unshakable loyalty to him. I in particular am deeply saddened. I have lost more in him than just the great role model he was to everyone. I loved him like a father. I was happiest when I was allowed to be with him ... Fate was too cruel.

The release of Germany's painstakingly assembled forces on 21 March must have come as a relief to pilots in JG1 and the millions of others involved, now heavily reinforced by men from the Eastern Front, minus nearly 10 per cent recorded as deserting on route. After a short, sharp barrage blasted holes in the British defences, the German troops rushed forward en masse, benefiting from a thick mist that lay across the battlefield. The enemy quickly fell back in disorder; thousands being killed or taken prisoner along the way.

It soon became apparent that the Germans had chosen a most opportune moment to strike. After the strain of almost continuous offensives since the Somme in 1916, the British Army's fighting capacity was at a low ebb and they could do little to stem the assault. They needed time to muster their strength and, in the meantime, could do little but retreat towards Amiens. For their part the French were equally battle weary and still trying to restore their forces to pre-mutiny levels – in both numbers and fighting spirit. In the circumstances it isn't surprising that Field Marshal Haig felt moved to issue his famous 'with backs to the wall and believing in the justice of our cause each one of us must fight on to the end' order to all ranks in the British Army on 11 April.

Reinforcements soon arrived and by 20 April the first and most important phase of Ludendorff's offensive had stalled, falling well short of Amiens let alone reaching the coast and breaking French and British resistance. Yet all this time the Royal Flying Corps and Royal Naval Air Service, now joined together as the Royal Air Force, vigorously resisted the enemy; low-level attacks on German troops, when the weather allowed, proving particularly effective. However, their aggression was met by an equally strong response from von Richthofen and his fellow fighter pilots.

If the Rittmeister had indeed been ordered to fly only when strictly necessary, the scale of the battle raging on the ground soon rendered this instruction impossible to enforce. And as the attacks stumbled and stalled a note of fatalism soon entered Ludendorff's vocabulary, quickly rendering most propaganda ineffective, even the deeds of its most gallant fighter ace.

For von Richthofen the days must have passed in a blur of action, less so the long nights of sleeplessness. To the general public reading of his ever growing score – reaching seventy-four by the end of March – the glory of the previous April and May seemed to have returned. But the man they idolised was now greatly changed from the hero of those heady days. He was now haunted by death, which became only too clear to Peter Lampel when visiting JG1 on one of several sojourns to the front he made in April for *Der Flieger*.

On the 2nd Lampel happened to meet and speak to von Richthofen over lunch shortly after he had shot down his seventy-fifth victim – an R.E.8 from 52 Squadron flown by 19-year-old Welshman Ernest Jones and his observer Robert Francis, a 24-year-old bank clerk from Bristol. In his combat report he simply recorded that:

At around 12.30 I attacked an RE 8 at an altitude of 800 metres, directly below the clouds, above the wood of Moreuil. As my adversary only saw me late, I managed to approach within 50 metres. From a range of ten metres I fired at him until he began to burn. When the flames appeared I was only five metres away from him. I could see how the observer and pilot were leaning out of their plane trying to escape the flames. The machine did not explode in the air but gradually burnt away. It fell out of control to the ground where it exploded and burnt to ashes.

When he spoke to Lampel the image of these men writhing in agony as flames enveloped them, unable to escape, was fixed in his mind, its awfulness clearly sickening him intensely. A murderer would feel no shame, but Manfred's conscience was clearly pricked by this dreadful event, even though he had sent many other men to oblivion before. The article that appeared in *Der Flieger*, part written by Lampel and Kurt Tucholsky, as editor, captured all of this and more:

The scene of this meeting was an abandoned English hut of 'elephant iron', in which it was just possible to stand. Light poured in through the open doors at either end. Richthofen and his officers sat on all four sides of a long table that occupied the centre and most of the room. The ace, himself, was sitting at the head of the table.

He was wearing a heavy grey wool sweater, which, being open in front exposed a leather vest beneath. He wore a pair of yellowish-brown riding breeches and leather putties. Other members of Staffel 11, including Leutnants Weiss, Wolff and Gussman, were wearing the coats of their grey service uniforms. None of them were wearing decorations, and not one of the coats was buttoned up. Some of the flyers still had smears of oil on their cheeks. They were all young, and tingling with excitement from the last flight over the lines.

With a wave of the hand toward a vacant chair, Richthofen invited Lampel to take a seat with him and a few others. And ordered another plate and some lunch for him. Evidently he stated in humour, 'It's not much, but you are welcome to the hospitality of our English bungalow. Our hosts left suddenly and forgot to leave a full larder.'

Lampel asked what success the squadron had had in the air that morning? 'I have just brought down my seventy-fifth enemy plane,' Richthofen replied simply. While Lampel congratulated him, Richthofen was staring intently out of the door. The pictures of burning planes are again in his mind revived by the hour-old memory of Jones and Newton's plunge earthwards in fire. 'Strange,' he began slowly, 'but the last ten I have shot down all burned. The one I got today also burned. I saw it quite clearly. At first it was only a small flame under the pilot's seat, but when the machine dived the tail stood up in the air and I could see that the seat had burnt through. The flames kept on showing as the machine fell down. It crashed with a terrible explosion – worse than I have ever witnessed before. It was a two-seater but its occupants defended themselves well.'

Grussman interrupted in a somewhat scolding way. 'You almost touched him in the air. We all saw you fly so close to him that it seemed a collision was inevitable. You scared me.' 'Yes it was close,' Richthofen replied with a grin, 'I had to come up quite close. I believe the observer, whoever he was, was a tough party – a first class fighting man. He was courageous and determined. I flew within 5 metres of him, until he had had enough, and this in spite of the fact that I believe I had hit him before. Even to the very last moment, he kept shooting at me. The slightest mistake, and I should have rammed him in the air.'

The conversation is interrupted by the appearance of a slim young officer in the doorway of the hut. He holds a telegram in his hand; it is the announcement that the Emperor has conferred on von Richthofen the third class order of the Red Eagle with Crown [in recognition of his seventieth victory on the 26 March]. There are boisterous congratulations, and Richthofen urges his comrades to continue doing their best.

A grateful nation's rewards can only go so far in recognising such gallantry, after a while they simply become trinkets. It would have been far better if the telegram had ordered a release from combat flying and so preserved the life of this brave, weary young man. Clearly those serving under him realised this, hence Grussman's observation and vocal criticism of his recklessness in pursuing an enemy aircraft to the verge of mutual destruction. Nevertheless, he was allowed to continue, his determination to do so, coupled to his continuing propaganda value, overriding all other considerations. In early April it didn't take a soothsayer to predict what would happen next if things were allowed to continue unchecked. Something akin to an ancient Greek tragedy was unfolding, all actors seemingly unable to change the script and avoid the inevitable calamity that would befall the leading actor.

And so, the battles continued to rage throughout April without let up and, increasingly, less chance of success. JG1 moved from Awoingt to Lechelle, a recently vacated British airfield where Lampel would meet von Richthofen a little later. Here they were placed under the direct authority of the Army High Command, 'to be deployed at the focal point of the battle', according to the War Diary. Then on the 12th they moved again, this time to an airfield on rising ground above Cappy. Here they overlooked the Somme as it wound its way past Corbie and Villers-Bretonneux, where the Germans had been fought to a standstill, with Amiens still 14 or so kilometres away.

This move, although tactically sound, was not popular, because the airfield only offered the most basic amenities – for the most part, personnel and aircraft were quartered in tents resting on wet and muddy ground and with little within easy reach that could offer more. There would soon be a number of temporary structures erected that the Geschwader carried with them all the time, but even these had their limits and added little comfort to the lives of weary airmen. And with the offensive now grinding to a halt in the face of stiff and ever-increasing opposition, a growing sense of foreboding must have settled on the heads of von Richthofen and his men. Nevertheless, each day when the weather allowed they ascended into the air to do battle with an enemy still pursuing a campaign of bombing and strafing, seeking combat in the air wherever and whenever they could.

The weather, as much as anything, dictated the ebb and flow of battle with rain, low clouds and high winds ruling out patrols most days, or, if flying was possible, making interceptions very difficult to achieve. But on the 6th JG1 claimed ten victories, nine of them Sopwith Camels, one despatched by von Richthofen himself. His seventy-sixth victim was 22-year-old Sydney Philip Smith, an experienced combat pilot from 46 Squadron, who was raised in Aldershot and whose body was consumed by fire and the explosion that followed his crash north-east of Villers-Bretonneux. Next day von Richthofen repeated the trick twice more by destroying what he thought to be an S.E.5 and a SPAD. Later research suggests that the first of these may have been a 73 Squadron Sopwith Camel flown by 22-year-old Ronald Adams. Surviving the crash and the war as a prisoner, he went on to become a noted actor and playwright. During the Second World War he re-joined the RAF, becoming a wing commander, and during the Battle of Britain was noted as a very skilled fighter controller at Hornchurch. In 1945–46 he returned to the stage and screen with increasing success and died at the age of 83 during 1979.

It was in 1972 that I was privileged to meet him in London and hear at first-hand his brief memories of that day:

Three of us were attacking an Albatros, if my memory serves me well, at a fairly low altitude when a 'tripehound' suddenly appeared on my tail. I twisted and turned but to no avail and was hit many times and wounded. With many of my controls shot away I had little or no control, crashed and was then dragged out of the wreck by a small party of German soldiers, who had to cut away some wreckage to do so and then carried me away on a stretcher to be treated. I was told by a German officer a little later that it was von Richthofen who had shot me down, though I cared little about this at the time.

When recovering in hospital, and still sedated, I was surprised to find a young officer, still dressed in flying kit and speaking to me in halting English by my cot. He remained for a few minutes, presented me with a box of cigars, wished me well and departed. I didn't realise at the time that it was von Richthofen, who we all knew by repute. I would have liked to have spoken to him longer – talking shop with other pilots, British or German, was always a pleasure – but he left before this could happen.

For me the war was over and when recovered I was soon in a prisoner of war camp, where I remained until repatriated in December '18.

Bad weather continued to curtail von Richthofen's flying activities for a time, but on the 20th he was again in action and scored a double victory by destroying two Sopwith Camels from 3 Squadron in quick succession. First of all, he shot down No. 3's 23-year-old commanding officer, Major Richard Raymond-Barker MC, whose body was consumed by flames. Then he turned his attention towards an aircraft piloted by the Rhodesian-born David Lewis, who survived the battle. In a letter to the author he described his close encounter with von Richthofen:

> During the evening of the 20th April 1918 I took off on a squadron patrol led by C flight commander Captain Douglas Bell. At the last moment Major Raymond-Barker decided to join us although as No. 3's CO he was generally encouraged not to do so and lead from the ground. However, I was told that he frequently ignored this instruction.
>
> We quickly climbed above the clouds to avoid anti-aircraft fire, but C flight lost touch with the rest and we flew on alone. About four miles over the German lines, we met some fifteen German triplanes, which tried to attack us from behind, but Bell frustrated this attempt by turning to meet them, so the fight started with the two patrols firing at each other head on. Major Barker's, who had pulled ahead of the rest, was hit by an incendiary bullet which caused his petrol tank to explode and his aircraft break up and go down. I doubt if he survived the blast.
>
> While this was happening I was attacking a bright blue triplane, which was on a level with me, and was just about to finish him off when I heard the rat-tat-tat of machine-guns coming from behind me and saw the splintering of struts just above my head. I quickly turned and found an all red triplane on my tail. I did what I could to avoid his fire, but he was too experienced a fighter, and only once did I manage to have him at a disadvantage, and then only for a few seconds, but in those few ticks of a clock I shot a number of bullets into his machine and thought I would have the honour of bringing him down, but in a second the positions were reversed and he had set my emergency petrol tank alight, and I was hurtling earthward in flames.

With flames licking all around me I hit the ground northeast of Villers-Bretonneux at a speed of sixty miles an hour and, by some miracle, was thrown clear of the wreckage. Except for minor burns and bullet holes in my flying coat and boots, I was completely unhurt. At that moment the red triplane commenced a low pass over the two wrecked Camels, coming to within one hundred feet of me and, as he did so, the pilot waved a greeting. I waved back.

Before being captured I walked the 50 yards over to the funeral pyre that was Major Barker's Camel. I couldn't get close to it because the fire was intense and, judging by the smell of burnt flesh and petrol fumes, was consuming man and machine entirely.

While Lewis fought for his life, Hans-Joachim Wolff looked on and recorded what he had seen that day:

Late in the evening, around half past seven, we took off again. A division lying near Villers-Bretonneux had asked for protection. We had hardly arrived when we encountered a whole bunch of Sopwith Camels; we immediately attacked, of course. Within a few seconds the first one was on fire, immediately afterwards the second, the third not long after that. I didn't get mine, unfortunately ... Herr Rittmeister must have been terribly pleased with his two kills.

After the dogfight he went down low so that everyone could see his red machine and waved to the infantrymen. Everyone knew who was flying the plane, and they had all seen the burning Englishmen shortly before. Everyone waved their hands and caps enthusiastically. When Herr Rittmeister landed, he clapped his hands together and rejoiced, saying, 'By golly, eighty is a decent number.' And we all celebrated with him and looked on admiringly.

News of his seventy-ninth and eightieth successes reached Manfred's mother a day later, thanks to the good offices of the 'ever courteous editor of the Rundschau'. In response she was seized by:

> A great and joyous excitement. I went outside and danced in the garden ... A longing for peace ran through my heart. Eighty aerial victories – a dizzying achievement. It must be enough now. Behind every summit yawns an abyss ... The sky became overcast, hard gusts of wind heralded a storm ... The sight depressed me ... I don't know why I am so pensive.

Her premonition, if that is what it was, took on solid form the next day, confirmed by a telegram from Albrecht simply stating that 'Manfred is living in English hands'. Inevitably she must have wondered what had happened and been sustained by the thought he was safe, although a prisoner of war? And for a time his comrades in France knew as little as she did, even though some had witnessed the events surrounding his 'capture'. Three of them, Karl Bodenschatz and Leutnants Richard Wenzl and Hans Joachim Wolff, later recorded their memories of that day's events and what follows draws together these recollections.

Dawn on 21 April saw the Somme valley shrouded in a mist. Although the pilots assembled at the airfield early in the morning there was little chance of flying until conditions improved. And while they waited von Richthofen, in an unusually light-hearted mood, joined in the fun and games of his young men. One can only assume that his success the previous day had cheered him. Added to this he would soon depart on leave, with Hans Wolff, to the Black Forest to hunt. And once this was over he planned to visit the Voss family in Krefeld, at the invitation of Werner's father. With passes and tickets already made out, all must have seemed set fair for the future and so allowed him to enjoy a few moments of fun before flying.

There was another issue that may have affected his mood that day. A.R. Weyl later recorded that the 'first example of the Fokker D.VII to go to the front went to von Richthofen's unit in early April and he was seen flying it when visiting neighbouring aerodromes'. If true, getting his hands on an aircraft so superior to the Dr.Is, Albatros D.Vs and the Pfalz D.IIIs in performance would probably have lifted his spirits and made a return to operational flying, when his leave was over, more tolerable. However, being aware of his exhausted state and propaganda value, it was more than likely that von Hoeppner intended to bring his front-line service to an end, whether Manfred wished it or not.

After waiting around the airfield for a couple of hours, a wind blowing from the east, coupled to a rising temperature, gradually thinned the mist, making flying possible. A phone call from a forward observer reported the enemy taking to the air and von Richthofen ordered his men to make ready for departure. A little earlier he'd received an order from 'The Group Commander of the Air Forces' (found on his body by the British later that day), which read:

> It has been reported to me by our airmen that strong enemy air forces have prevented them from flying across the Ancre in a westerly direction. You are ordered to force the enemy fighting aircraft back, so that a reconnaissance can be carried out over the lines between Marceux and Puchevillers.

He could now put this into action and ordered two flights to take off, one of these led by von Richthofen himself along with his newly arrived cousin, Wolfram, plus Walther Karjus, Wolff and Edgar Scholz. They quickly gained height and soon spotted seven Sopwith Camels below them on the German side of the lines and another seven above, some of which then dropped down to attack a group of fighters from Jasta 5 operating near Sailly le Sec. Then one or two, Wolff wasn't sure which, descended on von Richthofen's flight and a general melee developed in which Wolff occasionally spotted his leader's red triplane. While he and Karjus were fighting three Camels, von Richthofen came into view aiming at one of the enemy aircraft before diving away in a westerly direction.

As he disengaged from the battle for a few moments Wolff saw the Rittmeister's triplane at an 'extremely low height over the Somme near Corbie and instinctively shook my head and wondered why he was pursuing an opponent so far over the lines'. Suddenly he was attacked and forced to defend himself and when free from the attentions of this Camel pilot looked again for von Richthofen without success. Suspecting that something had happened to him, he and Karjus circled around at 900m hoping that he would soon reappear and return to Cappy with them. But it wasn't to be and when turning for home Wolff thought he spotted 'a small (red) machine on the ground that had not been there before' and reported this when he returned.

Worry soon turned to concern when they discovered that von Richthofen was missing and Bodenschatz quickly ordered some of the pilots to fly over the scene of the battle to see if they could spot the Rittmeister's aircraft on the ground. At the same time, observation units nearer the front were contacted to determine whether they had seen anything of importance. In response, Leutnant Fabian, a forward artillery observer, reported that a 'Red triplane landed on hill near Corbie ... Passenger has not left the aircraft' and so their worst fears were realised, but his eventual fate still awaited confirmation. This came on the 23rd when a Reuters report, containing the message that von Richthofen was indeed dead, and had been buried with full military honours in the village of Bertangles, was intercepted.

It was news his parents had dreaded to hear for a very long time and now the worst had happened. Very soon they were flooded with visitors offering their condolences, while telegrams and letters arrived from monarchs, politicians, military leaders, fellow pilots, friends and members of the general public. Newspapers in Germany were soon covered in headlines about this tragic loss and, amazingly, the same thing happened in France, Britain, the USA, Canada and Australia. In death even the enemy paid homage to a gallant foe, even though he bore personal responsibility for the deaths of so many Allied aircrew.

In many ways it was left to the journalists and writers in Germany, who were complicit in promoting von Richthofen's achievements for propaganda purposes, to spin a story that still exploited his name to further the country's cause. Foremost among them was Georg Ompteda:

> Richthofen is said to have preferred an aviator's death. He calmly considered this likely ending of life to be the finest, because it was for the Fatherland ... According to him a German should experience only a feeling of satisfaction, some joy and pride in falling for the purest ideal of all, namely his country. And when this reserved, calm man would become enthusiastic, his eyes sparkled and his voice rose when he spoke of the possibility of such a death. It greatly touched me. I found nothing to say in reply, but I was proud that our country possessed such men.

Even in death, as Ompteda realised, the von Richthofen name still held great currency as a propaganda tool and so the legend entered German folklore, in time to be picked up and exploited by the Nazi Party in pursuit of their own goals.

Chapter 9

Cause and Effect

Nothing in his life became him like the leaving of it.
                    William Shakespeare's *Macbeth*

For many decades, mystery and controversy surrounded von Richthofen's death. All that was known with any certainty was that a bullet punctured his chest and, in his dying seconds, he crash-landed his all-red triplane behind enemy lines, on Hill 102 above the Somme River. Of course, who killed him shouldn't have mattered in the least because the enormity of his achievements, as a fighter pilot, leader and, sadly, as a propaganda tool, easily surpasses all other considerations. And yet the question still lingers and will continue to do so because there will never be a definitive answer and mysteries always attract speculation.

The truth is that in manoeuvring over the lines at low altitude in pursuit of a Sopwith Camel from 209 Squadron, he entered a killing zone where skilled front-line soldiers and numerous machine gunners, in well-established positions with good fields of fire, were on high alert expecting another attack by German forces at any time. Extensive proof of their preparedness can be found in British and Australian Divisional, Brigade and 5th Army records. Here a simple examination of trench maps shows that when flying over the lines towards the village of Corbie, Manfred was within easy range of at least forty or more Vickers and Lewis machine guns and countless hundreds of rifles. And before that he had been pursued and fired at by another 209 Squadron Camel flown by the Canadian Captain

A.R. Brown. In the circumstances it is surprising that he wasn't hit many more times.

So, his 'means of leaving' life became, as mysteries do, a dominating factor in assessing his brief existence and, more importantly, why he had made such a basic mistake, which even his newest and least experienced pilots knew was wrong?

It was, in truth, a misjudgement with causes long in the making, perhaps dating back to his childhood when he was obliged by the Junker culture of his caste to pursue a military career and give all for his country without demur. Being a high-spirited, independent child, he fought against the petty restrictions, bullying and strict discipline of a military life, but his father's will, reinforced by Albrecht's frustrations at having to leave his beloved army due to ill health, prevailed. Forced to attend cadet school, Manfred suffered acute unhappiness and did not shine academically. Ultimately he survived and gradually accepted all the petty constraints and the personal and institutionalised bullying, though with little joy and minimal success. It was a behavioural pattern that followed him to the Military Academy in Berlin during 1909, though his passion for devil-may-care exploits, gymnastics, riding and hunting provided an outlet for his energies and, perhaps, true ambitions. However, academic success continued to elude him and it was only at the second attempt that he graduated to become an officer and join a Uhlan cavalry regiment.

And so he might have passed into obscurity, but war came and everything changed. Soon a conflict on two fronts, involving many millions of men, consumed its participants, inflicting a barely believable level of suffering and death.

For many young men such as Manfred the war may have come as a release from the monotony of peacetime life and he may have identified with the words of poet Rupert Brooke, who wrote in *1914:* 'Now God be thanked who has matched us with His hour, and caught our youth, and wakened us from sleeping.' This may be trite and, perhaps, blind to what lay ahead, but is hardly surprising in the wake of the pre-war indoctrination inflicted on innocent minds by all sides to encourage nationalistic jingoism and xenophobia. It was propaganda that sustained this deceit and continued to shape beliefs and ideologies for the next four years. All told, it might have been better if all the young men involved had taken heed of Wilfred Owen's words when he wrote, towards the end of the war, 'My friend, you would not tell with such high zest, to children ardent for some desperate glory, the old Lie: *Dulce et Decorum est, pro patria mori*' (loosely translated as 'it is sweet and glorious to die for one's country'.)

Sadly, there was no such restraining hand during 1914 and in August a war came that soon consumed the lives of young men at an alarming rate that few, if any, could have predicted. Some naively hoped it would end quickly, but the nature of this war was very different from those in the past. Trench warfare, heavy artillery, poison gas and the sheer number of machine guns held by two evenly matched sides on the Western Front ensured a static, siege-type of war that both sides found impossible to break down. Even so, it was attempted on a massive scale each year at huge cost in men and material.

For a time, Manfred 'enjoyed' a true cavalry role – scouting and skirmishing – before being forced to live a troglodyte existence in trenches and dugouts. Not one for enforced idleness, and a war without glory, his eyes soon turned skywards for a new mission and an aerial observer he became.

The glamour of this new form of warfare may not have been lost on him – nor was its obvious dangers, made worse by the lack of parachutes to escape a doomed aircraft and the flammable and toxic materials used in their construction. Aeroplanes were crude and flight was in its infancy, but their novelty soon attracted attention from the press. Images of knightly virtue and great chivalry were quickly conjured up, which, in the face of an entrenched life on the ground, soon found a ready audience in Germany, Britain and France. But, as any journalist knows, remaining newsworthy is a difficult trick to sustain because repetition soon becomes wearing. So the cult of the hero airman was born, allowing readers to follow and identify with an ever-evolving story and the men behind it.

All well and good, but the continued success of this propaganda relied on two things – an airman's ability to survive and ever more victories to be celebrated. Combat flying was too dangerous for the former, while the latter demanded luck and great resilience to help an individual withstand the stresses and strains barely understood at the time. The development of aircraft had quickly run ahead of a scientific appreciation of G forces, lack of oxygen at height and much more that flying exerted on human minds and bodies. And, of course, it took little or no account of the added pressures of combat flying – both physical and mental – and how quickly these could make even the strongest man weary, uncaring of their own safety and so reduce their value in front-line service. Then, added to all this, there were the long-term effects of injuries, particularly head wounds sustained in battle. Here surgery could restore the body, if the wounds were not too severe, but the science of psychiatry, still in its infancy, did not have the tools to heal psychological scars or the damage done to personality.

All the medics could do in the Great War was patch up physical wounds, mark them fit for duty and debate the reality and possible causes of 'shell shock'.

Now, after more than a century of research, and many more wars, specialists have finally reached firmer ground with the all-encompassing term Post-Traumatic Stress Disorder to describe the debilitating and crippling response to severe stress brought on by powerful external forces.

When von Richthofen, the sturdiest and most resilient of men, flew in combat for the first time all these effects were unknown and any failure of spirit marked down as cowardice in the face of the enemy. For most, the only escape was death, permanent injury or the intervention of a particularly well-informed and compassionate commanding officer seeking to have exhausted aircrew rested. But the pace and violence of such a bloody war made such a sympathetic response very difficult to achieve. And then you had the socially induced convention of stoicism to contend with, so carefully bred into men during this foolish age.

For the first few months, as his skill as an observer and then as a pilot grew, von Richthofen seemed to cope well with the effects of combat flying. However, at this stage the aircraft he flew, particularly the slow, cumbersome two-seaters, probably induced far fewer ill effects than those that would come later. But stepping up to fly higher-performance fighters in late 1916 introduced him to faster speeds, greater G forces and the effects of rapid atmospheric changes as he zoomed, twisted, turned and dived in combat. Here his physical fitness and robust constitution would have helped him cope. Nevertheless, it was a game of diminishing returns, with increasing levels of damage to the heart, the respiratory system, nasal and aural passages and the brain soon accumulating as the number of missions flown mounted.

The operational cycle introduced in late 1916, and carried through to the end of the war, was ultimately based on forward units observing enemy activity and then notifying the Jastas, which would be 'scrambled' to an intercept. Each time, and it could be three or four times a day, they climbed rapidly to 4,000 to 5,000m, or higher, to get above the enemy before diving down out of the sun to intercept them. These were tactics that worked well, but demanded constant vigilance and preparedness to be successful. In addition, they were generally interspersed with more general patrol duties to help create a 'barricade', as it was called. So each day contained a relentless cycle of work, with frequent combats, admittedly with inferior enemy aircraft most of the time. Nonetheless, it was a most demanding life in which you saw death close to and frequently suffered the loss of friends and comrades. And often these deaths were appalling to observe, especially when fire took hold and the airman's only alternative to burning to death was to jump or shoot themselves.

Nobody can stand these sorts of pressures forever and all would eventually crack to some degree, although the timing could vary from person to person. When this happened the breakdown could come in many forms – avoiding duty, becoming uncaring of one's own safety or the polar opposite, becoming too cautious, drinking too much, lethargic or manic behaviour, rapid mood changes, becoming irresponsibly argumentative and irrational and much more. These were all signs that medical science would eventually recognise and act upon, so introducing the idea of operational tours of particular lengths to counter the effect of combat fatigue. Sadly, this did not happen as a rule in the Great War, where for the most part aircrew suffered in silence and died when common sense and compassion should have proved more effective guides. But in a war when many thousands were killed and wounded needlessly every day the fate of a few airmen was of little consequences. Or as Cecil Lewis put it, 'Generals on all sides in that damnable war were very generous with other people's lives.'

Some squadron commanders did realise what was happening and sought to alleviate the problems wherever they could, but there was little they could do in the face of such a cold-blooded attitude to life. The more enlightened souls, such as the exceptionally experienced Major Lanoe Hawker, who von Richthofen killed in combat, believed each man, no matter how resilient, ceased to become truly effective after nine months at the front, some even less. As a result, this far-seeing and compassionate man sought to act upon this level-headed assessment, which strangely he did not apply to himself. Coupled to this, in 1919 a study conducted by members of the Air Service Medical Laboratory concluded that 80 per cent of groundings were nervous in origin. They also found 50 per cent of pilots had developed symptoms of serious neurosis during their time at the front with few, if any, escaping the ravages of such extreme stress. So attitudes were changing but at a perilously slow pace.

For von Richthofen there were two other issues to be added to this toxic mixture – celebrity and the long-term effects of a serious head wound.

Before Hindenburg and Ludendorff became supreme war lords, propaganda was an undeveloped art and what there was lacked punch. The more judicious British and French were far more advanced in these techniques, as Ludendorff was first to admit:

> Reports from the Army about the evil mood prevailing at home and reports from home about the low morale of the Army have become more frequent ... We are literally swamped by enemy propaganda, the serious danger of which is clearly recognised ... Disillusionment has come; it is impossible to gloss that over ... In the homeland itself we still fail to realise the mental attitude of the enemy. All parties represented in the Reichstag, with the exception of the right wing of the Centre, persistently echo the catch-words of hostile propaganda ... Is this the kind of influence calculated to restore flagging spirits, especially in times of stress when human weaknesses tend to assert themselves?

His anger is palpable and the actions he then took in 1916 to correct these shortcomings coincided neatly with the appearance of von Richthofen as a fighter pilot of note. To say he was a godsend to the teams of propagandists and censors, led by Walter Nicolai, might be thought an understatement. A handsome young Prussian hero brought up to believe in Kaiser and country, and be prepared to die for them both, while displaying knightly virtues, was almost too good to be true. But he was all that he seemed to be and more, because within him lay the seeds of a fine military leader, who with experience and training could have commanded much more than a Geschwader and served his country equally well in a later war. Though whether he might have been prepared to turn a blind eye to the Nazi excesses and fight for his country, like many of his comrades including Herman Goring, Karl Bodenschatz and Ernst Udet did, can only be guessed at. Nevertheless, the Nazis still managed to exploit his memory for their own purposes, such was the strength of his reputation.

As his fame spread, and his score grew ever larger, the exploitation of his image began in earnest. From the beginning there appeared to be little regard for Manfred's welfare or the burden celebrity placed on his already overloaded young shoulders. Cecil Lewis commented on the callous wastefulness of Great War generals, but I believe the purveyors of propaganda were equally guilty, most of them from the safety of their offices at Supreme Headquarters or in faraway Berlin. And so began a shameful episode, which would only end in disaster when the 'golden goose' was killed.

Of course, there were other pilots who attracted much attention, but all seemed to lack the 'X' factor that made von Richthofen stand apart, not simply because he had the highest score. Whether by luck or judgement, he managed to survive to become ever more famous at home and, most surprisingly of all, in the enemy's heartlands. This was the oddest of phenomena that found a voice in an article written by Charles Grey, writer and founder and editor of *The Aeroplane*, published in London following Manfred's death:

> Richthofen is dead. All airman will be pleased to hear that he has been put out of action, but there will be no one amongst them who will not regret the death of such a courageous nobleman ... every member of the Royal Flying Corps would also have been proud to shake his hand had he fallen into captivity alive.

Perhaps of the greatest significance when assessing von Richthofen's condition in the last few months of his life is the head wound he sustained on 6 July 1917 and the profound effects on behaviour and personality this had. Before it happened, his mother had observed a certain fatalism in his attitude to life, brought on by the constant battles he faced each day and the loss of so many comrades. This is an inevitable by-product of life on the front line and is a way of helping a soldier, sailor or airman face the unenviable prospect of death. Although worrying to observe for a loving mother, it is part of a defence mechanism, although one that is compounded by battle fatigue.

However, following his injury, Kunigunde noted more profound changes taking place within him. Realising this was happening, she attempted to turn her son, who seemed transfixed by a sense of duty and responsibility to his men, away from front-line service so that his life might be preserved. His response was uncompromising, even aggressive, and his uncharacteristic outburst to someone he loved and held in great respect perhaps revealed the true state of his mind. Knocked back by his response, Kunigunde grudgingly gave way. She sensed that there was no advice she could give that he would listen to and allowed fate take its course, hoping, one assumes, that his commanders would take steps to preserve her child.

When modern-day head injury and aviation medicine specialists have been asked to consider von Richthofen's condition in the last months of his life, they simply conclude that he was in no fit state to return to duty let alone combat flying. In later wars, when pressure to fight was equally intense, even the most gallant, hardy souls were rested no matter how hard they tried to remain operational and this should have so in 1918 as well. And if truth be told, the experienced Professor Paul Kraske, who treated Manfred when first injured, set out in his medical notes how the young aviator should be treated until considered fully recovered. He later wrote, after his initial examination had confirmed the severity of the wound, that, 'without a doubt there has been a severe concussion of the brain and even more probable cerebral haemorrhage. For this reason, sudden changes in air pressure during flight might lead to disturbances of his consciousness ... he must not resume flying before being given permission to do so by a physician.'

This should have been an end of the matter, especially since in 1916 the well-respected professor of neurology and psychiatry at the Institute for Research into the Consequences of Brain Injuries, Kurt Goldstein, had concluded that 20 per cent of patients with a skull wound and only 4 per cent of those with brain injuries were deemed fit for further combat service after treatment. His extensive research, which does not seem to have included aviators, was sufficient to give these figures true meaning. As a result, his advice seems to have been accepted by the medical profession and the army alike, which for the time was a major step forward. And yet Manfred seems to have ignored the medical advice he was given and the exhortations of his greatly respected mother. He even made light of military orders that effectively grounded him, leaving the unanswerable question. Why?

In truth it seems that he was overwhelmed by the extreme stresses involved in flying and fighting in such a testing environment, he was overcome by the demands of being Germany's greatest hero, and his daily existence became gripped by severe headaches and depression resulting from his head injury. And then there was his commitment to his men and a misplaced desire to see the battle through to an end no matter what the consequences. All in all, it was a toxic cocktail of physical and mental pressures that would have defeated anyone let alone a man whose fatigue was only too obvious to those around him. Only raw courage kept him going, plus a desire to lead his men no matter what the cost personally. However, he chanced his luck once too often on 21 April, made a simple mistake and met his end.

Despite public expressions of sorrow at his passing, the only true grief is found among those who genuinely loved that person. For Albrecht the loss of his much-loved son undoubtedly contributed to his early death in March 1920 – grief for a lost child being the most potent, consuming anguish that it is possible to imagine. Lothar, who returned to action in July, only to be wounded again a month later having increased his score to forty, was consumed by sorrow and guilt over his brother's death. He felt that if he had been flying as his brother's wingman on the 21st, a position he had often occupied, he would not have been shot down – a view of which his mother later wrote:

> I can only agree with him. The two brothers generally flew side by side; they never lost sight of one another and each was the other's best protection.

When the war ended Lothar found it difficult to settle back into a civilian life; a condition that afflicted many veterans, some for the rest of their lives. He married, then divorced in short order, siring two children, Viola and Wolf Manfred, along the way. Then in 1922, having returned to aviation, he crashed in a LVG C.VI when flying as a commercial pilot and died soon afterwards. Ilse and Bolko were much luckier, dying in 1963 and 1971 respectively, each, like Lothar, producing a son they called Manfred.

Kunigunde, now a widow and the mother of two dead heroes, continued on as best she could, remaining in her home at Schweidnitz supplementing her income by turning the house into a museum. In helping ends meet, she was assisted by royalties generated by Manfred's autobiography. The book sold in vast numbers on both sides of the Atlantic, even in peacetime, and so provided a valuable legacy that her son had hoped it would. And in time this strong, resilient woman wrote her own memoirs, then saw her son's legend purloined by the Nazis with whom, it is reported, she had little sympathy. Undoubtedly she carried grief to the end of her days and must have wondered what might have been if Manfred and Lothar had been spared? A fruitless pursuit and one that doesn't postpone grief for long, but still the thought persisted:

> I remained in front of Manfred's large oil portrait. He stood before me as if he could even now speak to me! No – those eloquent lips would never again open to tell me what I had, perhaps, already thought for myself; as if it was a continuation and feat of my own ego. In his clear head thoughts were put in order, his will was strong – he had achieved his goal. What would you say today – Manfred?

In her grief Kunigunde turned her home into a mausoleum through which she escorted many visitors each year, proudly recalling her sons in the process. One of her guests found this a very moving experience and later wrote:

> I left her sitting sad faced and alone in her garden, dreaming perhaps of those days when Manfred and Lothar laughed and played in this house of memories.

Late in the Second World War, with the Soviets advancing rapidly towards the Fatherland, she and Ilse, also widowed, were forced to leave Schweidnitz and move westwards to safety, leaving her home and the graves of her husband and son to be ransacked and defaced. But life goes on, some normality returned, and she settled in Wiesbaden, where she died on 24 April 1962, aged 93.

Shortly after the First World War Manfred's body was moved from the grave at Bertangles and taken a short distance to the communal German cemetery at Fricourt. But his stay there was a short one. In 1925, to great public acclaim, he returned to Germany. His mother wished to inter him with Albrecht and Lothar near the family home in Schweidnitz, but this was not to be. Unwilling to let a national hero go so easily, the state claimed his remains and arranged his funeral in Berlin and burial in the city's Invalidenfriedhof, attended by President Hindenburg and many other dignitaries.

When the 1939–45 war came to an end, and the Iron Curtain eventually descended on the city, von Richthofen's grave, now pockmarked by bullets, stood within a few feet of the Berlin Wall. Then in 1975 a more personal reinterment took place, which saw his family finally claim his remains, laying them to rest with his mother, sister and youngest brother in Wiesbaden. He was home at last and finally away from the strife and public gaze that had so plagued his short life.

References

Armstrong, Harry G., *The Principles & Practice of Aviation Medicine*, Balliere (1952).
Barbusse, Henri, *Under Fire*, Penguin Books (2003).
Bishop, W.A., *Winged Warfare*, Hodder & Stoughton (1918).
Bodenschatz, Karl, *Jagd in Flanderns Himmel*, Verlag Knorr & Hirth (1935).
Burrows, William E., *Richthofen*, Hart-Davis (1969).
Carisella, P.J., *Who Killed the Red Baron*, White Lion (1974).
Clark, Christopher, *The Iron Kingdom*, Penguin (2006).
Culpin, M., *Psychoneurosis of War and Peace*, Cambridge (1920).
Davies, Belinda J., *Home Fires Burning*, University of North Carolina (2000).
Fenton, N.R., *Shell Shock and its Aftermath*, St Louis (1926).
Ferko, A.E., *Richthofen*, Albatros (1995).
Fokker, Anthony, *Flying Dutchman*, George Routledge (1934).
Franks, Norman, *Jasta Boelcke*, Grub Street (2004).
Franks, Norman, *Sky Tiger*, William Kimber (1980).
Gibbons, Floyd, *The Red Knight of Germany*, Cassell (1930).
Grinker, Roy, *Men Under Stress*, Skilled Books (1945).
Hawker, Tyrrel, *Hawker VC*, Pen and Sword (2013).
Hegender, Heinz, *Fokker. The Man and His Aircraft*, Harleyford (1961).
Henden, H. & Haas, A.P., *Wounds of War. The Psychological Aftermath of Combat in the Vietnam War*, New York (1986).
Hillier-Graves, Tim, *Heaven High, Ocean Deep*, Casemate (2019).
Hillier-Graves, Tim, *Widowmaker*, Casemate (2020).
Italiander, Rolf, *Richthofen*, Verlag Berlin (1938).
Johnson, J.E., *Wing Leader*, Goodall Publications (1956).

Kilduff, Peter, *The Red Baron*, David & Charles (2007).
Kilduff, Peter, *Richthofen: Beyond the Legend*, Arms and Armour (1993).
Kilduff, Peter, *The Red Baron's Combat Wing*, Arms and Armour (1997).
Lasswell, Harold, *Propaganda in the World War*, Martono Publishing (1938).
Lee, Arthur Gould, *No Parachute*, Jarrolds (1968).
Lee, Arthur Gould, *Open Cockpit*, Jarrolds (1969).
Lee, John, *The War Lords*, Weidenfeld & Nicolson (2005).
Ludendorff, Erich, *The Concise Ludendorff Memoirs*, Hutchison (1935).
Marson, T.B., *Scarlet and Khaki*, Jonathan Cape (1930).
McKee, Alexander, *The Friendless Sky*, Souvenir Press (1962).
Nowarra, Heinz, & Brown, Kimborough, S., *Von Richthofen & The Flying Circus*, Harleyford (1965).
Robinson, Douglas H., *The Dangerous Sky*, Foulis (1973).
Rochford, Leonard H., *I Chose the Sky*, William Kimber (1977).
Schroder, Hans, *An Airman Remembers*, Aviation Book Club (1933).
Sheppard, Ben, *The War of Nerves*, Jonathan Cape (2000).
Stokes, Doug, *Paddy Finucane. Fighter Ace*, William Kimber (1983).
Taylor, A.J.P., *The First World War*, Hamish Hamilton (1963).
Taylor, P.M., *Munitions of the Mind*, Manchester University Press (1990).
Titler, Dale M., *The Day the Red Baron Died*, Ian Allan (1970).
Udet, Ernst, *Mein Fliegerleben*, Ullstein (1935)
'Vigilant', *Richthofen: The Red Knight of Germany*, John Hamilton (1935).
Von Richthofen, Kunigunde, *Mein Kriegstagebuch*, (1937).
Von Richthofen, Manfred, *Derr Rote Kampflieger*, Ullstein (1917).
Wenzl, Richard, *Richthofen Flieger*, Badische Zeitung (1918/1930).
Werner, Johannes, *Knight of Germany*, Greenhill Books (1991).
Weyl, A.R., *Fokker: The Creative Years*, Putnam (1965).
Williamson, Henry, *A Fox Under My Cloak*, MacDonald (1956).
Winter, Denis, *First of the Few*, Allen Lane (1982).
Wyngarden, Greg van, *The Richthofen Circus*, Osprey (2004).

Index

Abteilung IIIb, 150
Adams, Ronald, 248–9
Air Services Medical
    Laboratory, 261
Albatros Aviation Company,
    47, 147, 208, 232
Aldersdorf, 222, 230–1
Allmenroder, Karl, 158, 188
Althaus, Ernst von, 75
Anti-Richthofen Squadron, 171–2
Armstrong, H.G. (Surgeon General
    of the USAF), 199, 201
Arnim, Sixt von (General), 211
Arras, 167
Augusta Victoria, Kaiserin, 177
Australian Expeditionary Force
    (AEF), xii–xiii, xv
Avesnes le Sec, 236
Awoingt, 235

Bader, Douglas, 89, 145, 182
Bahr, 233
Ball, Albert, 125, 172, 175
Barlow, Harold, 187
Bauer, Rudolf, 158
Bell, Douglas, 250
Berlin, 13, 23, 54, 58, 126, 178,
    232, 237

Berlin Illustrated Company, 93
Bertangles, 139, 254, 267
Berthold, Rudolf, 75, 171
Bertincourt, 118, 120, 128
Beschow, 233
Bethmann Hollweg, Theobald von
    (Chancellor), 97, 114–15, 117,
    217
Bird, Algernon, 211–13, 219
Bishop, William Avery, 65
Bismarck, Chancellor, xvii, 2, 4, 12
Blume, 23
Bockelman, 159
Bodenschatz, Karl-Henrich, 134,
    187, 252, 254, 263
Boelke, Oswald, xiv, 55–7, 75,
    85–7, 93–5, 104, 111–13,
    118–19, 122–4, 128–35, 142,
    147, 165, 186, 234
Bohme, Erwin, 129, 130, 224
Brauneck, Otto, 204
Brieftauben Abteilung Metz, 85–8,
    92, 99
Brieftauben Abteilung Ostende
    (BAO), 73, 76–9, 84, 95
Breslau, 8, 10, 126
Brown, Arthur Roy, 256
Buddecke, Hans-Joachim, 75

Bulow, Karl von (General), 36–7
Bufe, Otto (KOFL 4th Army), 184–8, 204–205, 207, 209
Burkhard, Hans, 78
Busch, Arnold (Professor), 158
Busch, Wilhelm, 78

Cadet Institute (Wahlstatt), 16–21, 75, 178, 232
Cambrai, 167, 221, 225, 236
Cappy, 237, 253–4
Clutterbuck, Leonard, 235
Corbett, Dr Cyril Dudley (RAMC), 199–200
Cork, Richard, 64–5

Der Rote Kampflieger, 160, 180, 213, 220, 236
Doberitz, 54, 55, 92, 95
Douai, 54, 56, 86, 165, 167
Doughty, Georg, 136, 137
Doring, Kurt-Bertram von, 203, 213

Eberhardt, Colonel, 52
Ellis, Ralph, 187
Erzberger, Matthias, 217
Esser, 159
Euler, August, 47

Falkenhayn, Erich von (Chief of the General Staff), 96, 204
Falkenhayn, Fritz von, 204–205, 234
Feldflieger Abteilung No 18, 239

Feldflieger Abteilung No 62, 56, 86
Feldflieger Abteilung No 69, 70
Ferdinand, Archduke of Austria, 27
Ferko, A.E., 146
Festner, Sebastion, 159
Fischer, Fritz, 158
Flieger-Ersatz-Abteilung No 7, 62–3
Foster, Bill, 228–30
Fokker, Anthony, 46, 51–7, 89, 203, 208, 222–5, 231–2
Francis, Robert, 244
Franco Prussian War, 2, 33
Friedenskirche, 11
Freier, Hugo (4th Dragoons), 41

Gardner. Jimmy, 214
Garros, Roland, 46, 50–1, 53
German Air Service, 43–8, 58, 99, 183
German High Command, 35, 37, 131, 184
German 1st Army, 36–7
German 2nd Army, 36–7, 234
German 4th Army, 184–8, 204–205, 207
German 6th Army, 185
Gersdorff, Ernst von, 77, 104
Gerstenberg, Alfred, 111, 112
Godson, Mike, 228–30
Goldstein, Kurt, 265
Gontermann, Heinrich, 221–22
Goring, Hermann, 134, 231, 263
Graves, Albert Edward, xi–xiii
Grey, Charles, 263

Grieg, Oscar, 161, 165
Gussman, Siegfried, 245–7

Haehnelt, Wilhelm, 234
Haig, Douglas (Field-Marshall), 96, 244
Hall, Gilbert, 136–7
Hari, Mata, 151
Hawker, Lanoe, 137–41, 163, 261
Hay, Ronnie, 72–3
Hervey, Tim, 102–103, 107, 127
Hillier, Arthur, 40–1, 126–7
Hindenburg Line, 167
Hindenburg, Paul von (Field Marshall and Chief of the General Staff), 53, 96–8, 149, 177–9, 218, 262, 267
Hitler, Adolf, 109
Hoeppner, Ernst von (Commanding General of the Air Force), 53, 144, 183, 186, 204, 209, 212, 219, 223
Holck, Friedrich Eric von, 70–2, 101–102
Holzapel, Josef, 105–106
Howe, Hans, 159

Immelmann, Max, xiv, 56–7
Interrupter gear (development) 50–1

Jasta 1, 120
Jasta 2 (later renamed Jasta Boelke), 119–22, 128, 133, 136, 143, 165, 224

Jasta 4, 184, 187
Jasta 5, 253
Jasta 6, 184, 187
Jasta 7, 184
Jasta 10, 184, 187
Jasta 11, 66, 144, 150, 155, 160–2, 166, 172, 176, 182–5, 187, 221, 222, 239, 241, 245
Jasta 15, 184
Jasta 28, 182
Johnson, Johnnie, 83–4, 182
Jones, Ernest, 244

Kaiser Wilhelm II, xvi, 3, 6, 12–14, 27, 34, 97, 98, 131, 152, 201, 217, 262
Kaiser Prize (1913), 23
Kagohl 1, 99
Kagohl 2, 99
Kagohl 4, 103
Karjus, Walther, 253–4
Karl, Prince Friedrich, 19–20, 171
Kasta 8, 99, 100, 106–107
Kasta 20, 143
Kasta 23, 93, 103, 144
Kastner, H (Hauptman), 56
Kirmaier, Stefan, 133–4, 145
Klein, Hans, 204, 233
Kluck, Alexander von (General) 36, 37
Kommandeur der Flieger (KOFL), 146, 184-186
Kraske, Paul (Professor), 191, 193, 264–5
Krauth, Alfred, 158

Krebs, Fritz, 203
Krefeld, 210, 252
Kreft, Konstantin, 148, 159, 176, 222

La Brayelle, 147, 148, 163, 166
Lampel, Peter, 152, 155–6, 244–6
Lang, Rudolf Emil, 147–8
Lawrence, T.E., 149, 207
Le Petit Rouge, 160, 162, 174, 176
Lechelle, 247
Lee, Arthur Gould, 174–5
Leith-Thomsen, Hermann, 52–3, 55, 99, 183, 186
Lenin, Vladimir, 151, 226
Lewis, Cecil, 175, 261, 263
Lewis, David, 250–1
London Times, xiii
Loos, 85
Lossberg Fritz von (General) 211, 223
Lubbert, Friedrich-Wilhelm, 233, 239–40
Lubert, Hans-Georg, 239
Ludendorff, Erich (General), 49, 52–3, 97–8, 115, 148–9, 153, 173, 176–80, 206, 211, 216–19, 223, 244, 262
Luebbe, Heinrich, 53
Lynker, Bodo von, 92

Mackensen, August von (General) 67–9
MacClennan, John, 161–2, 165
MacNeill, 216–17

Madge, John, 211
Mannock, Edward, 125
Martin, Kingsley, 18
Massacre of civilians (Belgium and France), 31–3
Menzke, 92, 105, 238, 279
Messines, 167
Michaelis, Georg (Chancellor), 211, 217
Millington, Dave, 105–106
Mohnicke, Eberhard, 159–60, 233
Moritz, 78, 221
Morlancourt Ridge, xi–xii
Morris, Lionel, 125

Nicolai, Walter, 150–2, 157, 159, 173, 180, 183, 217–19, 226, 262

Olympics Games, 19–20
Ompteda, Georg von, 152–3, 162, 255
Osten, Hans-Georg von der, 66–7, 108–10, 220–1, 236–7
Ostend, 77–9
Osterroht, Paul von, 87
Otersdorf, Katie, 202
Overbeck, Professor, 94

Parschau, Otto, 55–7
Pastor, Gunther, 222
Patermann, Linus, 203
Peace Offensive (1918), 218, 232, 243
Percheid, Nicolai, 158
Post-Traumatic Stress Syndrome, 259–60

Raymond-Barker, Richard, 249–50
Rees, Tom, 125
Reichstag, xiv, 12–14, 97, 114, 152, 262
Reimann, Hans, 106, 110–11
Reimann, Leopold, 122
Regiment, 6th London, xi–xvi
Regiment, 8th London, 40, 127
Regiment, 1st (Alexander III) Uhlans, 22, 23, 26–30, 39
Regiment, 12th Uhlans, 3
Reinhard, Wilhelm, 225, 240–1
Reusing, Richard, 158, 236–8
Richthofen, Albrecht von, 3–11, 16, 18, 20, 22, 73–4, 92, 117, 143–4, 153, 225–6, 265–7
Richthofen, Elisabeth, Therese 'Ilse' von, 8, 11, 16, 74, 266–7
Richthofen, Ferdinand von, 155
Richthofen, Karl, Bolko von, 10, 17, 74, 232, 266
Richthofen, Karl von, 3–4, 11
Richthofen, Kunigunde von, 3–11, 16–18, 20, 24–5, 41, 43–4, 60–2, 66, 74, 75, 92, 93, 104, 106, 108, 113–14, 117, 132–3, 135–6, 142, 144, 170–1, 181, 214–16, 226, 228–9, 232, 238, 239, 252, 264–7
Richthofen, Lothar, Siegfried von, 8, 17, 25, 41, 45, 60, 74, 93, 95, 103, 143–4, 158, 171, 182, 214, 221–2, 224, 226–7, 232, 235–6, 243, 266–7

Richthofen, Manfred von,
Childhood, 1, 3, 7–11, 15
Education (Wahlstatt) 17–21
Military Academy (Lichterfelde), 19–21
1st Uhlan Regiment, 22–5
To war (Eastern Front), 28–31
To war (Western Front), 32–42
Air Service (training), 43–6, 58, 60
Active service as an observer, 67–74, 77–84
Pilot training, 85–91, 95–6
Western Front as a pilot, 100–108
Eastern Front as a pilot, 111–13
With Jasta 2, 118, 121–31, 133–43
With Jasta 11, 144, 146–9, 158–6
Bloody April 1917, 167–76
May to June 1917, 176–83
JG1, 184–8
Wounded, 189–209
Return to service, 210–16, 220, 221, 226–8, 230
1918, 233–9
Death, 252–3
Aftermath, 256–67
Richthofen, Wolfram von, 253
Rochford, Leonard, 64–5
Rocholl, Theodor, 158
Roucourt, 167, 204
Royal Flying Corps, 52, 58, 167
Royal Flying Corps Squadrons:
No 2, 82
No 3, 249–50
No 6, 138

No 8, 102
No 11, 82, 125
No 12, 102
No 20, 191–2
No 24, 139, 140
No 25, 161
No 46, 174–5
No 53, 187
No 56, 172–3, 175
No 59, 164
No 60, 102, 143
No 73, 248
No 209, 249–50
Royal Military Academy (Lichtherfelde), 19–22, 42, 150, 257

Salzmann, Erich von, 152, 154–5, 162, 165, 180
Sanke Cards (and Willi Sanke) 93, 158
Santuzza, 22–3
Saulnier, Raymond, 50–3
Schafer, Karl-Emil, 158, 182
Scheele, Franz Christian von, 111
Schickfus, Oscar, 188
Schickfus und Neudorff, Elfriede von, 3
Schickfus und Neudorff, Leopald von, 3, 10
Schickfus und Neudorff, Louise, 3–4
Schickfus und Neudorff, (nee von Falkenhausen) Maria Theresia von, 3

Scholtz. Edgar, 234, 253
Schorling, Adolf, 158
Schroder, Hans, 168–9, 190–1
Schweidnitz, 10–11, 16, 43, 73, 92, 113–14, 177–8, 181, 203, 214, 232, 267
Schweinichen, Hans von, 20
Schwerin, 92, 223
Siegert, Wilhelm, 146
Skauradzum, R., 233
Smith, Philip Sydney, 248
Somme, 96, 103, 111–12, 128, 218, 243–4, 247, 256
Sorg, Maximilian (KOFL 6th Army), 185
Sparks, Henry, 235
Stapenhorst, Eberhardt, 233

Taylor, A.J.P., 26–7, 37
Taylor, Philip, 14
Teichmann, Hulda von, 3
Thelin, Schubert and Gnadig, 121
Thuna, Rudolf von, 91
Traumatic Brain Injury (TBI), 193–4
Tritton, Mike, 145
Tucholsky, Kurt, 152, 156–7, 245–6
Turnip Winter, 116

Ullstein Verlag of Berlin, 180
Universum Film AG, 16
Verdun, 39, 96, 99, 103

Udet, Ernst, 263

Villers-Bretonneux, xi–xii, 247–8, 251
Vimy, 166
Voss, Werner, 143, 171, 210–14, 221, 252

Walz, Franz, 134
Wegener, Georg, 152, 155, 162–5
Weiss, Hans, 245
Wenzl, Richard, 241–3, 252
Weyl, A.R., 56–7, 222–3, 231–2, 253
Wilhelm, Crown Prince, 55, 206
Willberg, Helmuth, 207, 209
Williams, Coningsby, 210

Wilson, Woodrow (President), 122
Wintgens, Kurt, 57, 75
Wolff, Hans-Joachim, 242–3, 245, 251–4
Wolff, Kurt, 158, 203, 221
Wolff's Telegraphische Bureau (WTB), 173

Ypres, 188

Zander, Martin, 120
Zeppelin, Count Ferdinand von, 47
Zeumer, Georg, 69–71, 73–4, 77–8, 80–2, 84, 87–91, 101, 188